CRYPTOCURRENCY TECHNOLOGIES

CRYPTOCURRENCY TECHNOLOGIES

Shanmuga Prabha P.
Associate Professor,
Dept of CSE, Sathyabama Institute
of Science and Technology

Priya Lakshmi S.
Associate Professor,
Dept of CSE, Sathyabama Institute
of Science and Technology

Shanmuga Priya R.
Associate Professor,
Dept of CSE, Sathyabama Institute
of Science and Technology

KHANNA BOOK
PUBLISHING CO. (P) Ltd.
4C/4344, Ansari Road, Darya Ganj,
New Delhi, India

Sathyabama Institute of
Science and Technology
Jeppiaar Nagar, Rajiv Gandhi Salai,
Chennai, Tamilnadu, India

ISBN: 978-93-55383-61-7

CRYPTOCURRENCY TECHNOLOGIES

by **Shanmuga Prabha P.**
Priya Lakshmi S.
Shanmuga Priya R.

First Edition: 2026

To view complete list of books, please scan the QR Code:

Published by:
Khanna Book Publishing Co. (P) Ltd.
CIN: U22110DL1998PTC095547

Visit us at: www.khannabooks.com
Write us at: contact@khannabooks.com

Printed in Bharat.

Preface

The bitcoin industry is rapidly changing, with ongoing developments and legal considerations influencing its direction. This book explores the practical uses, legal issues, and wider societal ramifications of decentralized digital possessions in addition to their technological components. Learners, researchers, programmers, investors, and enthusiasts who want to comprehend the foundations of bitcoin technology are the target audience for this book. It bridges the distinction between knowledge and application by offering an organized investigation of the fundamental ideas, workings, and practical uses of digital assets.

Unit 1 describes about the physical money and digital money, history of money, interbank payment mode, cryptography etc.,

Unit 2 covers the hash function, digital signature, blockchain and its network etc.,

Unit 3 delivers the primitives of crypto, bitcoin, point of bitcoin, working of bitcoin, bitcoin in practice, bitcoin predecessor, bitcoin decentralization, bitcoin mining, ethereum, and case study on bitcoin cash etc.,

Unit 4 includes alternative approaches to mining and consensus, bitcoin and anonymity, programming smart contracts on ethereum, solidity language, cryptocurrencies & the real world, applications of cryptocurrencies and blockchains etc.,

Unit 5 covers cryptocurrency regulation such as stakeholders, legal aspects, cryptocurrency exchange, black market and global economy as well as blockchain applications includes internet of things, medical record management system, domain name service, future of blockchain etc.,

Our mission is to provide individuals with all the details they require to engage in and recognize the bitcoin system. We embrace innovative thinking, candid communication, and an ethical strategy to creation as you set out on this adventure within the complex realm of bitcoin technology. We expect this resource will be a useful tool for you whenever you investigate the emerging field of digital finance.

Contents

UNIT

1

DIGITAL MONEY AND CRYPTOGRAPHY

1.1 PHYSICAL MONEY AND DIGITAL MONEY

Understanding Digital Money

Digital money, or digital currency, signifies a substantial transformation in our understanding and utilisation of money. In contrast to physical cash or coins, digital money is wholly electronic, existing in the virtual domain. It is intangible and is accounted for and transferred through online systems and technologies. A prominent example of digital money is the pioneering cryptocurrency, Bitcoin.

The Evolution of Money

Currency has evolved significantly from the era of bartering and tangible money. Digital currency enhances the current financial framework, providing numerous significant benefits:

1. **Efficiency:** Digital currency optimises financial transactions, rendering them swifter and more economical. It obviates the necessity for physical storage and safeguarding, hence diminishing the risk of theft.
2. **Global accessibility:** The technological foundations of digital currency facilitate effortless international transactions, surmounting the obstacles inherent in conventional money transfer systems.
3. **Monetary policy:** Central banks can leverage digital currency as it facilitates the execution of monetary policies. Digital currencies can be tracked and monitored with more efficiency.
4. **Censorship resistance:** Certain types of digital currency, such as cryptocurrencies, provide censorship resistance, guaranteeing that transactions remain impervious to control or manipulation by governmental or private actors Digital currency has garnered considerable interest from governments globally. Sweden, progressing towards a cashless society, and China, with its digital yuan (DC/EP), exemplify nations adopting digital currency. A 2021 IMF poll indicates that approximately 111 nations are now investigating or intending to implement digital currency in the foreseeable future.

What Problems does Digital Money Solve?

Digital currency tackles numerous persistent challenges inside the banking system. It optimises transactions and diminishes operational expenses relative to conventional systems. For example, credit card transactions and wire transfers frequently utilise distinct processing systems, leading to delays and supplementary fees. The SWIFT system, utilised by banks worldwide, illustrates this inefficiency. The principal objective of digital currency is to eradicate these inefficiencies.

It accomplishes this via distributed ledger technology (DLT), wherein nodes or shared ledgers constitute a unified network to facilitate transaction processing. This network bypasses boundaries, reducing processing time and ensuring transparency. Moreover, digital currency utilises algorithmic consensus mechanisms to address the double-spending issue. This issue pertains to preventing the double expenditure of digital currency. Centralised systems employ serial numbers to avert duplication, but decentralised digital currency utilises encryption to uphold integrity and security.

Types of Digital Money

Digital currency exists in multiple forms, each designed for certain purposes:

1. **Central Bank Digital Currencies (CBDCs):** These are currencies issued by a nation's central bank, distinct from conventional fiat currencies. Central Bank Digital Currencies (CBDCs) enable direct interactions between governments and citizens, removing intermediaries such as banks. They can be categorised as retail CBDCs for everyday transactions and wholesale CBDCs for interbank purposes.
2. **Cryptocurrencies:** Cryptocurrencies, including Bitcoin and Ethereum, employ cryptographic technology to augment security and resist tampering. Their popularity has surged, with a market capitalisation surpassing $2 trillion in 2021.
3. **Stablecoins:** Stablecoins are engineered to alleviate price fluctuation and are typically tied to a stable asset, such as a fiat currency like the U.S. dollar or a composite of goods. Tether (USDT) is a widely used stablecoin intended to replicate the value of the U.S. dollar.

Advantages of Digital Money

Digital currency provides various benefits, revolutionising our approach to financial transactions:

- **Speed and cost-effectiveness:** Transactions are expedited and rendered more economical, diminishing the necessity for physical storage and safeguarding.
- **Simplified accounting:** Digital currency eradicates manual bookkeeping and the necessity for entity-specific ledgers, enhancing record-keeping efficiency.
- **Cross-border transfers:** Digital currency markedly enhances international money transfers, with the potential to transform the remittance sector.
- **Financial inclusion:** Digital currency enables even the unbanked to engage in the economy, promoting financial inclusion.
- **Censorship resistance:** Certain digital currency systems, such as cryptocurrencies, exhibit resilience against censorship and governmental surveillance.

Disadvantages of Digital Money

Although digital currency offers significant advantages, it also poses obstacles and risks:

- **Security vulnerabilities:** Digital currency is vulnerable to hacking, which may jeopardise a nation's financial system.
- **Privacy concerns:** In contrast to cash, digital currency transactions are traceable, which raises apprehensions regarding user privacy and the possibility for exploitation by entities or governments.

- **Additional costs:** Digital currency systems have expenditures, such as the requirement for digital wallets, custody solutions, and transaction fees.
- **Governance and policy challenges:** Policymakers encounter novel difficulties in regulating digital currency, as concerns over stability and integrity have already arisen.

Digital Money in Action: Real-life Examples

In the domain of digital currency, tangible instances demonstrate the revolutionary potential of electronic currencies. These instances illustrate the varied applications and effects of digital currency:

1. The Rise of Cryptocurrency

Cryptocurrencies such as Bitcoin, Ethereum, and Ripple have achieved significant acknowledgement as decentralised digital money. Bitcoin, the inaugural cryptocurrency, was established in 2009 by an unidentified individual or group known as Satoshi Nakamoto. The primary aim was to offer a substitute for conventional fiat currencies regulated by central authorities. Bitcoin's decentralised characteristic enables it to function on a peer-to-peer network, eliminating the necessity for intermediaries such as banks. Transactions are documented on a public ledger known as the blockchain, ensuring transparency and security. The price volatility and investment possibilities of Bitcoin have captivated both individual and institutional investors, establishing it as a global phenomenon with a market capitalisation over $2 trillion.

2. Central Bank Digital Currencies (CBDCs) in Action

Global central banks are investigating the creation of CBDCs to enhance their financial systems. A notable instance is the digital yuan (DC/EP) launched by the People's Bank of China. The DC/EP seeks to supplant physical currency and improve the efficacy of both domestic and international transactions. The Bahamas has entered the realm of CBDCs with the introduction of the sand dollar, a digital counterpart to the Bahamian dollar. This digital money streamlines financial transactions for the inhabitants of this island nation, providing a secure and convenient alternative to conventional currency.

3. Stablecoins: Bridging Volatility Gaps

Stablecoins have arisen as a solution to the price volatility linked to cryptocurrencies. These digital assets are generally linked to a stable asset, such as a fiat currency like the U.S. dollar or a collection of commodities. Tether (USDT) is a widely used stablecoin intended to replicate the value of the U.S. dollar. Stablecoins are being utilised throughout multiple sectors, including e- commerce and remittances. They offer stability, rendering them an appropriate option for routine transactions and as a conduit between conventional and digital financial systems.

Exploring the Future of Digital Money

As digital currency progresses, its potential applications and societal influence broaden. Here are several promising opportunities for the future of digital currency:

1. Financial Inclusion Initiatives

Digital currency has the capacity to close the financial inclusion gap by granting access to financial services for unbanked and underbanked individuals. Mobile money services, common in areas such as Sub-Saharan Africa, have illustrated how digital currency may empower individuals and enterprises with restricted access to conventional banking.

2. Decentralized Finance (DeFi)

The emergence of DeFi platforms and initiatives offers a novel application for digital currency. DeFi seeks to replicate conventional financial services, including lending, borrowing, and trading, through the utilisation of blockchain technology and cryptocurrency. Users can accrue interest on their digital assets, obtain loans without conventional intermediaries, and engage in decentralised exchanges.

3. Smart Contracts and Digital Identity

Smart contracts, facilitated by blockchain technology, permit self-executing agreements governed by predetermined rules. These contracts are utilised throughout multiple sectors, including legal, real estate, and supply chain management. Digital currency is essential for enabling transactions in smart contracts, automating procedures, and minimising the necessity for intermediaries.

Conclusion

Digital currency signifies not merely a change in transaction methods but a revolutionary influence upon the financial landscape. Digital currency, encompassing cryptocurrencies, CBDCs, and stablecoins, presents various benefits with issues that necessitate meticulous evaluation. Practical examples demonstrate its influence, and with technological progress, the future of digital currency offers prospects for financial inclusion, decentralised finance, and novel uses across several sectors.

Physical Money

Physical money is the most familiar form of currency. It includes coins and banknotes that people carry around in their wallets. Paper money has been in use for centuries and has undergone many changes over the years.

Here are some advantages of physical money:

- Wide Acceptance
- Tangible
- Easy to Use

On the other hand, here are some disadvantages:

- Can be Counterfeited
- Vulnerable to Theft
- Difficult to track

Cryptocurrency

Cryptocurrency is a new form of currency that uses mathematics and cryptography to secure transactions and create new units. It exists only in the digital world and has no physical form.

Here are some advantages of cryptocurrency:

- Decentralized

- Fast and Secure Transactions
- Offers Anonymity

Here are some disadvantages:

- Volatile Value
- Limited Acceptance
- Not Tangible

Comparison

In terms of acceptance, physical cash is widely accepted globally. Cryptocurrencies, on the other hand, still have limited acceptance. Although some businesses now accept cryptocurrencies as a form of payment, you still can't use it in most physical stores. Another point of comparison is security. Physical money can be stolen, but it's more difficult to hack, compared to cyber attacks on cryptocurrencies. Cryptocurrencies are secured using encryption and security protocols, but there's still the possibility of hackers stealing your digital currency. Lastly, there's the issue of volatility. Physical money, as we know it, is stable in terms of value. Cryptocurrency, on the other hand, is highly volatile. The value can fluctuate significantly in a short period, making it a high-risk investment.

Conclusion

In conclusion, both physical cash and cryptocurrency have their pros and cons. What's best for you depends on what you need. If you prioritize accessibility and stability in value, then physical money is the way to go. If you want faster transactions or anonymity, then cryptocurrency might be best for you. At the end of the day, both forms of money have their uses, and it wouldn't hurt to have both.

1.2 HISTORY OF MONEY

The terms "money" and "currency" are frequently used synonymously; however, various theories indicate they are not equivalent. Some theories posit that money is fundamentally an intangible concept, whereas currency represents the physical or tangible embodiment of this intangible notion. According to this perspective, money is imperceptible to touch or smell.

Currency, conversely, consists of coins, notes, or other physical representations of money. The fundamental form of money is numerical, while the basic form of currency includes paper banknotes, coins, or plastic cards such as credit or debit cards. Although this distinction between money and currency is significant in certain contexts, for the purposes of this analysis of the history of money, the terms are employed interchangeably.

What Is Money?

Currency does not consistently possess value, regardless of its form as a seashell, metal coin, paper note, or digital data generated by a computer. As of the end of 2023, worldwide wealth is estimated at approximately $432 trillion, and the value of currency is contingent upon the significance individuals attribute to it as a means of commerce, a unit of account, and a repository of wealth. Currency facilitates the indirect exchange of goods and services. It facilitates the communication of the price and value of commodities and offers individuals a means to preserve their riches. It serves as a unit of account—a socially recognised standard for pricing goods and facilitating payment. Nonetheless, the utilisation and structure of currency have transformed over time.

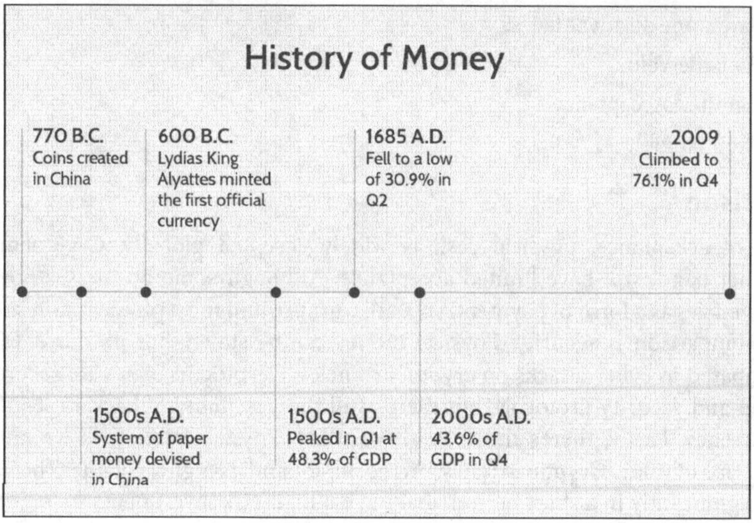

Fig. 1.1

From Bartering to Currency

Currency has been integral to human history for a minimum of 5,000 years in various forms. Prior to that period, historians commonly concur that a bartering system was probably employed. Bartering constitutes a direct exchange of commodities and services. A farmer might trade a bushel of wheat for a pair of shoes from a shoemaker. Nonetheless, these preparations require time.

To exchange an axe in an arrangement where the counterpart is expected to confront a woolly mammoth, one must locate an individual who deems the weapon a justifiable deal for facing the 12-foot tusks of the creature. If this fails, you must modify the agreement until a party consents to the terms.

A form of currency that gradually evolved over ages, encompassing easily tradable commodities like as animal pelts, salt, and weaponry. The exchanged goods functioned as a means of exchange, notwithstanding the negotiable value of each item in numerous instances. This trading mechanism has proliferated globally and persists in certain regions today. The introduction of money significantly enhanced the efficiency of business transactions, whether related to large-scale hunting or construction projects. at early August 2021, Chinese archaeologists from Zhengzhou University revealed the discovery of the world's oldest securely dated currency minting site at Guanzhuang, Henan Province, China. A mint is an establishment where coinage is produced. Circa 640 BCE, this establishment commenced the production of spade coins, among the earliest standardised metal currency types.

First Official Currency Is Minted

Concurrently, further west in 600 BCE, metal coinage was introduced when King Alyattes of Lydia minted what is regarded as the inaugural official currency, the Lydian stater. The coins were composed of electrum, a naturally occurring alloy of silver and gold, and were imprinted with images that served as denominations. Lydia's currency facilitated the enhancement of both its domestic and international commercial systems, establishing it as one of the wealthiest empires in Asia Minor. Today, the phrase "as rich as Croesus" alludes to the final king of Lydia, renowned for issuing the first gold coin.

Transition to Paper Currency

In 1260 CE, the Yuan dynasty of China transitioned from coinage to paper currency. When Marco Polo, a Venetian merchant, explorer, and writer who traversed Asia via the Silk Road, arrived in China about 1271 CE, the Chinese emperor had a comprehensive understanding of the money supply and its diverse denominations. Indeed, in the location where contemporary American currency states, "In God We Trust," the Chinese inscription of that era cautioned: "Those who counterfeit will be beheaded." Certain regions of Europe continued to utilise metal coins exclusively as cash until the 16th century. Colonial acquisitions of regions through European conquest yielded new sources of precious metals, allowing European powers to increase coin production.

However, banks ultimately began issuing paper banknotes for depositors and borrowers to utilise instead of metal coins. These notes could be presented to the bank at any time and redeemed for their nominal value in metal, typically silver or gold coins. This currency can be utilised to procure products and services. It functioned similarly to contemporary cash in the modern world. Nonetheless, it was issued by banks and private entities rather than the government, which currently oversees currency issuance in the majority of nations. The gold standard was instituted in the 1870s. This regulation allowed currency issuance proportional to a nation's gold holdings.

The first paper currency created by European countries was actually issued by their colonial administrations in North America. Due to the prolonged duration of supplies between Europe and the North American colonies, the colonies frequently experienced financial shortages. Rather than reverting to a barter system, the colonial rulers issued IOUs that functioned as cash. The initial occurrence was in Canada, then a French province, in 1685, when soldiers were provided with playing cards, designated and endorsed by the governor, to use as currency in lieu of coins from France.

The Emergence of Currency Wars

The shift to paper money in Europe increased the amount of international trade that could occur. Financial institutions and the elite began acquiring foreign currencies, so establishing the inaugural currency market. The stability of a certain monarchy or government influenced the value of the nation's currency, hence impacting its capacity to engage in an increasingly global currency market. Interstate competition frequently resulted in currency wars, wherein rival nations endeavoured to manipulate the value of each other's currencies—either by inflating it to render the adversary's goods prohibitively expensive, deflating it to diminish the opponent's purchasing power (and capacity to finance a conflict), or by obliterating the currency altogether.

Mobile Payments

The 21st century introduced a new payment method initiated by a fingertip touch. Mobile payments denote the monetary transactions utilised for the acquisition of products and services. They can also facilitate the transfer of funds to another individual, such as a family member or friend. This can be accomplished utilising a portable electronic device, such as a smartphone or tablet. This payment method initially gained prominence in Asia and Europe before transitioning to North America.

The technology has progressed from text message payments to enabling cheque deposits through the camera application on smart smartphones. Mobile payment providers such as Apple Pay are competing for retailers to adopt their platforms for point-of-sale transactions. Applications specifically designed for this payment mechanism include Venmo and PayPal.

Virtual Currency

Virtual currencies exist solely in electronic format. This currency, as a digital representation of money, is kept and exchanged through computer programs or specialised software. The allure of virtual money lies in its potential for reduced transaction fees compared to conventional online payment systems and its operation by decentralised entities, in contrast to government-issued currencies. Bitcoin rapidly established itself as the benchmark for digital currency. It was launched in 2009 by the anonymous entity Satoshi Nakamoto. As of August 7, 2024, the total value of all Bitcoin globally was $1.14 trillion. It is important to note that virtual currencies such as Bitcoin lack real coinage, as they are transacted on exchanges. While Bitcoin continues to be the most prominent and costly cryptocurrency, other digital currencies have emerged in the market. These comprise Ethereum, XRP, and Dogecoin.

What is the Historical Duration of Money's Existence, and What Were its Initial Methods of Value Exchange?

Currency has been integral to human history for a minimum of 5,000 years in various forms. Historians widely concur that a bartering system was probably employed prior to this period. Bartering entails the direct exchange of commodities and services. A farmer might trade a bushel of wheat for a pair of shoes from a shoemaker.

When and Where Did Coin Minting Begin?

The oldest accurately dated coin minting facility in the world is situated at Guanzhuang in China's Henan Province. The mint commenced the production of spade coins in 640 BCE, presumably the inaugural standardised metal currency.

When Were Coins Replaced by Paper Money?

The Chinese transitioned from coinage to paper currency in 1260 CE. When Marco Polo arrived in China about 1271 CE, the emperor possessed a comprehensive understanding of the money supply and its diverse denominations.

1.2.1 Forms Of Money

Situation Before Money

In the early ages, Indians used grains and cattle as money. The system where two parties exchange grains and cattle as money is called the Barter system. The main disadvantage of the barter system is Double coincidence, where both parties have to agree to sell and buy each other's commodities. Thereafter came the use of metallic coins - gold, silver, copper coins. [Refer Fig. 1]

Fig. 1.2: *Mettalic coins*

Money as a Medium of Exchange

Money acts as an intermediate in the exchange process, it is called a medium of exchange. A person holding money can easily exchange it for any commodity or service that he or she might want.

Modern Form of Money

Now, the modern forms of money include currency – paper notes and coins. The modern forms of money – currency and deposits – are closely linked to the workings of the modern banking system. It is authorised by the government of the country.

1. Currency

In India, the Reserve Bank of India issues currency notes on behalf of the central government. No other individual or organisation is allowed to issue currency. The rupee is widely accepted as a medium of exchange in India. [Refer Fig. 1.3]

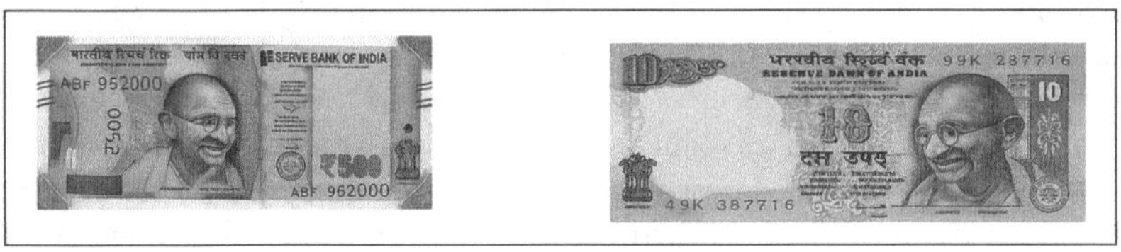

Fig. 1.3: *Modern forms of currency*

2. Deposits in Banks

The other form in which people hold money is as deposits with banks. People deposit their extra cash with the banks by opening a bank account in their name. Banks accept the deposits and also pay an amount as interest on the deposits.

The deposits in the bank accounts can be withdrawn on demand, these deposits are called demand deposits. The payments are made by cheques instead of cash. A cheque is a paper instructing the bank to pay a specific amount from the person's account to the person in whose name the cheque has been issued. [Refer Fig. 1.4]

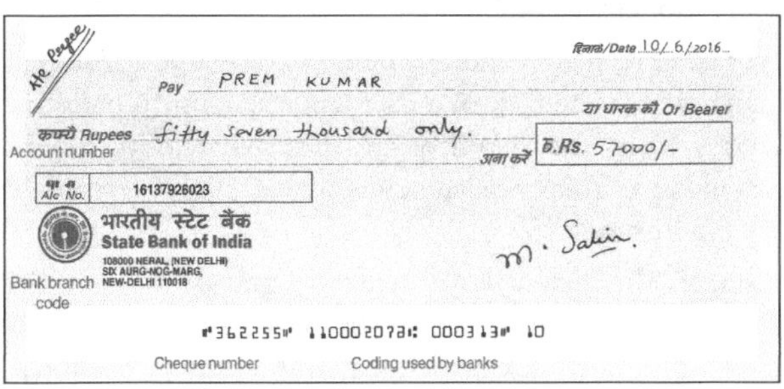

Fig. 1.4: *Cheque*

1.2.2 Fiat Currencies

What is Fiat money?

Fiat money is a type of currency not backed by a physical commodity, such as gold or silver, and is designated as legal tender by the issuing government through a regulatory authority. Its value is determined by supply and demand dynamics and the stability of the governing body that issues it. Contemporary paper currencies, such as the U.S. dollar and the euro, exemplify fiat money. In contrast to commodity money, which is linked to precious metals, and representative money, which signifies a claim on commodities, fiat money depends on the creditworthiness of the issuing government. Various elements, including inflation, governmental policies, and economic conditions, can influence the value of fiat money. It was introduced as an alternative to commodity money, representing a flexible yet government-dependent system where broader economic and political contexts dictate its value.

History of Fiat Money

Fiat money, starting in 10th-century China during the Yuan, Tang, Song, and Ming dynasties, originated as a currency not backed by precious metals. In China, paper drafts evolved as an alternative to metallic currency shortages, eventually becoming the first legal tender. The trend continued in the Yuan Dynasty when paper money became an exclusive legal tender, controlled by the Ministry of Finance in the Ming Dynasty. The West introduced paper money in the 18th century, facing concerns over inflation, notably in American colonies and France. Conflicts necessitated the adoption of fiat currencies, such as the American "greenbacks" during the Civil War. In the early 20th century, promises of convertibility were rescinded post-American Civil War due to economic exigencies. The Bretton Woods Agreement established a connection between gold's value and the U.S. dollar. In 1971, President Richard Nixon terminated direct convertibility, resulting in the extensive use of fiat currencies with interchangeability among principal currencies. This historical track underscores the adaptability of fiat currency to economic, political, and global monetary changes.

Advantages of Fiat Money

1. **Flexibility:** Governments can swiftly adapt to economic fluctuations through the utilisation of fiat currency. In contrast to commodity-backed currencies, which may have logistical difficulties in responding to changing economic conditions, fiat currency offers a versatile instrument for governments to successfully modify and execute monetary policies.
2. **Stability:** Fiat currencies generally demonstrate superior stability relative to asset-backed currencies. The lack of a direct connection to commodity value protects fiat currency from the volatility and unpredictability inherent in commodity market dynamics. This consistency fosters a more dependable and foreseeable monetary environment.
3. **Convenience:** The extensive acceptance and readily available access to fiat currency enhance its convenience. In contrast to asset-backed currencies, fiat currency is generally acknowledged and easily accessible, enabling smooth transactions and minimising possible obstacles associated with dependence on certain commodities.

4. **Control:** Governments exercise increased authority over monetary policy via the utilisation of fiat currency. This mechanism allows governments to regulate inflation rates and strategically promote economic growth. The adaptability provided by fiat currency enables policymakers to enact strategies that correspond with overarching economic goals.
5. **Cost-Efficient:** The production of fiat currency is more cost-effective than that of currencies directly linked to commodities. The lack of necessity to extract, refine, or safeguard particular assets leads to an efficient and cost- effective currency production process. This cost effectiveness enhances the usability and sustainability of fiat currencies.

Disadvantages of Fiat Money

1. **Inflation Risk:** Fiat currency is susceptible to inflation, which can initiate a harmful cycle of debt and inflation. This interaction may generate economic bubbles, presenting difficulties for enduring economic stability. The vulnerability of fiat money to inflation highlights the necessity of strong monetary measures to alleviate these dangers.
2. **Lack of Intrinsic Value:** In contrast to currencies supported by tangible goods, fiat currency possesses no intrinsic worth. The lack of solid assets backing its value leaves fiat currency potentially unstable and vulnerable to volatility. Comprehending this attribute is essential for assessing the stability and resilience of fiat currencies during economic difficulties.
3. **Unsuitability for Long-Term Savings:** The vulnerability of fiat currency to inflation renders it inappropriate for long-term savings. The value of fiat currency may decline over time, diminishing the purchasing power of savings. Individuals pursuing long-term financial stability may need to investigate alternate investing strategies to mitigate the effects of inflation on fiat currency.
4. **Hyperinflation Risk:** Governments possess the capacity to issue enormous quantities of fiat currency, resulting in the grave risk of hyperinflation. This situation might provoke economic volatility, affecting currency value and diminishing consumer and investor confidence. Meticulous supervision and judicious regulations are crucial for alleviating the risk of hyperinflation linked to fiat currencies.
5. **Dependency on Government Policies:** The worth of fiat currency is closely tied to governmental policies and activities, rendering it susceptible to political influences and various external causes. This dependency underscores the necessity for meticulous evaluation of economic policies, accentuating the significance of stable governance and prudent decision-making to sustain the legitimacy and robustness of fiat currencies.

Examples of Fiat Money

1. **U.S. Dollar:** The U.S. dollar functions as a fiat currency, its worth originating from the support of the U.S. government rather than a tangible commodity. This trait illustrates the dependence on the trustworthiness and stability of the U.S. government as a vital element in assessing the value and durability of the U.S. dollar in the global economy.

2. **Euro:** The euro, the fiat currency utilised by nations in the European Union, derives its worth not from a tangible product but from the endorsement of the European Central Bank. The dependence on a centralised monetary authority highlights the interrelation between Eurozone economies and the European Central Bank's function in preserving the stability and integrity of the euro.
3. **Indian Rupee:** The Indian rupee, utilised as a fiat currency in India, is not backed by a tangible commodity and depends on the endorsement of the Reserve Bank of India. The value and stability of the Indian rupee depend on the policies and choices enacted by the Reserve Bank of India, highlighting the central bank's pivotal role in influencing the currency's position within the Indian economy.

Why is Fiat Money Valuable?

1. **Government Backing:** Fiat currency is wholly dependent on the trust and confidence bestowed upon the issuing government. This support constitutes the basis for the currency's worth, fostering broad acceptability among the populace and guaranteeing its efficacy as a means of exchange.
2. **Legal Tender for Tax Payment:** Governments require that taxes be paid with the fiat currency they issue, so ensuring a continuous demand for the currency. This mandate necessitates that individuals and enterprises obtain and employ fiat currency to meet their tax responsibilities, thereby facilitating its ongoing circulation and acceptance.
3. **Chartalism:** Chartalism asserts that individuals voluntarily accept fiat currency due to its essential role in fulfilling tax obligations. The obligation to fulfil tax commitments, reinforced by possible penalties or legal repercussions, compels the widespread acceptance of fiat currency. This fundamental principle of capitalism highlights the essential function of tax liabilities in influencing the flow and acceptance of fiat currency.
4. **Credit Theory:** The credit theory contests the idea that money requires backing by a physical asset to preserve its value. This perspective posits that the core of money resides in its role as a credit-debt relationship, making the support of a physical object less significant in establishing its worth. This idea underscores the intrinsic credit-based characteristic of fiat currency.
5. **Government Control:** Governments utilise fiat currency as a means to promote economic stability, offering a framework to manage economic fluctuations. The value of fiat currency is closely connected to a nation's economic performance, governance practices, and their influence on interest rates.

   This interconnectedness enables governments to regulate economic swings, so enhancing general stability.
6. **Universal Acceptance:** The widespread acceptance of fiat currency, along with its comparatively steady value, enhances the control exerted by banks and lending institutions. The establishment of interest rates, supply, and liquidity is facilitated as the value of fiat currency is mostly affected by overarching economic variables. This widespread acceptance optimises financial processes and enhances the currency's function as a dependable means of exchange.

Why do Modern Economies Favor Fiat Money?

1. **Flexibility and Control:** Fiat currency grants governments exceptional latitude in regulating their monetary systems, formulating economic policies, and stabilising international markets. This financial system also supports fractional reserve banking, allowing commercial banks to increase their available funds to satisfy borrower demands, hence enhancing the economic influence of fiat currency.
2. **Economic Growth and Stability:** The fluid characteristics of fiat currency enable governments to adeptly address economic fluctuations, like boom phases, recessions, or demographic transformations. By judiciously managing the money supply, governments can affect essential economic factors such as loan accessibility, liquidity, and interest rates, promoting stability and conditions conducive to enduring economic growth.
3. **Global Acceptance and Trade:** Fiat currency has emerged as the predominant legal tender in almost all nations, guaranteeing widespread acceptance and a comparatively steady value. This prevalent acceptance facilitates the regulation imposed by banks and lending institutions on interest rates, supply, and liquidity.
4. **Government Backing and Confidence:** The basis of fiat currency is the steadfast trust and confidence in the issuing government. This backing not only enhances the currency's value but also ensures its broad adoption. The stability of fiat currency is closely associated with the stability of the issuing nation. In the modern financial environment, nearly all nations have embraced fiat currency as their recognised and sanctioned legal tender, highlighting the essential role of governmental support in sustaining the currency's value and legitimacy.

What are Some Alternatives to Fiat Money?

1. **Commodity Money:** Commodity money is a real currency made from a tangible commodity such as gold or silver, with its value stemming directly from the intrinsic worth of the substance. Commodity money, which has inherent worth, functions as a medium of exchange, with its recognised value in transactions dictated by the material from which it is made.
2. **Representative Money:** Representative money serves as a substitute that signifies a claim on a physical product, redeemable upon request. This occurs when a currency is supported by a tangible commodity, such as gold, and can be redeemed for the equivalent commodity. The worth of representative money is fundamentally linked to the guarantee of convertibility.
3. **Cryptocurrencies:** Cryptocurrencies, which include digital or virtual currencies, utilise cryptographic methods for security and function independently of central bank regulation. Bitcoin, Ethereum, and Ripple serve as prime examples of decentralised digital currency. The valuation of cryptocurrencies is governed by the fundamental economic laws of supply and demand, providing a dynamic and decentralised aspect to currency.
4. **Barter System:** The barter system involves the direct exchange of products and services without the use of currency. In this system, transactions are conducted via the mutual exchange of goods, preceding the use of cash. The barter system, although less common in contemporary countries, continues to exist in specific situations, demonstrating a direct trade method that eliminates the necessity for traditional cash.

1.2.3 Currency Pages

What Is Quantitative Easing?

Quantitative easing (QE) is a form of monetary policy in which a central bank, like the U.S. Federal Reserve, purchases securities in the open market to reduce interest rates and increase the money supply. Quantitative easing creates new bank reserves, providing banks with more liquidity and encouraging lending and investment. In the United States, the Federal Reserve implements QE policies.

Understanding Quantitative Easing

Quantitative easing is frequently employed when interest rates are close to zero and economic growth is stagnant. Central banks possess constrained instruments, such as interest rate decrease, to affect economic growth. In the absence of the capacity to further reduce rates, central banks must tactically augment the money supply. Central banks implement quantitative easing by purchasing government bonds and other securities, thereby infusing bank reserves into the economy. Augmenting the money supply enhances liquidity inside the banking sector and further reduces interest rates. This enables banks to extend loans under more favourable conditions. A government's fiscal policy may be executed simultaneously to augment the money supply. The Federal Reserve can affect the money supply in the economy, but the U.S. Treasury Department has the authority to generate new currency and establish tax policies through fiscal policy. This injects capital, either directly or indirectly, into the economy. Quantitative easing may encompass a blend of monetary and fiscal policy.

Does Quantitative Easing Work?

Many economists contend that the Federal Reserve's quantitative easing program aided in salvaging the U.S. and worldwide economies after the 2007– 2008 financial crisis; yet, the outcomes of QE remain challenging to measure. Worldwide, central banks have sought to implement quantitative easing to avert recession and deflation in their nations, yielding similarly ambiguous outcomes. Although quantitative easing (QE) policy effectively reduces interest rates and stimulates the stock market, its overall effect on the economy remains unclear. Quantitative easing typically advantages borrowers over savers and investors over non-investors, presenting both advantages and disadvantages, as noted by Stephen Williamson, a former economist at the Federal Reserve Bank of St. Louis.

Risks of Quantitative Easing Inflation

The introduction of additional currency into an economy heightens the danger of inflation. As liquidity circulates through the system, central banks maintain vigilance, given that the delay between the augmentation of the money supply and the inflation rate typically spans 12 to 18 months. A quantitative easing policy that fails to stimulate the anticipated economic growth while inducing inflation may result in stagflation, characterised by elevated inflation and unemployment rates.

Limited Lending

Despite a rise in liquidity for banks, a central bank such as the Fed cannot compel banks to augment lending activity, nor can it mandate individuals and businesses to borrow and invest. This results in a credit crunch, when liquidity is retained by banks or firms accumulate cash due to an unpredictable economic environment.

Devalued Currency

Quantitative easing can lead to the depreciation of the native currency due to an increase in the money supply. A devalued currency benefits domestic producers by making their exports cheaper in the global market; yet, it also raises the cost of imports, hence escalating production costs and consumer price levels.

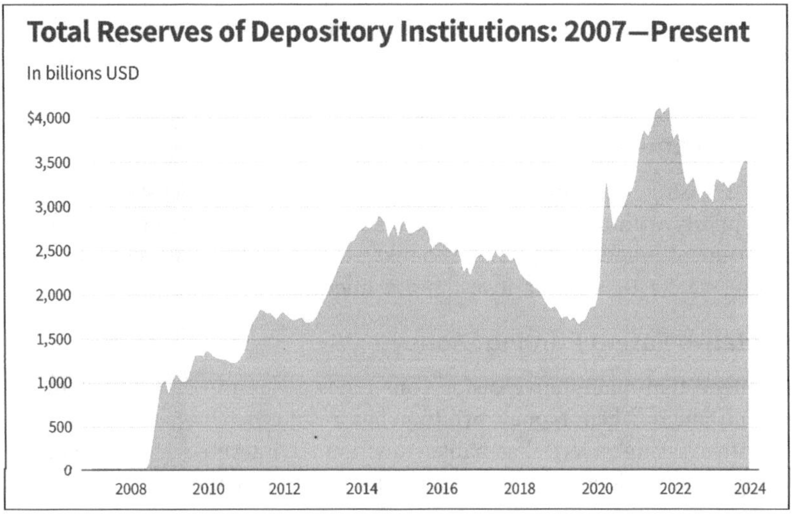

Fig. 1.5

In response to the Great Recession, the U.S. Federal Reserve implemented a quantitative easing program from 2009 to 2014. The Federal Reserve's balance sheet expanded due to the acquisition of bonds, mortgages, and various other assets. By 2017, U.S. bank reserves exceeded $4 trillion, facilitating the lending of such reserves and promoting general economic expansion. Nonetheless, banks retained $2.8 trillion in surplus reserves, an unforeseen consequence of the Federal Reserve's quantitative easing policy. In 2020, the Federal Reserve declared its intention to acquire $700 billion in assets as an emergency quantitative easing action in response to the economic and market disruption caused by the COVID-19 shutdown. In 2022, the Federal Reserve substantially altered its monetary policy by implementing considerable interest rate increases and reducing its asset holdings to counteract the ongoing trend of elevated inflation that began in 2021. Federal Reserve System Board of Governors. "The Federal Reserve's Reactions to the Post-COVID Era of Elevated Inflation."

Europe and Asia

Subsequent to the Asian Financial Crisis of 1997, Japan entered an economic recession. The Bank of Japan initiated an assertive quantitative easing campaign to combat deflation and invigorate the economy, transitioning from the acquisition of Japanese government bonds to the procurement of private debt and equities. The impact of the quantitative easing initiative proved ephemeral, as Japan's gross domestic product (GDP) increased from $4.1 trillion in 1998 to $6.27 trillion in 2012, but subsequently declined to $4.44 trillion by 2015. The Swiss National Bank (SNB) implemented a quantitative easing approach after the 2008 financial crisis, resulting in asset ownership surpassing the nation's yearly economic production. While economic growth was stimulated, the extent to which the ensuing recovery can be ascribed to the SNB's quantitative easing program remains ambiguous.

In August 2016, the Bank of England (BoE) initiated a quantitative easing program to mitigate the anticipated economic consequences of Brexit. The strategy involved purchasing £60 billion in government bonds and £10 billion in corporate debt to prevent interest rates from increasing and to promote business expansion and employment. As of June 2018, the Office for National Statistics in the United Kingdom indicated that gross fixed capital formation was increasing at a compound average quarterly rate of 0.2% over the preceding decade, although excluding the economic downturn, the rate was 0.8%, in contrast to 0.6% for the decade prior to the slump. U.K. economists could not ascertain whether growth would have occurred in the absence of this quantitative easing policy.

How Does Quantitative Easing Work?

Quantitative easing is a monetary policy employed by a nation's central bank to enhance liquidity within its financial system, primarily through the acquisition of long-term government bonds from major banks, thereby fostering economic growth by incentivising banks to lend or invest more liberally.

Is Quantitative Easing Printing Money?

Critics contend that quantitative easing constitutes a variant of money printing and cite historical instances when money printing has resulted in hyperinflation. Proponents of quantitative easing assert that banks function as intermediaries instead of directly distributing cash to individuals and companies, so mitigating the risk of excessive inflation.

How Does Quantitative Easing Increase Bank Lending?

Quantitative Easing substitutes bonds in the banking system with cash, hence augmenting the money supply and facilitating banks in liberating capital. Consequently, they are able to underwrite additional loans and acquire other assets.

1.3 INTERBANK PAYMENT MODE

How do Banks Pay each Other?

In most countries, when banks want to transfer money to each other, perhaps upon instruction from a customer, they don't put bundles of banknotes in vans, they pay each other digitally. How does this work? This topic is intended as a primer about payment systems and explains correspondent banking, nostros, real time gross settlement (RTGS) systems and deferred net settlement (DNS) systems. It supports other posts where I discuss decentralisation of these systems using distributed ledgers.

1.3.1 Same Bank or Intra Bank Transfer (Third Party Transfer)

Intra Bank transfers, commonly known as Third Party Transfers, involve sending funds within the same bank. For example, if you aim to transfer Rs 1 Lakh to Mr. B, who also holds an account with SBI, this transaction falls under the category of Intra Bank transfer.

Requirements

Unlike Inter Bank transfers, Intra Bank transfers do not require an IFSC code. The process is simplified, necessitating only the account number and the payee's name for successful transactions within the same bank.

Comparison

1. Amount Limits

- **Inter Bank Transfer:** RTGS requires a minimum transfer of Rs 2 Lakh, while NEFT has no such minimum requirement. Intra Bank Transfer: No minimum transfer amount is mandated.

2. Working Hours

- **Inter Bank Transfer:** NEFT and RTGS operate during SBI's working hours. IMPS provides flexibility with 24/7 transaction processing.
- **Intra Bank Transfer:** Transactions within the same bank, whether online or offline, are often more flexible in terms of processing times.

3. Requirements

- **Inter Bank Transfer:** Requires recipient's account number and IFSC code for accurate transactions.
- **Intra Bank Transfer:** Simplified process with only the account number and payee's name needed, eliminating the need for an IFSC code.

Advantages and Risks Related to Intra Bank and Inter Bank Transfers

Advantages

1. InterBank Transfer

- **Reduced Delays:** InterBank transfers ensure quicker availability of funds to beneficiaries.
- **Quick Clearing Cycles:** Expedited clearing processes with a maximum of three days for completion.
- **CostEffective:** No additional costs or taxes are imposed on customers.
- **Reduced Paper Movement:** Minimizes physical movement of paper cheques, offering potential efficiency in the settlement process.

2. IntraBank Transfer

- **Simplified Process:** Transactions within the same bank are often more straightforward.
- **No IFSC Code Needed:** Eliminates the requirement for an IFSC code, streamlining the transfer process.
- **Flexible Processing Times:** Transactions within the same bank may offer more flexibility in processing times.

Risks

1. InterBank Transfer

- **Operational Risks:** The clearinghouse must trust that the data provided by the local bank branch is accurate for the day's clearing.
- **Verification Challenges:** The drawee must verify the image of the signature, presenting potential challenges.

2. IntraBank Transfer

- **Internal Risks:** IntraBank transfers may still involve operational risks that banks need to address adequately.

1.3.2 Different Bank or Inter Bank Transfer

Inter-Bank transfers involve the movement of funds between accounts held in different banks. For instance, if you possess an account with State Bank of India and wish to transfer Rs 1 Lakh to Mr. A, who holds an account with Axis Bank, this transaction is classified as an Inter-Bank transfer.

Methods

1. **NEFT (National Electronic Funds Transfer):** This method facilitates the transfer of funds between banks and operates during SBI's working hours.
   It provides a secure and efficient way to transfer money to accounts in other banks.
2. **IMPS (Immediate Payment Service):** IMPS allows for instant transfers, offering flexibility as it operates 24/7.
   This method is particularly convenient for transactions that need to be processed at any time, irrespective of banking hours.
3. **RTGS (Real-Time Gross Settlement):** RTGS is suitable for larger transactions, with a minimum amount requirement of Rs 2 Lakh. Similar to NEFT, it operates during SBI's working hours, ensuring real-time settlement of funds.

Amount Limits

- **RTGS:** Requires a minimum transfer amount of Rs 2 Lakh.
- **NEFT:** No minimum transfer amount is mandated.

Working Hours

- **NEFT and RTGS:** Operate during SBI's working hours.
- **IMPS:** Allows for transactions round the clock.

Requirements

To execute an Inter Bank Transfer successfully, you need the recipient's account number and IFSC code. These details ensure accurate and secure transactions between different banking entities.

Interbank Payments: The problem

Annie who banks at Bank A wants to transfer $10 to Clarabel who banks at Bank C.

What do the customers see? We see that Annie's account goes down by $10, and Clarabel's account goes up by $10.

- **The problem.** But if that's all that happened, can you see the problem from the banks' perspective? Remember that your "account balance" with a bank is how much the bank owes you – it's how much you can attempt to withdraw from a cash machine. The more you have in your account, the more the bank owes you.

So, after this transfer:

- Bank A now owes Annie less money! It's really happy ☺
- Bank C is not happy at all – it now owes $10 more to Clarabel ☹

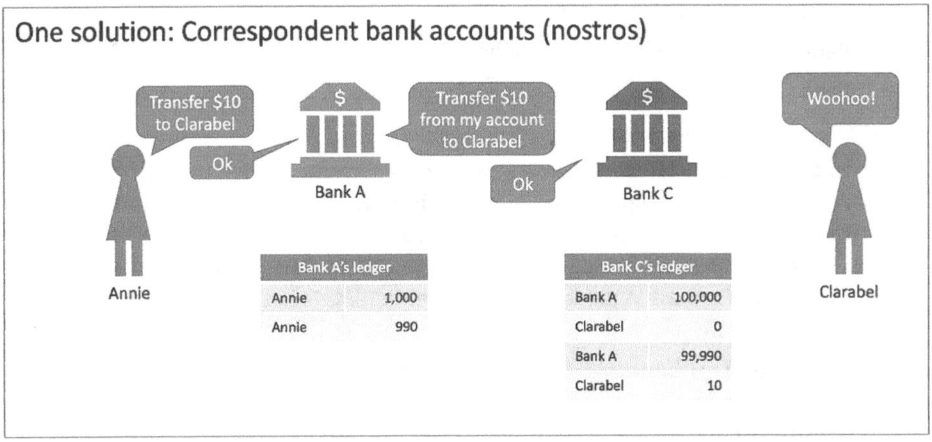

Fig. 1.6

Essentially Bank A is better off and Bank C is worse off. So this payment instruction must be balanced by a bank to bank transfer: Bank A needs to pay Bank C $10 to balance out the customer account movements.

- **Settling up:** So how do banks pay each other? Banks don't tend to put banknotes in vans and dispatch them to other banks. How does it work digitally? There are two main ways:
  - Correspondent bank accounts
  - Central bank payment systems

1.3.3 Correspondent Bank

If Bank A opened an account with Bank C, it could instruct Bank C to transfer the $10 from its account to Clarabel's account:

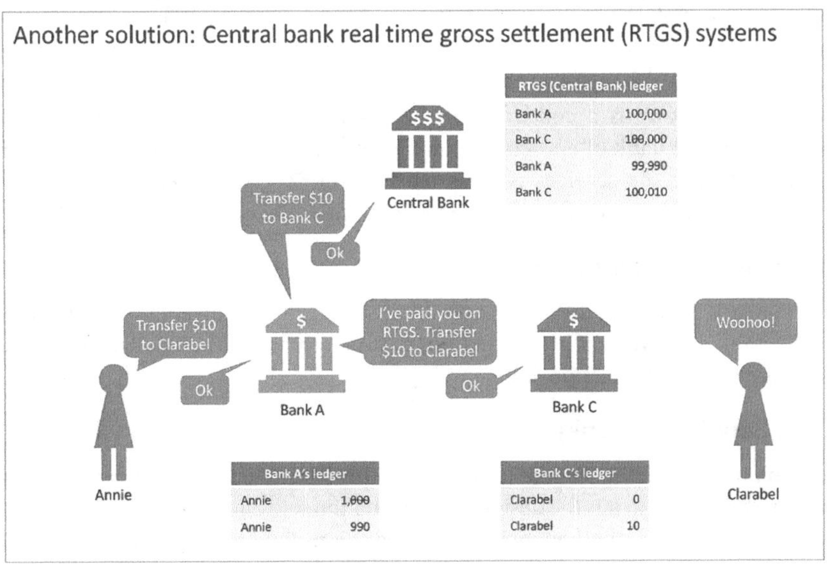

Fig. 1.7

In this way, neither bank is better or worse off:

- Bank A owes Annie $10 less ☺ but has $10 less in its account with Bank C ☹
- Bank C owes Clarabel $10 more ☹ but owes Bank A $10 less ☺

So that's all neatly squared off.

- **Initial funding:** How might Bank A fund its account at Bank C in the first place? Perhaps the banks opened accounts with each other at the same time, funded with the same amounts: Bank A opens an account at Bank C, and Bank C opens an account at Bank A, and they both agree "Let's start off by owing each other $100,000.". Or Bank A could sell an asset to Bank C "Here's a bond, please pay me by crediting my account".
- **Correspondent banking:** This is called correspondent banking – Bank A calls Bank C its correspondent bank, and calls its account there it's "nostro" account. (Nostro is Latin for "our", so using the word nostro is basically a pretentious way of saying "our account". If you felt like it, you could refer to your bank accounts as your nostros, but you would lose your friends.)
- **Pain point:** However, if you were a bank, maintaining accounts at every single other bank that your customers might want to transfer money to would be quite a pain, and expensive (they have to have money sitting there doing nothing, in anticipation of payment instructions, and as we all know, current accounts pay very low interest). And risky! What if the other bank went bankrupt? You'd lose your money.
- **There is another way:** The Difference Between Correspondent, Intermediary and Beneficiary Banks Regardless of whether you are a corporation with worldwide connections or an individual requiring insight into global transactions, comprehending the functions of Correspondent, Intermediary, and Beneficiary Banks is essential. These three entities are crucial to international commerce. Understanding their distinct functions and the underlying processes of foreign payments will enhance your ability to make smart financial decisions.

What is Correspondent Banking?

Correspondent banking is a collaboration between two banks, typically from separate nations, wherein one bank offers services on behalf of the other. In this configuration, the institution providing the services is designated as the "correspondent bank," whilst the institution receiving them is referred to as the "respondent bank."

What is an Intermediary Bank?

An intermediary bank functions as a conduit between the originator bank and the beneficiary bank. It serves a crucial function, particularly when the two banks engaged in transactions lack a direct relationship.

What is a Beneficiary Bank?

A beneficiary bank is a financial institution where the designated recipient of a cash transfer maintains a bank account. It is the designated destination for funds in financial transactions. In banking terminology, the beneficiary denotes the individual or entity that ultimately receives the payments.

Distinction between Correspondent and Intermediary Banks

In the complex domain of international banking, correspondent banks and intermediate banks are essential, particularly in facilitating cross-border payments. Correspondent banks generally act as representatives for other financial institutions, particularly when those institutions lack a presence in a particular region. Their principal function is to facilitate foreign monetary transfers, managing funds and immediately executing transactions on behalf of the financial institutions they represent. A bank in the US may utilise its correspondent banking relationship with a UK bank to enable USD- denominated payments between the two countries. Conversely, intermediary banks function as a third party, serving as a conduit when the source and beneficiary banks lack a direct connection. Functioning as intermediaries in the financial network, they guarantee the secure transfer of funds to their designated destination, even when many intermediaries are required due to a lack of direct banking connections.

A tiny regional bank may require support from larger institutions to facilitate an overseas transfer. Essentially, although both entities facilitate the seamless execution of a cross-border transaction, their functions differ at the operational level. The correspondent bank directly provides its services in areas lacking the presence of its partner banks. Simultaneously, the intermediary bank facilitates indirect pathways, guaranteeing that transactions proceed uninterrupted despite the absence of direct bank-to-bank connections. A transaction involving an intermediary bank indicates the presence of three or more players in the chain.

What are Nostro and Vostro Accounts?

Nostro and vostro are banking terminologies that denote distinct account types maintained between banks, primarily for foreign transactions. An nostro account is a bank account maintained in a foreign country, denominated in that country's currency; it essentially represents "our account with you." A US bank may possess a nostro account in the UK denominated in pounds sterling. A vostro account is, conversely, defined as "your account with us." In this instance, the UK bank would classify the account as a vostro account, indicating it is maintained by the US bank in the UK. These accounts enable seamless international transactions and settlements.

What are the Advantages and Disadvantages of Correspondent Banking?

Correspondent banking relationships denote an arrangement between two financial organisations in which one executes services on behalf of the other. This is frequently employed to enable international financial transactions, wherein local banks forge connections with foreign banks to offer services in those nations. Below is an analysis of the benefits and drawbacks of correspondent banking relationships:

Advantages

Access to Foreign Markets

Correspondent banking offers local banks access to international financial markets and currency exchange without necessitating the establishment of abroad branches.

Cost Efficiency

Establishing and sustaining a physical presence for a bank in a foreign nation can be expensive. By establishing correspondent relationships, banks can provide services to clients in overseas marketplaces while avoiding substantial expenditures.

Risk Management

Participating in direct international operations entails significant risks. Correspondent banking enables domestic banks to transfer foreign currency and offer international services while transferring a significant portion of the operational risks to the correspondent bank.

Expedited Transactions

Correspondent banks frequently facilitate transactions between financial institutions, so diminishing the duration clients must await overseas payments or transactions.

Local Expertise

The correspondent bank in the other nation generally possesses greater expertise regarding local legislation, market conditions, and customs. This information can be crucial for national banks and their clientele.

Disadvantages

Dependence

Operational, financial, or legal issues faced by a correspondent bank might adversely affect the financial services provided by domestic banks, financial institutions, or payment service providers to their consumers, perhaps resulting in the closure of customer accounts.

Diluted Customer Relationship

The direct relationship between a beneficiary bank and a correspondent bank may become weakened. For example, if a transaction encounters an issue, the domestic bank may need to coordinate with the correspondent bank, introducing additional communication levels and possible delays.

Operational Risks

Although certain risks are assigned to the correspondent bank, novel operational hazards arise. These may arise from possible errors, fraudulent activities, or inefficiencies attributable to the correspondent bank.

Compliance and Regulatory Challenges

Correspondent banking may provide compliance problems, particularly in relation to anti-money laundering (AML) and combatting the financing of terrorism (CFT). Global regulators are increasingly concentrating on these domains, potentially imposing additional compliance obligations on banks worldwide.

Limited Control

Domestic banks may possess restricted oversight of the correspondent bank's operations, potentially resulting in inconsistencies in service quality and client experience.

Reduction in Correspondent Relationships

In response to heightened regulatory scrutiny and the related expenses, banks worldwide have persistently diminished their correspondent banking links, a behaviour termed "de-risking." This may restrict the alternatives accessible to banks seeking to form new partnerships.

1.3.4 Central Bank

- **One bank to bank them all.** So there is a more efficient way. If all banks held a bank account with a super bank, they wouldn't need to hold accounts with each other any more, they would just need to maintain that account at the super bank, and instruct the super bank to make payments from it, to any of the other banks with an account there.

Central Banks

This is one of the roles of a central bank, and we call this system a settlement system – perhaps a Real Time Gross Settlement (RTGS) system if the -10/+10 adjustments were made during the day, or a Deferred Net Settlement (DNS) system if payments were queued up for a period of time and then net adjustments were made, perhaps every hour, or at the end of every day.

How Does Annie Pay Clarabel if Both Banks are on a RTGS?

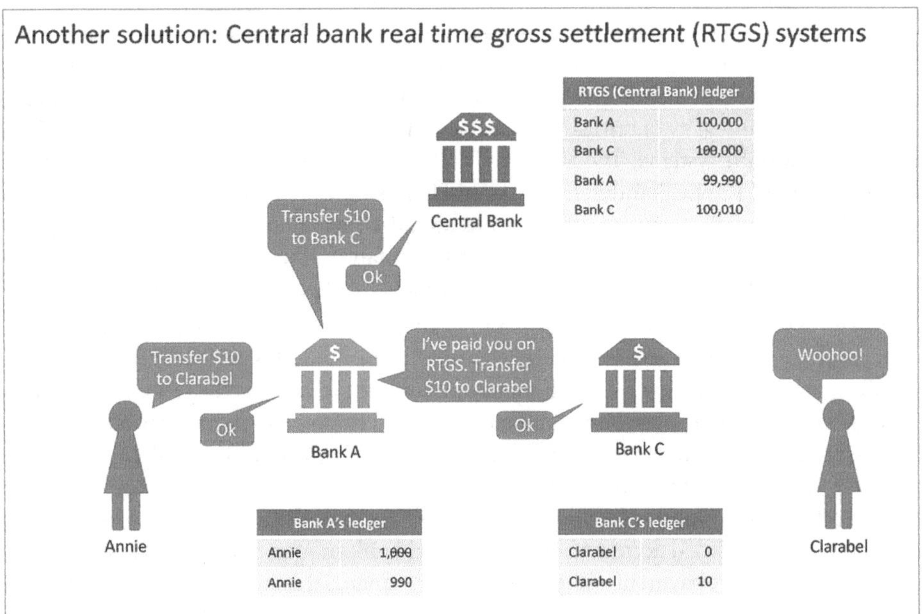

Fig. 1.8

Clearing

So the final settlement where the banks pay each other and everyone is happy, is done at the central bank. You'd say that the central bank clears the transaction because there is no further action needed. (NB Just to confuse everyone, the word clearing in payments means something different to the word clearing in securities trading).

- If both customers bank with the same bank, then that bank clears the transaction.

- If there is a correspondent banking relationship, then the receiving bank clears the transaction.
- If there is a central bank system – a RTGS or DNS, then the central bank clears the transaction.
- Basically, whoever does the -10/+10 adjustment to their ledger is the clearer.

The accounts that each bank holds with the central bank for this purpose is sometimes called their clearing account. (In reality banks hold multiple accounts at the central bank, for different purposes). This is much more efficient than maintaining lots of nostros.

However, it only works within one country and in one currency. So most advanced countries will have a centrally cleared RTGS or DNS system for clearing interbank payments within that country for the domestic currency. Banks who participate in the RTGS and have accounts with the central bank are known as "clearing banks" for that currency and they have a higher status than non-clearing banks – because the non-clearing banks need to use clearing banks to participate in the RTGS/DNS. Financial institutions possess many avenues for settling their payment commitments. Private sector and central bank- operated payment systems frequently compete to secure payment business from banks. Central bank policies significantly influence the competitive payment environment. The emergence of new technologies, such as distributed ledger technology, will further strengthen this function. Central banks fulfil four critical functions in payment systems.

Initially, as operators, they each possess and manage the payment system utilised to execute the monetary policy of their respective jurisdiction or currency region, known as Real-Time Gross Settlement (RTGS) systems. Secondly, as regulators, they aim to guarantee the security and integrity of critical payment systems, including their own Real-Time Gross Settlement (RTGS) systems. The Statute of the European Central Bank (ECB) exemplifies these two roles: "The ECB and national central banks may offer facilities, and the ECB may establish regulations, to ensure efficient and sound clearing and payment systems within the Community and with other nations." Third, as catalysts, they promote innovation in the payments sector, encompassing payment instruments and payment systems.

Central banks may possess a comparative advantage in several domains; nevertheless, none of these functions are inherently required to be undertaken by central banks. The RTGS system may be owned and managed by the private sector, as exemplified by Switzerland. Oversight may be conducted by an alternative governmental body, such as the Payment Systems Regulator (PSR) in the United Kingdom. The catalytic function is similarly applicable. The fourth function of central banks, however, cannot be fulfilled by any other institution or group. Central banks furnish the settlement asset as central bank money to qualified account holders. Central bank money represents the most secure settlement asset for payment systems and other financial market infrastructures (refer to CPSS, 2003). The selection of settlement assets in a payment or settlement system, especially one managing substantial values or interbank transactions, is critical due to the potential exposures between the settlement institution and system participants, as well as the essential operational function of the settlement institution within the system.

Consequently, it is unsurprising that, from a financial stability standpoint, proficient regulators favour the use of central bank money as the settlement asset in Financial Market Infrastructures (FMIs). Principle 9 of the CPMI- IOSCO Principles for FMIs asserts that "An FMI should execute its money settlements in central bank money when feasible and accessible." If central bank money is not utilised, a financial market infrastructure (FMI) must minimise and rigorously manage the credit and liquidity risks associated with the use of commercial bank money. The dual functions of central banks as both operators and regulators of payment networks may provide potential challenges. The central bank supervises its own payment system (the RTGS system) and also monitors private sector payment systems that may compete with it.

Such possible conflicts of interest seem to be exclusive to payment systems. In banking supervision, such tensions are absent because supervisors do not compete with banks in delivering financial services to households and enterprises. Central banks recognise the necessity of preventing any conflicts of interest through robust internal governance and rules. In larger economies, payment systems in the commercial and governmental sectors frequently coexist. The regulatory requirements specifically mandate the provision of a level playing field for all systems, known as the "equal treatment" principle.

An illustration of this type of co-existence inside the euro area is Target2 (owned by central banks) and Euro1 (owned by the private sector). In the United States, there exist two primary large-value payment systems: Fedwire, which is held by the central bank, and CHIPS, which is owned by the private sector. The primary distinction between public sector and private sector systems is generally the broader array of participating financial institutions in publicly operated RTGS systems compared to Euro1 and CHIPS. Private sector systems have arisen primarily due to the efficiency improvements in settlement systems for financial institutions with substantial bilateral settlement responsibilities. However, they also enhance operational resilience for participating financial institutions and mitigate overall systemic risk by functioning as alternatives to RTGS systems and vice versa.

Recently, we have observed the introduction of novel private sector systems propelled by market demand for "instant" payment solutions, such as RT1 in the eurozone and RTP in the United States. Additionally, other private sector initiatives are seeking account access from prominent central banks. Central banks recognise the value of competition among financial market infrastructures as part of their function as catalysts. Competition can serve as a crucial element for enhancing efficiency. Effective competition, coupled with significant choices among FMIs, may contribute to the efficiency of FMIs" (CPMI-IOSCO PFMI Principle 21).

In evaluating applications of innovative large-value payment systems, central banks should maintain their established criteria, prioritising financial stability along with competitive and technological neutrality. We contend that it is essential to scrutinise any assumption that new payment technologies may result in less efficient settlement processes owing to heightened liquidity fragmentation. Liquidity fragmentation occurs when liquidity is "trapped" in multiple locations, hindering its swift and constant transfer from one site to another. This may result in excessively high and expensive liquidity holdings for financial institutions. In contemporary, interconnected large-value payment systems such as those of FnGP, which function on a 24/7, real-time basis, this is no longer applicable. Capital, including foreign money, can transfer instantaneously and virtually without impediment among individuals situated in several jurisdictions. In FnGP, where settlement balances are pre-funded via central bank accounts, transfers to and from the RTGS system can occur in real- time within the operational hours of the corresponding RTGS system. The implementation of FnGP can eliminate liquidity fragmentation rather than exacerbate it.

Furthermore, consumer selection ought to be entrusted to the customers themselves. Financial institutions are optimally positioned to determine which payment methods are most appropriate for their requirements. They recognise that any liquidity retained for settlement purposes incurs significant costs. Thus, they are incentivised to allocate it efficiently across the many forms of settlement arrangements. Internationally engaged institutions assess the costs of settlement balances comprehensively. This encompasses not only the expenses associated with their account balances at the central bank but also the costs (and hazards) of maintaining deposits with correspondent banks and other settlement entities.

1.3.5 International Payments

International currency accounts. In fact, correspondent banking is how banks can give customers accounts in non-domestic currencies where they don't have a banking licence. For example, a Singapore bank may not have a banking licence in the UK, and so it will maintain a GBP denominated nostro with a big bank in the UK, and it would use that as a mega-account for all its customers' GBP currency. A Singapore bank customer might log in to her account and see that she has £200, but the £200 is actually sitting in a UK bank account under the name of the Singapore bank, mixed up with all the other Singapore Bank customers' GBP.

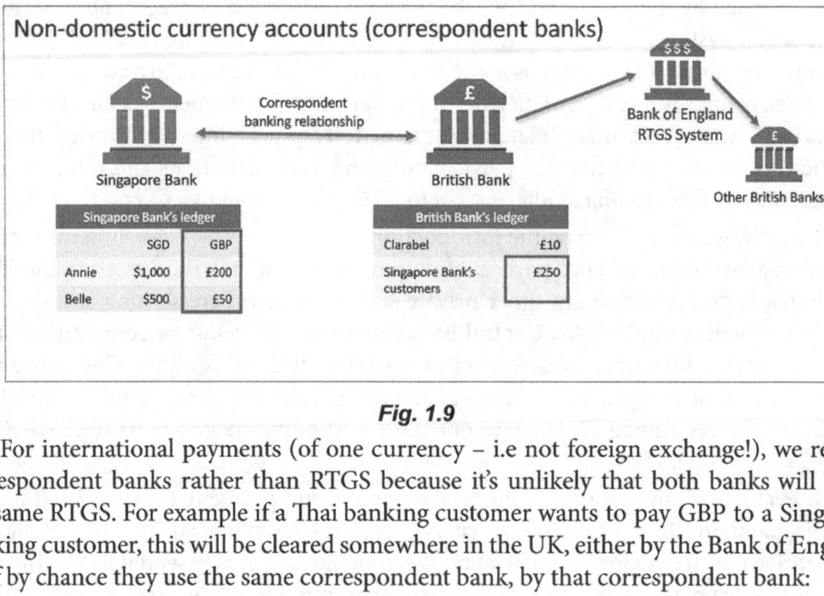

Fig. 1.9

For international payments (of one currency – i.e not foreign exchange!), we rely on correspondent banks rather than RTGS because it's unlikely that both banks will be on the same RTGS. For example if a Thai banking customer wants to pay GBP to a Singapore banking customer, this will be cleared somewhere in the UK, either by the Bank of England, or, if by chance they use the same correspondent bank, by that correspondent bank:

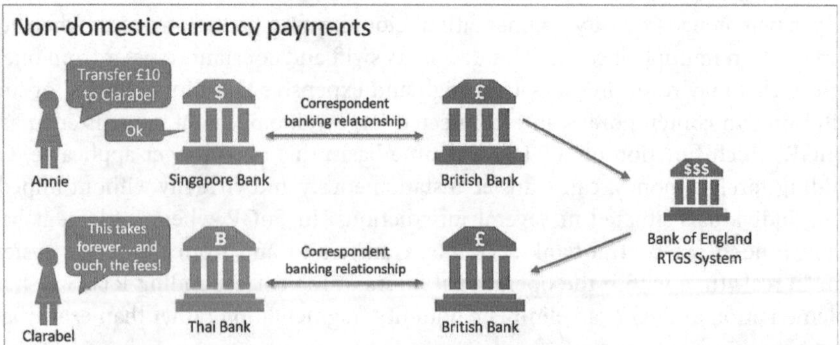

Fig. 1.10

And that's the happy scenario! Sometimes smaller banks or banks in poorer countries might not be able to establish banking relationships with big foreign banks, as I have written about. Then the small banks need to open accounts with larger local banks and use their facilities... So payments take longer and fees accumulate.

Best International Payment Methods

Without further ado, here are our top 6 picks for the best international payments on the market.

For each option, we'll give you a detailed description, including:

- what they are
- how customers use them
- how vendors accept them
- the average cost for vendors and/or customers
- pros and cons

International Transfer Providers

International transfer providers are companies that specialize in transferring money between different countries. They offer lower fees and better exchange rates than traditional banks. This makes them an attractive option for international payments.

How Customers Use Them

Customers can use these providers by signing up for an account online. They can also do so through their mobile app. They can then start transfers from their bank accounts to the recipient's bank account in another country.

How Vendors Accept Them

Vendors must also have an account with the transfer provider to receive payments. The funds will be transferred to their local bank account in their currency of choice.

Average Cost

International transfer providers often are a subscription-based service. They also need a transfer fee for each transaction.

For example, a transfer of 1,000 USD with a currency exchange to Euros could cost $0-$6.82 in extra charges. But it's important to note that up to almost 39 EUR is lost in transition. Wise is one of the best options for retaining funds and they charge a one time fee. The payer is the one who pays for this service most often.

Pros

- Lower fees compared to traditional banks
- Faster transfer times
- Better exchange rates than banks

Cons

- Some providers may have limits on amount that can transferred at once
- Not all countries and currencies are supported

1.4 CRYPTOGRAPHY

Cryptography is a method of safeguarding information and communications by employing codes, ensuring that only intended recipients can comprehend and utilise the data. Consequently, inhibiting unauthorised access to information. The prefix "crypt" signifies "hidden," while the suffix "graphy" denotes "writing."

In cryptography, approaches employed to safeguard information derive from mathematical principles and a series of rule-based computations known as algorithms, which transform signals to render them difficult to decipher. These algorithms facilitate cryptographic key generation, digital signing, and verification to safeguard data privacy, secure internet browsing, and protect secret transactions, including credit and debit card transactions.

Features of Cryptography

- **Confidentiality:** Information is accessible solely to the designated individual, with no other person permitted access.
- **Integrity:** Information must remain unaltered during storage or transmission between the sender and the intended recipient, with any modifications being detectable.
- **Non-repudiation:** The originator of information cannot later deny their intention to transmit that information.
- **Authentication:** The identities of both the sender and receiver are verified. The destination and origin of the information have been verified. Interoperability: Cryptography facilitates secure communication among diverse systems and platforms.
- **Adaptability:** Cryptography perpetually evolves to outpace security threats and technical progress.

Applications of Cryptography

- **Computer passwords:** For the purpose of ensuring the safety of computers, cryptography is utilised extensively, particularly in the process of generating and storing passwords. Upon user login, the password is hashed and compared to the previously stored hash. Passwords are subjected to hashing and encryption before to storage. This approach encrypts passwords, rendering them unreadable even if a hacker accesses the password database.
- **Digital Currencies:** Digital currencies such as Bitcoin employ encryption to safeguard transactions and minimise fraud. Intricate algorithms and cryptographic keys are employed to protect transactions, rendering it exceedingly difficult to manipulate or counterfeit them.
- **Secure web browsing:** The security of online browsing is ensured using encryption, which protects users from eavesdropping and man-in-the-middle attacks. Public key cryptography is employed by the Secure Sockets Layer (SSL) and Transport Layer Security (TLS) protocols to encrypt data transmitted between the web server and the client, thereby creating a secure communication channel.

- **Electronic Signatures:** Electronic signatures function as the digital counterpart to handwritten signatures and are utilised for document execution. Digital signatures are generated by cryptography and can be authenticated via public key cryptography. In numerous countries, electronic signatures are legally binding, and their adoption is rapidly increasing.
- **Authentication:** Cryptography is employed for authentication in various contexts, like accessing bank accounts, logging into computers, or utilising secure networks. Authentication protocols utilise cryptographic technologies to verify the user's identity and ascertain their access permissions to the resource.
- **Cryptocurrencies:** Cryptocurrencies, such as Bitcoin and Ethereum, utilise cryptography extensively to safeguard transactions, prevent fraud, and uphold the integrity of the network. Complex algorithms and cryptographic keys are employed to safeguard transactions, making it nearly hard to tamper with or counterfeit the transactions.
- **End-to-end Internet Encryption:** End-to-end encryption safeguards bidirectional communications such as video calls, instant messaging, and email. Even if the message is encrypted, it guarantees that only the designated recipients can access its content. End-to-end encryption is extensively employed in communication applications such as WhatsApp and Signal, offering a significant degree of protection and anonymity for users.

Types of Cryptography Algorithm

- **Advanced Encryption Standard (AES):** AES (Advanced Encryption Standard) is a widely utilised encryption method that employs a singular key for both encryption and decryption processes. It is a symmetric block cypher algorithm having block sizes of 128 bits, 192 bits, or 256 bits. The AES algorithm is widely considered a successor to the DES (Data Encryption Standard) algorithm.
- **Data Encryption Standard (DES):** DES (Data encryption standard) is an older encryption method that is used to convert 64-bit plaintext data into 48-bit encrypted ciphertext. It employs symmetric keys, indicating that the same key is utilised for both encryption and decryption. Although it may be considered outdated by contemporary standards, it can serve as a fundamental foundation for acquiring knowledge of more advanced encryption techniques.
- **RSA:** RSA is a fundamental asymmetric cryptographic method that employs two distinct keys for encryption. The RSA algorithm relies on a block cipher notion that converts plain text into cipher text and vice versa.
- **Secure Hash Algorithm (SHA):** SHA is used to generate unique fixed-length digital fingerprints of input data known as hashes. SHA variants such as SHA- 2 and SHA-3 are routinely employed to assure data integrity and authenticity. A minimal alteration in input data significantly alters the hash output, signifying a compromise of integrity. Hashing is the method of storing key-value pairs utilising a hash function within a hash table.

Advantages of Cryptography

- Cryptography can facilitate access control to guarantee that only authorised parties can access a resource.

- It provides secure methods for communicating confidential information such as passwords, bank account numbers, and other sensitive data online.
- It aids in the protection against diverse forms of attacks, including replay and man-in-the-middle assaults.
- Cryptography assists organisations in complying with many legal obligations, including data protection and privacy regulations.

1.4.1 Encryption and Decryption

What are Encryption and Decryption?

Encryption is the procedure of transforming ordinary data into an incomprehensible format. Decryption is the process of transforming encoded or unreadable data back into its original format. Encryption is performed by the sender of the data, while decryption is executed by the recipient. The identical algorithm and key are employed for both encryption and decryption processes.

What is Cryptography?

Cryptography safeguards and preserves data throughout communication. It aids in blocking unauthorised individuals or groups from accessing confidential information. Encryption and decryption are the two fundamental functions of cryptography. A message transmitted over the network that is converted into an indecipherable encrypted format is referred to as data encryption. At the recipient's end, the received communication is transformed back to its original form, a process referred to as decryption.

What is Encryption?

Encryption is a method that converts original information into an unrecognisable format.

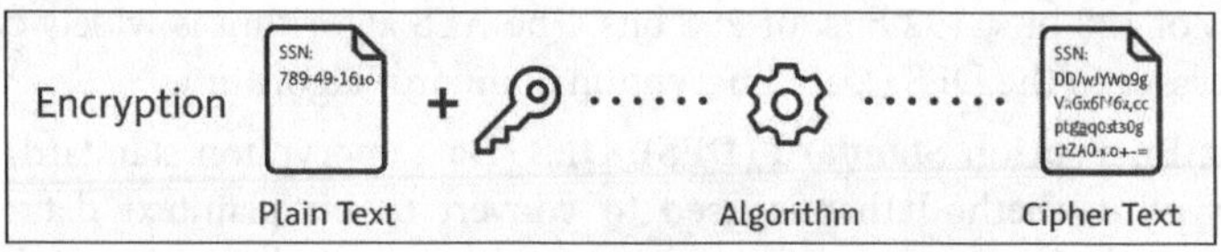

Fig. 1.11: Encryption Process

This revised version of the message is fundamentally distinct from the original. from competitors. A hacker cannot access the data since senders employ an encryption method. Encryption is typically performed with key algorithms. The data is encrypted to safeguard it against theft. Nonetheless, some established organisations also employ encryption to safeguard their trade secrets.

What is Decryption?

Decryption is the procedure of transforming encoded or encrypted data into a format that is comprehensible to humans or computers. This method involves decrypting the text either manually or by employing the keys utilised to encrypt the original material.

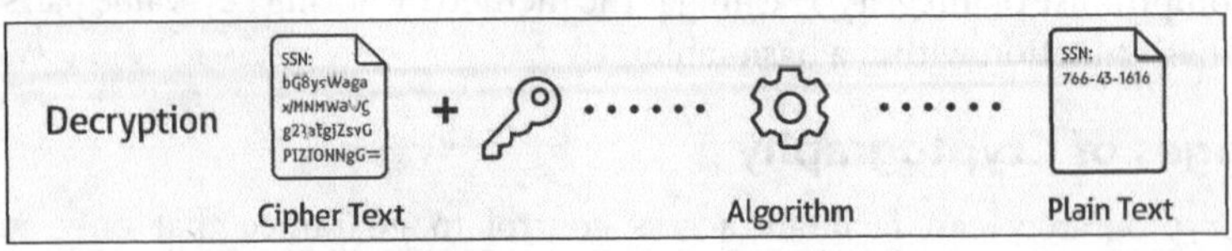

Fig. 1.12: Decryption process

Applications of Encryption and Decryption

Based on my experience, the essential reasons for utilising encryption are as follows:

- It assists in safeguarding your sensitive information, including passwords and login identifiers.
- Ensures confidentiality for sensitive information.
- It assists in verifying that the document or file is unaltered.
- The encryption process also deters plagiarism and safeguards intellectual property.
- Beneficial for network communication, such as the internet, and when a hacker may readily obtain unencrypted information.
- This technology is crucial as it enables the secure protection of data that should remain inaccessible to others.

Examples of Encryption and Decryption

I have included instances of encryption and decryption for your review.

- **Secure Online Banking:** Financial institutions employ encryption to safeguard communication between clients and their systems. Decryption is feasible solely with authorised access, ensuring transaction confidentiality.
- **Email Encryption:** Email encryption use technologies such as PGP or S/MIME to safeguard sensitive communications from unauthorised access. The recipient decrypts the message utilising a private key that corresponds to the sender's public key.
- **Digital Signatures:** Encryption facilitates the authentication of documents. A digital signature, generated with the signer's private key, is decrypted by others utilising the public key to authenticate its validity.
- **Cloud Storage Security:** Files stored on cloud services are encrypted to avert data intrusions. Users locally decrypt these files via a key supplied by the cloud provider following successful authentication.

Types of Keys

- **Symmetric Key:** Symmetric-key encryption algorithms utilise identical cryptographic keys for the encryption of plaintext and the decryption of ciphertext.
- **Asymmetric Key:** Asymmetric encryption employs two key pairs: the Public Key and the Private Key. The Public Key is accessible to all, whereas the Secret Key is exclusively available to the message's recipient, thereby enhancing security.
- **Public Key:** Public-key cryptography is an encryption system that utilises two pairs of keys. Public keys encrypt communications for a recipient.
- **Private Key:** The private key may belong to a public or private asymmetric key pair. It can be utilised in asymmetric encryption, as the identical key may be employed for both encryption and decryption of data.
- **Pre-Shared Key:** In cryptography, a pre-shared key (PSK) is a confidential secret that was previously exchanged between the two parties through a secure channel before to its utilisation.

Difference between Encryption and Decryption

Based on my in-depth knowledge, the main difference between encryption and decryption is as follows:

Parameter	Encryption	Decryption
What is	It is the process of converting normal data into an unreadable form. It helps you avoid unauthorized access to data.	It is a method of converting the unreadable or encoded data back into its original form.
Process	Whenever the data is sent between two separate machines, it is encrypted automatically using a secret key.	The receiver of the data automatically allows you to convert the data from the codes into its original form.
Location of Conversion	The person who is sending the data to the destination.	The receiver receives the data and converts it.
Example	An employee is sending essential documents to his/her manager.	The manager is receiving the essential documents from his/her employee.
Use of Algorithm	The same algorithm with the same key is used for the encryption- decryption process.	The only single algorithm is used for encryption and decryption is a pair of keys, each used for encryption and decryption.
Major function	Transforming humanly understandable messages into an incomprehensible and obscure form that can not be interpreted.	It is the conversion of an obscure message into an understandable form which is easy for a human to understand.

Conclusion

Cryptography is employed to safeguard and preserve data during transmission.

In my work, encryption is employed to transform original data into an unrecognisable form. Decryption is the procedure of transforming encoded or encrypted data into a format that is comprehensible to humans or computers. The encryption approach safeguards your sensitive information, including passwords and login identifiers. Public, private, pre-shared, and symmetric keys are essential components utilised in cryptography. "An employee is sending essential documents to his/her manager" is an example of an encryption approach. The manager is obtaining the requisite encrypted documents from the employee and decrypting them.

1.4.2 Hashed Function

What is Cryptography Hash Function?

A cryptographic hash function (CHF) is a mathematical algorithm commonly employed to authenticate data integrity. It has numerous applications, especially in information security (e.g., user authentication). A CHF converts data of varying message lengths into a fixed-size numerical string known as a hash. A cryptographic hash function is a unidirectional process, rendering it very challenging to reverse-engineer the original data utilised in its creation.

How Does a Cryptography Hash Function Work?

The hash function accepts data of a predetermined length. The size of the data block differs among algorithms. If the blocks are insufficiently sized, padding may be employed to occupy the void. Regardless of the hashing method employed, the result, or hash value, consistently maintains a fixed length. The hash function is thereafter applied a number of times according to the quantity of data blocks.

What Does a Cryptography Hash Function Do?

A cryptographic hash function accepts a textual input and generates a fixed-size hashed output that is irreversible. Nevertheless, from a macro perspective, their contributions are greater.

- **Secure against unauthorized alterations:** It assists you in even minor changes to a message that will result in the generation of a whole new hash value.
- **Protect passwords and operate at various speeds:** Numerous websites permit the storage of passwords, eliminating the need for recollection at each login. Storing unencrypted passwords on a publicly accessible server is perilous as it exposes the data to potential theft. Websites typically employ hashed passwords to generate hash values for storage.

Applications of Cryptographic Hash Functions

Here are several applications of cryptographic hash algorithms.

Message Authentication

Message authentication is a mechanism that ensures the integrity of a communication. It guarantees that data is received exactly as transmitted, without alterations, insertions, or deletions; a hash function is employed for message authentication, and the resultant value is often termed a message digest.

Message authentication frequently necessitates the utilisation of a message authentication code (MAC). Message Authentication Codes (MACs) are extensively utilised by two parties possessing a shared secret key for the purpose of authentication. A MAC function employs a secret key and data block to produce a hash value that signifies the secured communication.

Data Integrity Check

Hash functions are mostly utilised to generate checksums for data files. This tool provides the user with confidence in the accuracy of the data. The integrity check enables the user to identify any alterations to the original file. It does not guarantee uniqueness. Rather than modifying file data, the attacker can replace the entire file, calculate a new hash, and transmit it to the recipient.

Digital Signatures

The digital signature application is analogous to message authentication. Digital signatures function analogously to Message Authentication Codes (MACs). Digital signatures encrypt hash values of messages utilising a user's private key. The digital signature can be authenticated by anyone possessing the user's public key.

Conclusion

This article discusses cryptographic hash functions. A cryptographic hash function is a mathematical algorithm that transforms various inputs, such as messages or data, into fixed-length character strings, ensuring that inputs of any length yield a consistent output size.

1.4.3 Digital Signature

What is Digital Signature?

A digital signature is a method of verification. It does not facilitate secure communication. To ensure confidentiality, both the message and the signature must be encrypted utilising either a symmetric key or an asymmetric key cryptosystem. This supplementary security layer can be integrated into a fundamental digital signature framework.

Assume we Possess

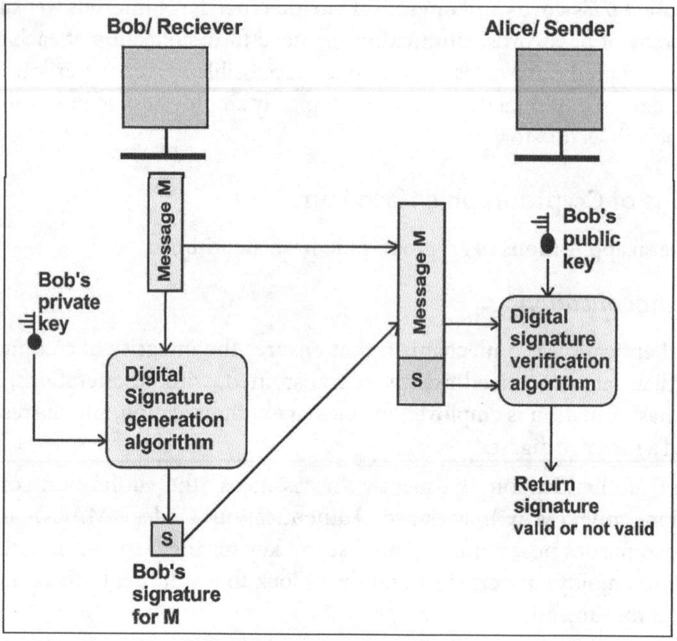

Fig. 1.13

Alice is the agent that transmits a message or commences communication. Bob signifies the recipient of the message. Eve symbolises an eavesdropper or antagonist who may seek to intercept or manipulate the message. In Public Key cryptography, also referred to as Asymmetric cryptography, the communication procedure is as follows: Alice encodes the message utilising Bob's public key. The encrypted communication arrives at Bob. Bob decodes the message transmitted by Alice utilising his private key. When Alice transmits a message to Bob, he will verify the sender's authenticity to confirm that it was indeed Alice who sent the message, rather not Eve. To accomplish this, Bob may request that Alice electronically sign the communication. An electronic signature can verify Alice's authenticity as the sender of the communication. We refer to this form of signing as a digital signature.

Method of Digital Signature

These two are standard Approaches to implement the Digital Signature:

- Rivest-Shamir-Adleman (RSA)
- Digital Signature Algorithm (DSA)

Rivest-Shamir-Adleman (RSA)

In the Rivest-Shamir-Adleman method, the message requiring a signature is initially input into a hash function that produces a safe, fixed-length hash code. The sender's private key is subsequently employed to encrypt the hash code, thereby creating the signature. The subsequent step is transmitting both the signature and the message to the designated recipient. For validation purposes, upon receiving the message, the recipient initially calculates its hash code. The recipient utilises the sender's public key to decrypt the previously encrypted signature. If the decrypted signature matches the hash code generated by the receiver, the signature will be deemed valid. As only the sender possesses the private key, they alone could have generated a valid signature.

you can refer the below diagram for RSA, here,

- M = Message or Plaintext
- H = Hash Function
- || = Group the plantext and hash function (hash digest)
- E = Encryption Algorithm
- D = Decryption Algorithm
- PUa = Public key of sender
- PRa = Private key of sender

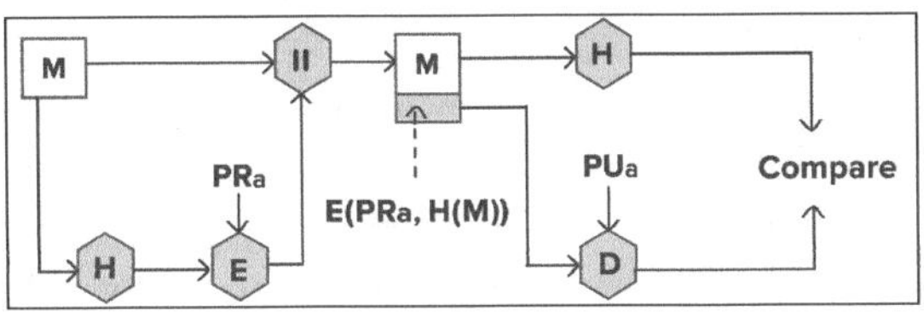

Fig. 1.14

Digital Signature Algorithm (DSA)

The Digital Signature Algorithm (DSA) employs a hash function to generate a hash code, analogous to RSA. The hash code is amalgamated with a randomly generated number k as input to a signature function. The signature function relies on the sender's private key (PRa) and a collection of parameters known to a group of communicating principals. This collection may be regarded as a global public key (PUG). The signature function produces a signature of two components: s and r. A hash code is created upon the receipt of an incoming message. The hash code is subsequently amalgamated with the signature and inputted into a verification mechanism. The verification mechanism relies on the global public key and the sender's public key (PUa), which is associated with the sender's private key. The verification function outputs a value equivalent to the signature's component r, provided the signature is genuine. The signature function is constructed so that only the sender, with the private key, may generate a valid signature.

You can refer below diagram for DSA, where,

- M = Message or Plaintext
- H = Hash Function
- || = Group the plantext and hash function (hash digest)
- E = Encryption Algorithm
- D = Decryption Algorithm
- PUa = Public key of sender
- PRa = Private key of sender
- Sig = Signature function
- Ver = Verification function
- PUG = Global public Key

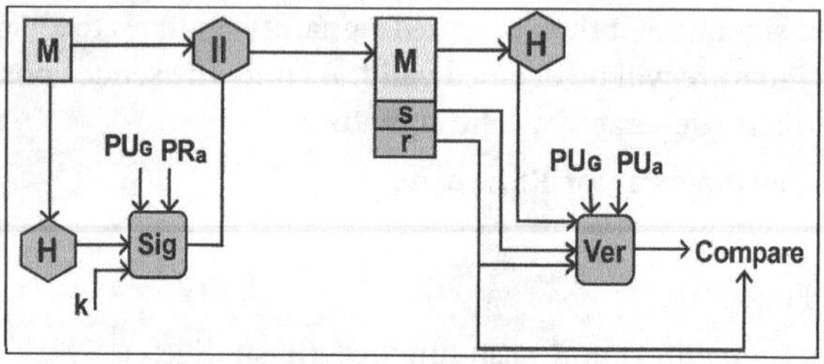

Fig. 1.15: DSA Approach

Primary Termologies

- **User Private Key (PR):** A secret cryptographic key only possessed by the user, used to sign messages. It's used to verify digital signatures created with a corresponding private key.
- **User Public Key (PU):** A publicly known key that can be shared with anyone, used for signature verification. As it is, the private key must be kept secret and secure because it proves that a given user is genuine.
- **Signing (Sig):** Signing involves creating a digital signature with the help of a user's private key. In case of DSA, this process requires mathematical operations to be performed on the message that should be signed using a given private key in order to generate a unique signature for that message.
- **Verifying (Ver):** Verifying is the process of verifying whether or not a digital signature has been forged using its corresponding public key. In DSA, this involves comparing the messages hash against the verification value through mathematical operations between two binary strings – one representing an encrypted data and another one representing plain-text original message.

Advantages of DSA

- **Authentication:** At some point, digital signatures ensure strong identity authentication for the sender. The recipient can be sure that the message or document was signed by the purported signatory.
- **Integrity**: Digital signatures ensure the integrity of the content. If something is altered in the content after the signature is made, then it becomes invalid with respect to verifying the content.

- **Non-Repudiation:** A digital signature gives non-repudiation, meaning the sender cannot disclaim his creation of that document post factum. Most relevant in legal and contractual issues.
- **Efficiency:** Digital signatures make the process of signing electronic and automate it, giving way to fast online transactions free from the need of manual verification, paperwork, and a physical signature.
- **Security:** As long as the whole digital signing process is well organized, digital signatures may prove to be secure. Cryptographic public key cryptography and hashing algorithms prevent unauthorized parties from forging digital signatures.
- **World Acceptance:** Such a mechanism (digital signatures) to represent the conclusion of the related transaction in case of legal or contractual terms is known and widely accepted all over the world.
- **Time stamping:** Time stamping would also make another secure layer against replay attacks and against the freshness of the signature.
- **Cost Savings:** The digital signing process discontinues the need for transporting documents, thereby saving on costs to be done with printing, courier services, and manual handling.

Disadvantages of DSA

- **Key Management Complexity:** Cryptographic keys that are used for signing documents must be properly managed. Generating, storing, and distributing keys in a secure manner are all complicated procedures that need to be attended to, and revocation has to be handled carefully.
- **Infrastructure Dependence:** Digital signatures are built on a secure and reliable infrastructure of Public Key Infrastructure (PKI) and Certificate Authorities. If the infrastructure is compromised or becomes unavailable, it may compromise trust in digital signatures.
- **Legal and Regulatory Challenges:** Although many people are increasingly using digital signatures, there might still be legal and regulatory challenges in some places. It will be very important to observe local laws and standards.
- **Initial Setup Costs:** A proper setup of an extensive digital signature system may include the cost of obtaining certificates for digital certificates, putting in place safety measures, and training of the users.
- **Offline Usability:** In the event of not having access to the signer's private key, digital signatures are found to be challenged. Solutions of hardware tokens and secure elements add to the complexity.
- **User Education:** Education of the proper application and value of digital signatures is necessary in order that the users should be educated in use. The correct measures to be taken against vulnerability, as well as being aware of any possible threat, are important in successful implementation.
- **Vulnerability to Key Compromise:** Private keys need to be safeguarded from unauthorized access since one compromised private key can initiate fraudulent signatures.

Conclusion

The Digital Signature Algorithm (DSA) is a dependable and standardised method for digital signatures that guarantees message authenticity, integrity, and non-repudiation. DSA offers numerous advantages, including enhanced security, worldwide acceptance, and cost efficiency; nevertheless, it also presents disadvantages such as the complexity of key management and dependence on infrastructure. Comprehending and surmounting these limitations is essential for the efficient application of DSA in securing digital communications.

UNIT 2 CRYPTOGRAPHY AND BLOCKCHAIN TECHNOLOGY

2.1 CRYPTOGRAPHY

Cryptography is a method of safeguarding communication by transforming plaintext into incomprehensible ciphertext. It encompasses multiple techniques and protocols to guarantee data secrecy, integrity, authentication, and non-repudiation. The two principal categories of cryptography are symmetric key cryptography and asymmetric key cryptography. These methods are essential for safeguarding the security and privacy of information in the contemporary digital landscape, facilitating secure online transactions, protecting sensitive data in databases, and ensuring the confidentiality of communications. With the advancement of technology, cryptography remains an essential instrument in the persistent struggle to safeguard our information from hackers.

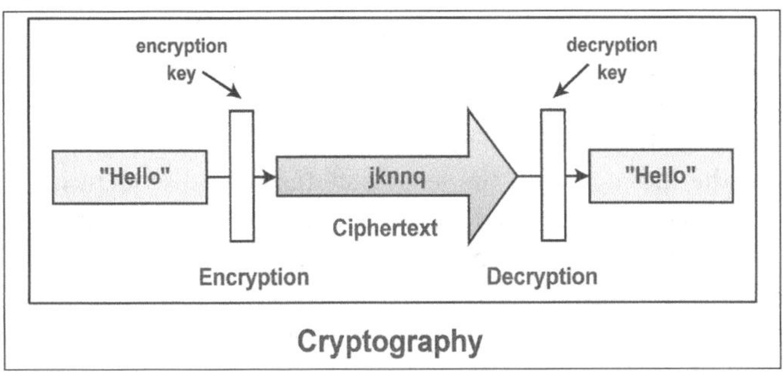

Fig. 2.1

What is Cryptography?

Cryptography is a technique of securing information and communications through the use of some algorithms so that only those persons for whom the information is intended can understand it and process it.

2.1.1 Hash Function – Digital Signature

Hash Functions - Definition

Hash functions accept a possibly lengthy message as input and produce a distinct output value derived from its content. The result of a hash function is typically termed the message digest. Hashing is a unidirectional function, and with a suitably designed algorithm, it is impossible to reverse the hashing process to disclose the original input. Contrast this with encryption (a bidirectional function) that facilitates both encryption and decryption using the appropriate key or key combination.

A particular application of hash functions is in data structures such as hash tables or Bloom filters. The objective here is not security, but expeditious data retrieval. Hash functions utilised in digital signatures are designed to yield identical outputs for identical inputs (deterministic). This allows the message recipient to recalculate the message digest using the identical hash function and compare it to the sent digest to confirm that the message was unaltered throughout transmission. A little alteration in spacing, punctuation, or text will result in a wholly distinct message digest. One cannot ascertain the extent of disparity between two messages by analysing the digest. A minimal variation in the input will yield a significantly different digest value.

Five criteria exist for a cryptographic hash function:

- The input may vary in length.
- The output possesses a predetermined length.
- The hash function is very simple to compute for any input.
- The hash function is unidirectional, indicating that it is exceedingly difficult, if not impossible, to ascertain the input from the result.
- The hash algorithm is collision-resistant (no two distinct messages may provide the identical hash value).

SHA – Secure Hash Algorithm

The Secure Hash Algorithm (SHA) and its successors, SHA-1, SHA-2, and SHA-3, are hash functions standardised by the National Institute of Standards and Technology (NIST). SHA-1 accepts an input of nearly any length and generates a 160-bit hash. It handles messages in 512-bit increments. If a message length is not a multiple of 512 bits, the SHA algorithm appends data to the message until the length attains the subsequent highest multiple of 512 bits. SHA-1 is no longer deemed secure against financially robust attackers. In 2017, all prominent online browser developers ceased the acceptance of SHA-1 SSL certificates. Google even exhibited a collision in SHA-1. SHA-2 was introduced in 2001 in response to the vulnerabilities identified in SHA-1. It encompasses substantial modifications from its predecessor and features four primary variants:

- SHA-256 generates a 256-bit hash value utilising a 512-bit block size.
- SHA-224 employs a truncated variant of the SHA-256 hash, yielding a 224-bit digest with a 512-bit block size.
- SHA-512 generates a 512-bit message digest utilising a 1,024-bit block size.
- SHA-384 employs a truncated variant of the SHA-512 hash, yielding a 384-bit digest with a block size of 1,024 bits.

The cryptography community usually regards SHA-2 algorithms as secure; yet, they could exhibit the same vulnerability as the SHA-1 method. SHA-3 was released in 2015 and, although it belongs to the same family of standards, it is fundamentally distinct from the MD5-like architecture of SHA-1 and SHA-2. SHA-3 is a component of the larger cryptographic primitive family known as Keccak. It was created as a direct substitute for SHA-2, providing identical variants (SHA3-256/SHA3-224/SHA3-512/SHA3-384) and hash lengths while employing a more safe algorithm.

MD2 – Message Digest

The MD2 Message-Digest Algorithm was created by Ronald Rivest, a co- founder of RSA Security, in 1989 to offer a safe hash function for 8-bit processors.

MD2 extends the message to a length that is a multiple of 16 bits and calculates a 16-byte checksum, which is appended to the end of the input message. A 128- bit message digest is produced by utilising the original message in conjunction with the appended checksum. Cryptanalytic assaults on the MD2 method are documented, and it has been demonstrated that MD2 does not qualify as a one- way function. Consequently, it should be discontinued. MD4, an advancement of MD2, was introduced in 1990 and is compatible with 32-bit processors. It elevates the security level using an improved algorithm. MD4 appends padding to the message to achieve a length that is 64 bits less than a multiple of 512 bits. The MD4 algorithm processes 512-bit message blocks through three computational cycles to generate a 128-bit message digest. An 8-bit message is augmented with 440 supplementary bits to get a total of 448 bits, which is 64 bits less than a 512-bit message.

Numerous vulnerabilities have been identified in the MD4 algorithm, rendering it no longer secure. Utilisation should be eschewed whenever feasible. MD5 was introduced in 1991 as the subsequent iteration of the message-digest algorithm. It processes 512-bit blocks of the message while employing four rounds of calculation to yield the identical 128-bit message digest length as in MD2 and MD4. MD5 shares identical padding criteria with MD4; the message length must be 64 bits smaller than a multiple of 512 bits. MD5 incorporated enhanced security protections that lowered the speed of message-digest generation.

Recent cryptanalytic assaults have revealed that MD5 is vulnerable to collisions. In 2005, it was proved that two digital certificates associated with distinct public keys possess identical MD5 hashes. All algorithms within the MD family are no longer deemed appropriate as hashing functions. Nevertheless, they may still be utilised today.

Digital Signatures

Secure hash functions enable the implementation of a digital signature system.

A digital signature infrastructure serves two objectives:

- Digitally signed messages guarantee to the recipient that the message originated from the asserted sender. This ensures nonrepudiation.
- Digitally signed messages assure the recipient that the message remained unaltered during transmission. This safeguards against malicious (man-in-the-middle) and inadvertent (communication interference) alterations.
- Digital signatures depend on the integration of public-key cryptography and hash functions.

Alice is transmitting a digitally signed, albeit unencrypted, message to Bob:

1. Alice creates a message digest of the original plaintext using a secure hash algorithm such as SHA3-512.
2. Alice subsequently encrypts the message digest with her private key. The result is the digital signature.
3. Alice attaches the digital signature to the textual message.
4. Alice subsequently transmits the added message to Bob.

5. Bob eliminates the digital signature from the attached message and decrypts it using Alice's public key.
6. Bob computes the hash of the textual message using SHA3-512.
7. Bob subsequently contrasts the decrypted message digest obtained from Alice with the message digest he generated. Should the two digests correspond, he can be confident that the message he received originated from Alice.

The digital signature procedure inherently lacks privacy. It just guarantees the fulfilment of the cryptographic objectives of authentication, integrity, and nonrepudiation. If Alice seeks to guarantee the confidentiality of her message to Bob, she may encrypt the added message produced in step 3 using Bob's public key. Bob must first decrypt the encrypted communication using his private key before to proceeding to step 5. Digital signatures are employed not only for messages; software companies frequently utilise digital signature technology to authenticate code distribution across insecure networks such as the internet. Checksums do not necessitate any encryption key; they are straightforward digests of fingerprints that reflect specific data.

HMAC – Hashed Message Authentication

The hashed message authentication code (HMAC) algorithm provides a partial digital signature and ensures message integrity, but it does not offer nonrepudiation. HMAC is predicated on the integration of two principles: private-key encryption and hash functions. HMAC can be integrated with any secure hash function, including SHA3. The resultant message authentication code (MAC) is termed HMAC-SHA3. HMAC integrates a confidential key with a hash function, serving as an intermediary between the unencrypted application of a message-digest algorithm and the resource-intensive digital signature techniques reliant on public-key cryptography. HMAC does not perform encryption on the message. The message, whether encrypted or not, must be transmitted with the HMAC hash. Entities possessing the secret key will independently hash the message, and the received and computed hashes will correspond if the message is legitimate.

DSS – Digital Signature Standard

This standard mandates that all officially sanctioned digital signature algorithms utilise the SHA-3 hashing mechanism. The DSS delineates the encryption techniques permissible for facilitating digital signature infrastructure. The following are currently accepted in version 186-4:

Digital Signature Algorithm (DSA)

- RSA - Rivest-Shamir-Adleman Algorithm
- Elliptic Curve Digital Signature Algorithm (ECDSA)

Key Confusion

Public-Key Cryptography and Digital Signatures may induce perplexity. Encryption, decryption, digital signatures, and signature verification all employ identical methods with varying key inputs. Presented below are several fundamental guidelines:

- A communication is encrypted using the recipient's public key.
- You utilise your private key to decrypt a communication.

- You authenticate a message using your private key.
- The signature of a message is authenticated using sender's public key.

2.1.2 ECDSA

Blockchain serves as the foundational technology for the cryptocurrency Bitcoin. The blockchain is a decentralised database that maintains a record of all transactions or digital events that have transpired and is accessible to all participants. The bulk of system members validate each transaction. It encompasses every individual transaction record. Bitcoin is the most prominent cryptocurrency and serves as an exemplar of blockchain technology. Examples of blockchains include:

- **Public Blockchain:** It is an unrestricted public ledger that allows any individual to participate and conduct transactions, with a decentralised copy for each participant. This indicates that any individual with internet connection can engage with the public Blockchain. A private blockchain operates within a restricted environment, sometimes governed by a singular entity, and is typically hosted on a local network within an organisation, rather than being accessible to anybody willing to contribute computing resources.
- **Hybrid Blockchain:** Organisations seeking to leverage the advantages of both private and public blockchains utilise a hybrid blockchain, which facilitates the establishment of a private, permissioned system alongside a public, permissionless framework, enabling them to determine access to specific data and the information that is disclosed publicly.
- **Consortium Blockchain:** The consensus mechanisms of a consortium blockchain are governed by designated nodes. A validator node is responsible for initiating, collecting, and validating transactions. Member nodes are capable of initiating or receiving transactions.

What is ECDSA?

The Elliptic Curve Digital Signature Algorithm is a Digital Signature Algorithm (DSA) that use elliptic curve cryptography keys. This equation is highly efficient and grounded on public key cryptography. ECDSA is employed in numerous security systems, is prevalent in encrypted messaging applications, and underpins Bitcoin security, with Bitcoin "addresses" functioning as public keys. Elliptic Curve Digital Signature Algorithms (ECDSA) have garnered considerable attention recently, especially from standards developers, as alternatives to established cryptosystems like integer factorisation and discrete logarithm problem systems. In security applications, cryptographic algorithms are the most critical foundational tool.

Digital Signature of ECDSA

A digital signature is the electronic counterpart of a handwritten signature, enabling the recipient to convince a third party that the message was authentically dispatched by the sender. Handwritten signatures are far less secure than digital signatures. A digital signature is impervious to forgery. One additional benefit of digital signatures compared to handwritten signatures is its applicability across the entire communication. Every component of the digital communication is influenced by the signature key. A handwritten signature is affixed at the bottom of a paper document. The wording above the signed signature may be modified without altering the signature itself. Digital signatures preclude such modifications. Contemporary digital signature techniques can be classified according to a mathematical problem that underpins their security.

- **Integer Factorisation (IF) Schemes:** Their security is predicated on the intractability of the integer factorisation problem. RSA signature schemes represent one instance.
- **Discrete Logarithm (DL) Schemes:** Their security relies on the intractability of the discrete logarithm problem within a finite field.
- **Elliptic Curve (EC) Schemes:** Their security is predicated on the intractability of the elliptic curve discrete logarithm issue. The Elliptic Curve Digital Signature Algorithm is utilised in this study and is undoubtedly the most recent among many designs.

Domain Parameter of ECDSA

An elliptic curve E defined over a discrete space Fq with characteristic p and a base point G Domain parameters might be distributed by a group of entities or unique to a single user.

Domain Parameter Generation Methods

One method for generating cryptographically safe domain parameters is as follows:

- **Step 1:** Select coefficients a and b from F_q verifiable using a random method.
- **Step 2:** Compute the value of Number N.
- **Step 3:** Verify N is divisible by the large prime number if not go to step 1.
- **Step 4:** Verify N does not divisible by q^k-1 for each k where k ranges from 1 to 20.
- **Step 5:** Verify N is not equal to q if not then go to step 1.
- **Step 6:** Select an arbitrary point G'∈ N_q and set G=(N/n).

Domain Parameter Validation

Validation of domain parameters ensures that the domain parameters have the necessary arithmetic features. In practice, domain parameter validation is performed for two reasons:

1. To prevent the intentional insertion of erroneous domain parameters, which may enable some attacks
2. To detect inadvertent coding or transmission mistakes.

The use of an improper set of domain parameters can render all intended security attributes null and void. A concrete (though implausible) attack that can be conducted if domain parameter validation for a signature scheme is not done was demonstrated. The attack is directed at a key agreement protocol that uses the ElGamal signature technique.

Steps for Domain Parameter Validation

- **Step 1:** usage of a specific algorithm is used to do explicit domain parameter validation.
- **Step 2:** D is generated by A utilizing a trustworthy system.
- **Step 3:** A obtains confirmation from a trusted party T, a certification authority, that T validated D's explicit domain parameters using a specified Algorithm.

- **Step 4:** A obtains assurance from a trustworthy third party T that D was generated using a trustworthy system.

ECDSA Key Pair

An ECDSA key pair is linked to a specific set of EC domain settings. The public key is a randomly generated multiple of the base point, whereas the private key is the integer used to generate the multiple points.

Key Pair Generation

The key pair of entity A is associated with a certain set of EC domain parameters D = (q, FR, a, b, G, n, h). This relationship can be ensured cryptographically (e.g., with certificates) or contextually (e.g., by using the same domain parameters by all organizations). Prior to key generation, entity A must be confident that the category parameters are correct. Creation of an ECDSA key pair. Every item A does these things:

1. Choose an integer d at random or a pseudo-random number within the range [1, n1].
2. Determine Q = dG.
3. A's private key is d, and A's public key is Q.

Algorithm for Explicit Validation of an ECDSA Public Key

Input for the algorithm: A public key Q=(xQ, yQ) associated with valid domain parameters (q, FR, a, b, G,n,h).

Output for the algorithm: Acceptance or rejection of the validity of h.

1. Check that Q does not equal O.
2. Check that xQ and yQ are properly represented elements of Fq(i.e., integers in the interval |0, p-1| in case q = p, and bit strings of length A bits in the case $q = 2^m$).
3. Check that h lies on the elliptic curve defined by a and b.
4. Check that nQ = O.
5. If any check fails, then Q is invalid; otherwise Q is valid.

Proof of Possession of a Private Key

- An organization can assert that signed messages came from it if it can certify another entity's public key as being its own. To prevent this, before the CA verifies the public key as belonging to A, it should demand that all entities show proof of ownership of the private keys that match their public keys.
- It should be noted that private key possession evidence offers distinct guarantees from public key verification. The former proves that a private key is in your possession even though it might correlate to an invalid public key, whereas the latter proves that a public key is legitimate but that you do not own the associated private key. With both, a great level of assurance is offered.

ECDSA Signature Generation

The steps for creating and verifying signatures with the ECDSA are described in this section. An entity A with domain attributes D=(q, FR, a, b, G, n, h) and associated key pair (d, Q) performs the following actions to sign a message m.

1. Select a random or pseudo-random integer k, where k ranges from 1 to n c – 1.
2. Transform x1 to an integer by computing kG = (x1, y1).
3. Compute r = x1 mod n and if r = 0 then go to step 1.
4. Compute k – 1 mod n.
5. Compute s = k – 1(e + dr)mod n. If s is equal to 0 then follow step1
6. The message m bears the signature of A. (r,s).

ECDSA Signature Verification

B receives an authentic copy of A's domain parameters D = (q, FR, a, b, G, n, h) and related public key Q in order to validate A's signature (r, s) on m. It is advised that B verifies D and Q as well. Next, B performs the following:

1. Check if the integers r and s fall inside the range [1, n – 1].
2. Transform the bit string to a number e and perform SHA – 1(m).
3. Compute w = s^{-1} mod n.
4. Compute u1 = ew mod n and u2 = rw mod n.
5. Compute X = u1G + u2Q.
6. If X = O, then reject the signature. If not, compute v = x1 mod n and convert X's x coordinate x1 to an integer.
7. Accept the signature if and only if v = r.

Benefits of ECDSA

- **High Security:** It is an equation based on public key cryptography (PKC) that is particularly successful. ECDSA underpins the security of Bitcoin and is extensively employed in encrypted messaging applications. Smaller keys are favoured over larger keys for many reasons. Smaller keys provide simpler mathematics, enabling faster methods to generate signatures.
- **Good application performance:** The key pairs required for the signing and verification of digital signatures are generated using ECC through the ECDSA digital signature algorithm. Elliptic Curve Cryptography (ECC) is commonly employed to authenticate transactions or events in blockchain applications because of its superior attributes compared to other public-key methods.
- **High speed of verification:** The signed message msg, the signature components r and s produced by the signing algorithm, and the public key pubKey, corresponding to the signer's private key, serve as inputs for the ECDSA signature validation procedure. The outcome is a boolean value, either valid or invalid.
- **Support government standards:** The Digital Signature Standard (DSS), a Federal Information Processing Standard (FIPS) of the United States Government, encompasses the requirements for the Digital Signature Algorithm (DSA). The computational intractability of the discrete logarithm problem (DLP) in prime-order subgroups of Z underpins its security.
- **Complaints with modern requirement:** ECC adheres to FIPS since ECDSA is among the FIPS-approved methods for asymmetric key functions in FIPS 140-2, alongside RSA and DSA. It is a highly successful equation based on public key cryptography (PKC).

Limitations of ECDSA

- **Standard curve:** Secure implementation is difficult and challenging, particularly for conventional curves. Contemporary standards are antiquated, particularly ECDSA, which pales in comparison to Schnorr signatures.
- **Signing verification error:** The key is compromised if a defective or compromised random number generator is employed for signing. Binary curves continue to present specific patent challenges. It may be costly. **Problem with curves:** In particular for binary curves, it still has certain patent issues. It may be costly. The rising utilisation of elliptic curves has intersected with the continuous advancement of quantum computing research.
- **The size of encryption process:** The principal disadvantage of ECC is that it significantly enlarges the size of the encrypted message in comparison to RSA encryption. Furthermore, the ECC method is more intricate and difficult to implement compared to RSA, heightening the likelihood of implementation errors and diminishing the technique's security.
- **The same random value:** Bitcoin private key acquired with ECDSA signatures. The employment of a same nonce value across several messages constitutes one of the deficiencies.

Applications of ECDSA

A Bitcoin address is generated by hashing an ECDSA public key through cryptographic methods. The individual possessing the ECDSA private key is the legitimate owner of the account. This indicates that ECDSA offers equivalent security to RSA with the utilisation of smaller keys. Smaller keys are favoured over larger keys for many reasons. Smaller keys provide easier mathematics, enabling the generation of signatures by more rapid algorithms. To establish a TLS connection, smaller public keys result in smaller certificates, necessitating the transmission of less data.

2.1.3 Memory Hard Algorithm

In cryptography, a memory-hard function (MHF) is a function that requires substantial memory for efficient evaluation. It contrasts with a memory-bound function, which incurs expenses by decelerating computation due to memory latency. Memory-hard functions (MHFs) are utilised in key stretching and proof of work due to their heightened memory demands, which considerably diminish the computational efficiency benefit of specialised hardware relative to general- purpose hardware, in contrast to non-MHFs.

Introduction

MHFs are engineered to utilise substantial memory resources on a computer to diminish the efficacy of parallel computing. To assess the function with reduced memory usage, a considerable time cost is involved. The resource-intensive nature of each MHF computation restricts the simultaneous execution of function computations to the available memory capacity. This diminishes the efficacy of specialised hardware, including application-specific integrated circuits and graphics processing units, which employ parallelisation in computing an MHF for numerous inputs, such as during brute-force password hash attacks or cryptocurrency mining.

Motivation and Examples

Bitcoin's proof-of-work relies on the iterative assessment of the SHA-256 function; however, contemporary general-purpose processors, including standard CPUs, exhibit inefficiency in executing a fixed function repeatedly. Application-specific integrated circuits (ASICs) engineered for Bitcoin mining can utilise 30,000 times less energy per hash compared to x86 CPUs, while achieving significantly higher hash rates. This raised apprehensions regarding the centralisation of mining for Bitcoin and other cryptocurrencies. Due to the disparity between miners employing ASICs and those utilising CPUs or standard hardware, developers of subsequent proof-of-work systems implemented hash functions that posed challenges in creating ASICs capable of evaluating the hash function substantially faster than a CPU.

Due to the platform-independent nature of memory costs, MHFs have been utilised in cryptocurrency mining, exemplified by Litecoin, which employs scrypt as its hashing algorithm. They are advantageous in password hashing as they substantially elevate the expense of attempting numerous potential passwords against a compromised database of hashed passwords, without considerably augmenting the computation time for legitimate users.

Measuring Memory Hardness

Multiple methods exist to assess the memory difficulty of a function. A frequently observed metric is cumulative memory complexity (CMC). In a parallel architecture, CMC represents the total memory necessary to compute a function over each time step of the calculation. Alternative effective strategies encompass the integration of memory utilisation over time and the assessment of memory bandwidth consumption on a memory bus. Functions that necessitate substantial memory bandwidth are occasionally termed "bandwidth- hard functions."

Variants

Memory-hard functions (MHFs) can be classified into two distinct categories based on their evaluation patterns: data-dependent memory-hard functions (dMHF) and data-independent memory-hard functions (iMHF). In contrast to iMHFs, the memory access pattern of a dMHF is contingent upon the function input, such as the password supplied to a key derivation function.

Instances of dMHFs include scrypt and Argon2d, whereas instances of iMHFs comprise Argon2i and catena. Numerous of these Memory Hard Functions (MHFs) have been engineered for utilisation as password hashing functions due to their memory hardness. A significant issue with dMHFs is their susceptibility to side-channel attacks, including cache timing assaults. This has led to a predilection for employing iMHFs in password hashing. Nonetheless, iMHFs have been analytically demonstrated to possess inferior memory hardness characteristics compared to dMHFs.

2.1.4 Zero Knowledge Proof

A zero-knowledge proof or zero-knowledge protocol in cryptography is a technique wherein one person (the prover, Peggy) can demonstrate to another party (the verifier, Victor) that she possesses knowledge of a value x, without disclosing any information beyond the mere fact of her knowing of x. Another perspective on this concept is that interactive zero-knowledge proofs necessitate engagement between the entity (or computational system) demonstrating their knowledge and the entity verifying the proof. If substantiating the assertion necessitates the prover's access to confidential information, the definition indicates that the verifier will be incapable of subsequently validating the assertion to others, as the verifier lacks the confidential information. It is essential that the statement under proof explicitly asserts that the prover possesses the requisite knowledge; otherwise, the proof would not qualify as zero-knowledge, as the verifier would acquire supplementary information regarding the prover's possession of the necessary secret information by the conclusion of the protocol.

If the assertion solely indicates that the prover possesses confidential information, it is classified as a zero-knowledge proof of knowledge. This exemplifies the fundamental concept of zero-knowledge proofs: demonstrating possession of specific knowledge is straightforward if one can disclose that information; the difficulty lies in substantiating that one possesses such knowledge without disclosing the confidential information or any additional details. In zero-knowledge proofs of knowledge, the protocol must inherently necessitate interactive input from the verifier, typically manifested as a challenge or challenges, whereby the prover's responses will persuade the verifier solely if the statement is true (i.e., if the prover possesses the asserted knowledge). This is evidently true, as otherwise the verifier could document the protocol's execution and subsequently replay it to another party. If the new party accepts this as evidence that the replayer possesses the secret information, then their acceptance is either warranted—indicating that the replayer indeed knows the secret, thus compromising the protocol's zero-knowledge property—or it is fallacious, resulting in a party erroneously accepting proof of knowledge from someone who does not actually possess it. Certain types of non-interactive zero- knowledge proofs exist; nonetheless, the proof's validity is contingent upon computational assumptions, notably those associated with an ideal cryptographic hash function.

The Ali Baba Cave

A renowned narrative illustrates the core concepts of zero-knowledge proofs, initially published by Jean-Jacques Quisquater and colleagues in their paper "How to Explain Zero-Knowledge Protocols to Your Children." In a zero- knowledge proof, it is customary to designate the two participants as Peggy (the statement prover) and Victor (the statement verifier). Peggy has discovered the incantation required to unlock a mystical portal within a cave. The cave is circular, including an entrance on one side and a magical door obstructing the opposite side. Victor seeks to ascertain if Peggy is aware of the secret word; however, Peggy, valuing her privacy, is unwilling to disclose her knowledge of the secret word or acknowledge her awareness to anyone. The walkways to the left and right from the entrance are designated as A and B.

Initially, Victor remains outside the cave while Peggy enters. Peggy selects either option A or way B; Victor is prohibited from observing her choice. Victor then enters the cave and vociferously calls out the name of the road he desires her to choose on her return, either A or B, selected arbitrarily. Assuming she genuinely knows the incantation, this is straightforward: she unlocks the door, if required, and retraces the intended route. However, assume she was unaware of the term. She could only return along the designated way if Victor provided the name of the identical route she had taken to enter. Given that Victor would randomly select either A or B, she would possess a 50% probability of making an accurate prediction.

Should they replicate this feat numerous times, approximately 20 consecutively, her probability of accurately predicting all of Victor's requests would diminish to an infinitesimal level (around one in a million). Consequently, if Peggy consistently emerges at the exit designated by Victor, he can deduce that it is quite plausible — exceedingly probable — that Peggy possesses knowledge of the secret phrase. A pertinent observation regarding third-party observers: even if Victor is equipped with a concealed camera that captures the entire transaction, the camera will only document either Victor exclaiming "A!" with Peggy manifesting at A, or Victor exclaiming "B!" with Peggy appearing at B. A recording of this nature would be facile for any two individuals to fabricate, necessitating simply that Peggy and Victor prearrange the sequence of A's and B's that Victor will vocalise. Such a recording will undoubtedly fail to persuade anyone other than the original participants. Indeed, even a spectator of the initial experiment might remain unconvinced, as Victor and Peggy may have meticulously staged the entire "experiment" from inception to conclusion.

Additionally, if Victor selects his A's and B's by conducting an on-camera coin flip, this protocol forfeits its zero-knowledge attribute; the recorded coin flip would likely appear persuasive to any subsequent viewer. Consequently, while this does not disclose the secret word to Victor, it enables him to persuade the public that Peggy possesses that information, contrary to her expressed desires. Nonetheless, digital cryptography typically employs a pseudo-random number generator, which functions similarly to a coin exhibiting a predetermined sequence of heads and tails known exclusively to its owner. If Victor's coin exhibited this behaviour, it would again be feasible for Victor and Peggy to have fabricated the "experiment," so employing a pseudo-random number generator would not disclose Peggy's knowledge to the public in the same manner that utilising a flipped coin would. Peggy can demonstrate to Victor her knowledge of the magic phrase without disclosing it to him in a single attempt. If Victor and Peggy proceed together to the cave's entrance, Victor can observe Peggy entering through A and exiting through B. This would unequivocally demonstrate that Peggy possesses knowledge of the key word, without disclosing the magic word to Victor. Nonetheless, such evidence may be witnessed by an external party or documented by Victor, rendering it persuasive to any observer. Peggy could not disprove the evidence by asserting collusion with Victor, thereby relinquishing control over who is informed of her knowledge.

Two Balls and ahe Colour-Blind Friend

This example necessitates two similar objects of differing colours, such as two coloured balls, and is regarded as one of the simplest elucidations of the functioning of interactive zero-knowledge proofs. The initial live demonstration was conducted by software engineers Konstantinos Chalkias and Mike Hearn at a blockchain conference in September 2017, drawing inspiration from the work of Professor Oded Goldreich, who utilised two differently coloured cards. Envision a scenario where your friend is colour-blind, and you own two identical balls: one red and one green. Your acquaintance perceives them as entirely identical and is doubtful that they can be differentiated. You aim to demonstrate to him that they are, indeed, of different colours, without disclosing which is red and which is green. This is the proof system. You hand the two balls to your pal, who then conceals them behind his back.

Subsequently, he retrieves one of the balls from behind his back and presents it. The ball is thereafter positioned behind his back once more, after which he opts to disclose only one of the two balls, switching to the alternate ball with a probability of 50%. He will enquire, "Did I change the ball?" This entire process is subsequently reiterated as frequently as required. One can definitively ascertain whether he altered them by examining their colours. If they were identical in colour and hence indistinguishable, it would be impossible to get a probability of right guessing above 50%. By repeatedly executing this "proof" with your friend, such as 128 iterations, your friend should be persuaded of the distinct colouration of the balls ("completeness"); otherwise, the likelihood of randomly identifying all switch/non-switch instances approaches zero ("soundness"). The aforementioned proof is zero-knowledge as your friend does not ascertain which ball is green and which is red; in fact, he acquires no information on the differentiation of the balls.

Definition

A zero-knowledge proof must satisfy three properties:

1. **Completeness**: if the statement is true, the honest verifier (that is, one following the protocol properly) will be convinced of this fact by an honest prover.
2. **Soundness**: if the statement is false, no cheating prover can convince the honest verifier that it is true, except with some small probability.
3. **Zero-knowledge**: if the statement is true, no verifier learns anything other than the fact that the statement is true. In other words, just knowing the statement (not the secret) is sufficient to imagine a scenario showing that the prover knows the secret. This is formalized by showing that every verifier has some simulator that, given only the statement to be proved (and no access to the prover), can produce a transcript that "looks like" an interaction between the honest prover and the verifier in question.

The first two of these are properties of more general interactive proof systems. The third is what makes the proof zero-knowledge. Zero-knowledge proofs are not proofs in the mathematical sense of the term because there is some small probability, the soundness error, that a cheating prover will be able to convince the verifier of a false statement. In other words, zero-knowledge proofs are probabilistic "proofs" rather than deterministic proofs. However, there are techniques to decrease the soundness error to negligibly small values. A formal definition of zero-knowledge has to use some computational model, the most common one being that of a Turing machine. Let {\displaystyle P},{\displaystyle V}, and {\displaystyle S} be Turing machines. An interactive proof system with {\displaystyle (P,V)} for a language {\displaystyle L} is zero-knowledge if for any probabilistic polynomial time (PPT) verifier {\displaystyle {\hat {V}}} there exists a PPT simulator {\displaystyle S} such that{\displastyle \forall x\in L,z\in \{0,1\}^{*},\operatorname {View} _{\hat {V}}\left[P(x)\leftrightarrow {\hat {V}}(x,z)\right]=S(x,z)} where {\displaystyle \operatorname {View}_{\hat {V}}\left[P(x)\leftrightarrow {\hat {V}}(x,z)\right]} is a record of the interactions between {\displaystyle P(x)} and {\displaystyle {\hat {V}}(x,z)}. The prover {\displaystyle P} is modeled as having unlimited computation power (in practice, P usually is a probabilistic Turing machine).

Intuitively, the definition states that an interactive proof system {\displaystyle (P,V)} is zero-knowledge if for any verifier {\displaystyle {\hat {V}}} there exists an efficient simulator {\displaystyle S} (depending on {\displaystyle {\hat {V}}}) that can reproduce the conversation between {\displaystyle P} and {\displaystyle {\hat {V}}} on any given input. The auxiliary string {\displaystyle z} in the definition plays the role of "prior knowledge" (including the random coins of {\displaystyle {\hat {V}}}). The definition implies that {\

displaystyle {\hat {V}}} cannot use any prior knowledge string {\displaystyle z} to mine information out of its conversation with {\displaystyle P}, because if {\displaystyle S} is also given this prior knowledge then it can reproduce the conversation between {\displaystyle {\hat {V}}} and {\displaystyle P} just as before. The definition given is that of perfect zero-knowledge. Computational zero-knowledge is obtained by requiring that the views of the verifier {\displaystyle {\hat {V}}} and the simulator are only computationally indistinguishable, given the auxiliary string.

2.2 BLOCKCHAIN

2.2.1 Introduction

Cryptography is a technique for safeguarding data against unauthorised access. Cryptography is employed in the blockchain to safeguard transactions occurring between two nodes inside a blockchain network. As previously said, a blockchain encompasses two primary concepts: cryptography and hashing. Cryptography encrypts messages in a P2P network, whereas hashing secures block information and links between blocks in a blockchain. Cryptography generally emphasises the security of participants, transactions, and protection against double-spending. It facilitates the security of various transactions within the blockchain network. It guarantees that only the designated persons may access, comprehend, and process the transaction data.

Role of Cryptography in Blockchain

Blockchain is constructed using several cryptographic principles. The advancement of cryptographic technology imposes limitations on the continued evolution of blockchain. In blockchain technology, encryption is primarily employed to safeguard user privacy and transaction data while ensuring data integrity. The fundamental technologies of cryptography encompass symmetric encryption and asymmetric encryption. Asymmetric cryptography employs digital signatures for verification, with each transaction recorded in the block being verified by the sender's digital signature, so ensuring data integrity. Cryptography is essential for ensuring the security of public networks, hence preserving the integrity and security of blockchain technology.

Benefits of Cryptography in Blockchain

Numerous advantages of cryptography in blockchain are outlined below:

- **Encryption:** Cryptography employs asymmetric encryption to safeguard transactions on its network, protecting information and communication from unauthorised disclosure and access.
- **Immutability:** This characteristic of cryptography is crucial for blockchain, facilitating the secure linkage of blocks and ensuring the integrity of data stored within the blockchain. It also prevents attackers from deriving valid signatures for unposed queries based on previous queries and their associated signatures.
- **Security:** Cryptography facilitates transaction record management through data encryption and access via public and private keys. Cryptographic hashing renders data manipulation infeasible, hence enhancing the security of blockchain technology.
- **Scalability:** Cryptography renders transactions irreversible, ensuring that all users can depend on the integrity of the digital ledger. It enables the secure recording of an unlimited number of transactions within the network.

- **Non-repudiation:** The digital signature offers a non-repudiation service to prevent any denial of a message transmitted by the sender. This advantage pertains to collision resistance; specifically, each input value possesses a distinct hash function, hence preventing any overlap across messages, allowing for clear differentiation between them.
- **Prevent hackers:** The digital signature inhibits hackers from modifying the data, as any alteration renders the digital signature invalid. Cryptography safeguards data from hackers and renders blockchain cryptography impervious.

Limitations of Cryptography in Blockchain

The following are certain limitations of cryptography in blockchain technology:

- **Information difficult to access:** Strongly encrypted and digitally signed information can be difficult to access even for a legitimate user at the most critical time of decision-making. An intruder can compromise the network, rendering it non-functional.
- **High availability:** It is one of the fundamental aspects of information security, and cannot be ensured through the use of cryptography. Alternative solutions are required to protect against threats such as denial of service or total failure of information systems.
- **No protection against vulnerabilities:** Cryptography does not guard against the vulnerabilities and threats that emerge from the poor design of protocols, procedures, and systems. These challenges must be resolved by the appropriate design of the defence infrastructure.
- **Expensive:** Cryptography needs huge time and money investments. Public key cryptography necessitates the establishment and upkeep of a public key infrastructure, which demands substantial investment. The incorporation of cryptographic algorithms during message transmission and information processing contributes to the delay.
- **Vulnerability:** The security of cryptographic methods relies on the intricacy and challenge of the mathematical problem. A breakthrough in resolving such mathematical issues could render cryptography systems susceptible.

2.2.2 Advantage over Conventional Distributed Database

Distributed databases essentially offer the benefits of distributed computing inside the realm of database administration. A distributed database is defined as a collection of interrelated databases dispersed across a computer network, while a distributed database management system is a software system that manages this distributed database, rendering the distribution transparent to the user. Distributed database management is primarily proposed for reasons such as organisational decentralisation, economic efficiency, and enhanced autonomy. The following are some of these advantages:

1. **Management of data with different level of transparency:** Ideally, a database should be distribution transparent in the sense of hiding the details of where each file is physically stored within the system. The subsequent categories of transparency are fundamentally achievable in the distributed database system:
    - **Network transparency:** This basically refers to the freedom for the user from the operational details of the network. There are two categories of these. Transparency in location and nomenclature.

- **Replication transparencies:** Replication transparencies render users oblivious to the existence of duplicates, as data copies may be kept at many locations to enhance availability, performance, and reliability.
- **Fragmentation transparency:** It renders the user oblivious to the existence of fragments, whether they are vertically or horizontally fragmented.

2. **Increased Reliability and availability:** Reliability is defined as the likelihood that a system is operational at a specific moment, while Availability refers to the probability that the system remains continuously accessible for a designated time period. When data and DBMS software are dispersed over multiple locations, one site may fail while others remain operational, restricting access solely to the data at the failed site, hence enhancing reliability and availability.
3. **Easier Expansion:** In a distributed environment expansion of the system in terms of adding more data, increasing database sizes or adding more processor is much easier.
   - **Improved Performance:** We can achieve interquery and intraquery parallelism by executing multiple queries at different sites by breaking up a query into a number of subqueries that basically executes in parallel which basically leads to improvement in performance.

Distributed databases are computer databases that are geographically dispersed across numerous physical sites, usually interconnected by a network. Here are some of the advantages of distributed databases:

- **Improved scalability:** Distributed databases can be scaled horizontally by adding more nodes to the network. This enables for increasing capacity and performance as data and user demand increases.
- **Increased availability:** Distributed databases can provide increased availability and uptime by distributing the data across multiple nodes. Should one node fail, data remains accessible from alternative nodes inside the network.
- **Increased flexibility:** Distributed databases can be more flexible than centralized databases, allowing data to be stored in a way that best suits the needs of the application or user.
- **Improved fault tolerance:** Distributed databases can be designed with redundancy and failover mechanisms that allow the system to continue operating in the event of a node failure.
- **Improved security:** Distributed databases can be more secure than centralized databases by implementing security measures at the network, node, and application levels.

Distributed databases offer numerous benefits compared to centralised databases, such as enhanced scalability, availability, performance, flexibility, fault tolerance, and security. The benefits of distributed databases render them a favoured option for large-scale applications requiring data access by several users or applications across geographically diverse locations.

Features of Distributed Databases Include

- **Scalability:** Distributed databases can be effortlessly expanded by incorporating additional nodes into the system. This enables the database to manage substantial data volumes and elevated traffic loads.

- **Fault tolerance:** Distributed databases are designed to be resilient to failures, which means that if one node fails, the database can continue to operate without interruption.
- **Data replication:** Distributed databases often replicate data across multiple nodes to ensure data availability and reduce the risk of data loss.
- **Distributed query processing:** Distributed databases can perform queries across multiple nodes, allowing for faster and more efficient data retrieval.
- **Data consistency:** Distributed databases must ensure data consistency across all nodes. This can be accomplished through multiple approaches, including the implementation of a consensus protocol or a distributed locking mechanism.
- **Location transparency:** Distributed databases enable users to access data irrespective of the data's or user's geographical location. This indicates that users can retrieve the necessary data from any node inside the system.
- **Security:** Distributed databases must guarantee that data is safeguarded against unauthorised access. This can be accomplished using diverse security measures, including encryption and access control.

2.3 BLOCKCHAIN NETWORK

Core Components of Blockchain Networks

The fundamental elements of blockchain networks are crucial for their operation and efficacy. Every component is essential for preserving the integrity, security, and efficiency of the blockchain. The fundamental elements of the blockchain network are as follows:

1. **Nodes:** Nodes are distinct computers that engage in the blockchain network. Each node retains a complete or partial copy of the whole blockchain.
   - **Full Nodes:** It retains a complete record of all transactions. It possesses the ability to validate, accept, and reject transactions.
   - **Partial Nodes:** it often referred to as Lightweight Nodes, do not retain a complete copy of the blockchain ledger. It retains solely the hash value of the transaction. The entire transaction is available solely through its hash value. These nodes possess limited storage capacity and minimal processing power. **Mining Nodes:** Nodes that authenticate transactions and incorporate them into the blockchain, usually via a process known as mining (in Proof of Work systems).
2. **Ledger:** The blockchain functions as a decentralised ledger that securely and permanently records all transactions. The ledger consists of blocks, each encompassing a collection of transactions, a timestamp, and a reference (hash) to the preceding block, therefore creating a chronological chain.
   - **Public Ledger:** It is accessible and transparent to everyone. Any participant in the blockchain network can access or modify information.
   - **Distributed Ledger:** In this ledger, every node possesses a local copy of the database. A consortium of nodes collaboratively performs the task of verifying transactions and appending blocks to the blockchain.
   - **Decentralised Ledger:** In this ledger, no single node or collective of nodes possesses central authority. Each node engages in the execution of the task.

3. **Transactions:** Transactions constitute the essential data units within a blockchain, signifying the exchange of value or information. A transaction is generated, authenticated by nodes, and subsequently documented on the blockchain. It generally comprises the sender's and recipient's addresses, the amount, and a digital signature for verification.
4. **Consensus Mechanisms:** Consensus mechanisms are algorithms that enable the network to concur on the legitimacy of transactions and uphold a uniform state of the ledger.
    - **Proof of Work (PoW):** Necessitates participants to resolve intricate mathematical equations to authenticate transactions (e.g., Bitcoin).
    - **Proof of Stake (PoS):** Validators are selected according to the quantity of coins they possess and are prepared to "stake" as collateral (e.g., Ethereum 2.0).
    - **Delegated Proof of Stake (DPoS):** Participants elect a limited number of delegates to authenticate transactions on their behalf.

Auxiliary Elements of Blockchain Networks

Supporting components collaborate to establish a resilient framework for diverse uses of blockchain technology. This is a summary of the auxiliary elements:

1. Cryptography

Cryptography is vital for safeguarding transactions, ensuring data integrity, and preserving privacy inside the blockchain network.

- **Hash Functions:** Produce a distinctive fixed-size output (hash) for any input data. This guarantees that even a minor alteration in the input will yield an entirely distinct hash, so safeguarding the data against manipulation.
- **Digital Signatures:** Employed to authenticate the legitimacy of transactions. A digital signature is generated with the sender's private key and can be authenticated by others with the sender's public key, thereby verifying the transaction's integrity and origin.
- **Public and Private Keys:** Every user possesses a pair of cryptographic keys. The public key is disseminated, whereas the private key remains confidential, facilitating safe transaction authentication.

2. Smart Contracts

Smart contracts are self-executing agreements with terms encoded directly in software, operating on the blockchain.

- **Automation:** They provide contract execution autonomously, eliminating intermediaries, hence decreasing costs and enhancing efficiency.
- **Conditions:** Smart contracts can perform activities when specified circumstances are satisfied, such as transferring funds or issuing tokens.
- **Use Cases:** Widely utilised in diverse applications, including as supply chain management, insurance claims, and decentralised finance (DeFi).

3. Tokens

Tokens are digital assets established on a blockchain that signify diverse utilities, rights, or properties.

- **Utility Tokens:** Grant users access to a particular product or service within a blockchain ecosystem (e.g., Ethereum's Ether).
- **Security Tokens:** Indicate ownership of a tangible asset, such as equities or real estate, and are subject to regulatory oversight.
- **Stablecoins:** Cryptocurrencies engineered to preserve a consistent value, frequently linked to a fiat currency (e.g., USDT, USDC).

2.3.1 Mining Mechanism

What is Blockchain Mining?

In the context of bitcoins or other cryptocurrencies, blockchain mining is the procedure that authenticates each phase of the transaction. Individuals engaged in this process are referred to as blockchain miners, whose principal objective is to validate the transfer of funds between computers inside the network via a complex array of hardware and software. The nomenclature of blockchains derives from their 'blocks' and 'chain' configuration. The blocks consist of many bitcoins, which are discrete entities containing all data code individually. The links that join one neighbourhood block to another are termed the chain. Each blockchain signifies a distinct code authentication that is securely maintained within the network software and is explicitly encrypted.

From The term "blockchain mining" refers to the fundamental process of incorporating transaction data into the Bitcoin blockchain. These blockchain miners configure and operate specialised blockchain mining software on their PCs, enabling secure interaction among themselves. A system that downloads software, connects to the network, and commences bitcoin mining is termed a 'node.' All of these nodes collaborate to communicate and execute transactions to include new blocks into the blockchain, commonly referred to as the Bitcoin network. The Bitcoin network operates continuously, 24 hours a day. Since its establishment in 2009, it has remained impervious to hacking and has not experienced downtime while facilitating millions of dollars in bitcoin transactions. A centralised authority—such as a regulatory agency, governing body, or bank—does not exist in Blockchain to guarantee the completion of bitcoin transactions.

Any individual possessing mining hardware and an Internet connection may join the mining community and engage in participation. Proof of work is a complex mathematical problem employed to facilitate the process. Proof of labour is necessary to authenticate the transaction and obtain remuneration for the miner. The miners compete to mine a particular transaction, with the first miner to solve the puzzle winning the reward. Miners are participants in the network possessing the necessary hardware and computational power to authenticate transactions.

Types of Mining

Utilising a regular desktop or PC is impractical owing to the complexity of resources and work required in the mining process. The blockchain mining process requires specialist computer hardware and software to meet the necessary expertise. It is neither the endeavour of an individual or a machine. When these two converge, the intelligence and data decryption velocities will integrate to function within a singular transaction authentication process. Possessing dedicated mining hardware and software specifically designed for block mining would be beneficial. Participate in a mining pool to gain access to your Bitcoin wallet. To prevent fraudulent transactions of bitcoin mining rewards, ensure the security of your wallet. The mining process can be conducted individually, in a group, or via cloud mining.

Individual Mining

An individual must first register as a miner before commencing mining activities. Upon the completion of a transaction, all individual users inside the blockchain network are tasked with solving a mathematical puzzle. The individual who resolves it first is rewarded. Upon discovering the solution, all other miners in the blockchain network will validate the decrypted value prior to its incorporation into the blockchain. The transaction is confirmed.

Pool Mining

A collective of users collaborates to authorise a transaction in pool mining. The complexity of the data encoded in the blocks may occasionally render it impossible for a user to independently decrypt the information. Consequently, a consortium of miners collaborates to devise a solution. Upon the verification of the result, the award is distributed among all participants.

Cloud Mining

Cloud mining no longer necessitates computer hardware and software. It is an uncomplicated method to eliminate obstructions. Cloud mining alleviates the ongoing concerns associated with managing machines, order scheduling, and sales revenue. Although it is advantageous, it entails certain disadvantages. The operational capacity is constrained by bitcoin hashing limitations. The meagre incentive earnings lead to an increase in operating expenditures. Software upgrades are restricted, as is the validation process.

Use of Blockchain Mining Validating Transactions

Bitcoins are decentralised digital currencies managed and exchanged among users using a peer-to-peer computer network. Bitcoin transactions are substantial on a daily basis. Nonetheless, there exists a delay inside the entire framework. The transactions entail considerable risk as these cryptocurrencies function without a central authority. The legitimacy of printed currency is determined by the numerical codes inscribed on each note. Consequently, how are such cryptocurrencies authenticated? Blocks are appended to the blockchain with every transaction. Outcomes of blockchain miners function as verification.

Confirming Transactions

Bitcoins are distinctly embedded within the blocks of the blockchain network.

A transaction occurs within the blocks of the Bitcoin network. Miners employ the blockchain mining process to establish the authenticity of a transaction. Upon the completion of the block, the transactions receive confirmation.

Maintaining Safe Channels

Bitcoin miners cooperate to maintain the security of the transaction network. As the quantity of operators engaged in blockchain mining increases, network security correspondingly enhances. In instances of attack, duplicity, or deceit, the decentralised network renders the attribution of culpability to any individual unfeasible. The security of cryptocurrency networks ensures the prevention of fraudulent activities.

Conclusion

The path to achieving ubiquitous and accessible blockchain technology for all individuals globally is complex. Blockchain, as to any emerging technology, seems to hold significant promise. Upon its inception, the internet generated significant excitement and was acclaimed as the most groundbreaking technology ever created. It transformed our communication methods, yet necessitated time for maturation and enhancement.

2.3.2 Distributed Consensus

What is Distributed Consensus in Distributed Systems?

Distributed consensus in distributed systems denotes the mechanism via which several nodes or components within a network reach an agreement on a singular value or course of action, notwithstanding possible failures or variations in their initial states or inputs.

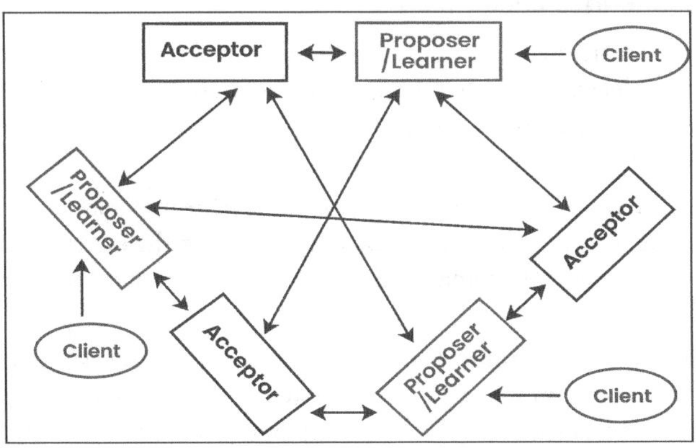

Fig. 2.2

Ensuring consistency and dependability in decentralised environments, where nodes may function autonomously and encounter delays or failures, is crucial. Widely utilised algorithms such as Paxos and Raft are engineered to accomplish distributed consensus efficiently.

Importance of Distributed Consensus in Distributed Systems

The following delineates the significance of distributed consensus in distributed systems:

- **Consistency and Reliability:** Distributed consensus guarantees that all nodes within a distributed system concur on a unified state or decision. This consistency is essential for preserving data integrity and averting conflicting updates.
- **Fault Tolerance:** Distributed consensus algorithms allow systems to maintain correct functionality despite the failure of certain nodes or the occurrence of network partitions. By establishing a uniform state, the system can recuperate and maintain activities seamlessly.

- **Decentralisation:** In decentralised networks, where nodes function independently, distributed consensus facilitates coordinated actions and guarantees that decisions are made collectively rather than centrally. This is crucial for scalability and resilience.
- **Concurrency Control:** Consensus protocols facilitate the management of simultaneous access to shared resources or data among distributed nodes. Consensus establishes the order of processes or transactions, so preventing conflicts and preserving data integrity.
- **Blockchain and Distributed Ledgers:** In blockchain technology and distributed ledgers, consensus algorithms (e.g., Proof of Work, Proof of Stake) are fundamental. They facilitate consensus among participants on transaction authenticity and uphold a decentralised, immutable transaction record.

Challenges of Achieving Consensus

Reaching consensus in distributed systems poses numerous obstacles due to the intrinsic complexities and possible uncertainties inside networked contexts.

The Primary Challenges Encompass

- **Network Partitions:** Network partitions can occur due to communication failures or delays between nodes. Consensus algorithms must guarantee that, notwithstanding the occurrence of partitions, nodes can ultimately converge on a consistent state or outcome.
- **Node Failures:** Nodes inside a distributed system may have failures or become inaccessible, resulting in possible inconsistencies in the system's state. Consensus protocols must adeptly manage these errors and guarantee the system's continued functionality.
- **Asynchronous Communication:** Nodes within distributed systems can engage in asynchronous communication, resulting in potential delays, reordering, or loss of messages. Consensus algorithms must account for such communication issues to enable accurate and speedy decision-making.
- **Byzantine Faults:** Byzantine faults occur when nodes exhibit arbitrary or malicious behavior, such as sending incorrect information or intentionally disrupting communication. Byzantine fault-tolerant consensus techniques are essential for ensuring correctness amongst such defects.

Distributed Consensus Algorithms in Distributed Systems

Distributed consensus algorithms are fundamental in ensuring that nodes in a distributed system can agree on a single value or decision despite potential failures, delays, or differences in their initial states. These algorithms play a crucial role in maintaining consistency, reliability, and coordination across decentralized networks. Here's an in-depth explanation of key distributed consensus algorithms:

1. Paxos Algorithm

Paxos is a classic consensus algorithm which ensures that a distributed system can agree on a single value or sequence of values, even if some nodes may fail or messages may be delayed. Key concepts of paxos algorithm include:

Paxos Algorithm

- **Roles:**
  - **Proposer**: Initiates the proposal of a value.
  - **Acceptor**: Accepts proposals from proposers and communicates its acceptance.
  - **Learner**: Learns the chosen value from acceptors.

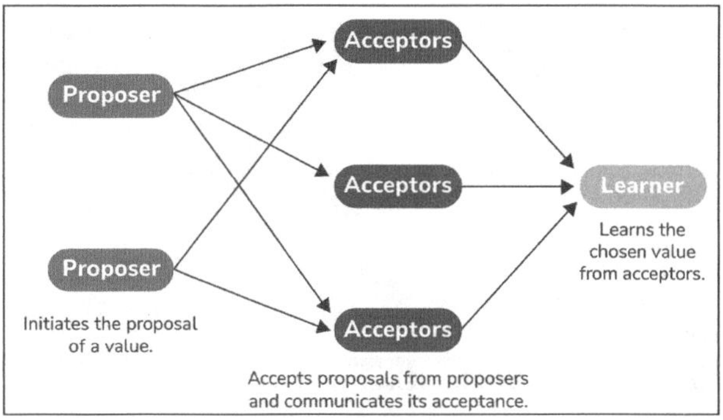

Fig. 2.3

- **Phases:**
  - **Phase 1 (Prepare):** Proposers send prepare requests to a majority of acceptors to prepare them to accept a proposal.
  - **Phase 2 (Accept):** Proposers send accept requests to acceptors with a proposal, which is accepted if a majority of acceptors agree.
- **Working**:
  - **Proposers:** Proposers initiate the consensus process by proposing a value to be agreed upon.
  - **Acceptors:** Acceptors receive proposals from proposers and can either accept or reject them based on certain criteria.
  - **Learners:** Learners are entities that receive the agreed-upon value or decision once consensus is reached among the acceptors.
- **Safety and Liveness:**
  - Paxos ensures safety (only one value is chosen) and liveness (a value is eventually chosen) properties under normal operation assuming a majority of nodes are functioning correctly.
- **Use Cases:**
  - Paxos is used in distributed databases, replicated state machines, and other systems where achieving consensus among nodes is critical.

2. Raft Algorithm

The Raft algorithm is a consensus algorithm designed to achieve consensus among a cluster of nodes in a distributed system. It simplifies the complexities of traditional consensus algorithms like Paxos while providing similar guarantees. Raft operates by electing a leader among the nodes in a cluster, where the leader manages the replication of a log that contains commands or operations to be executed.

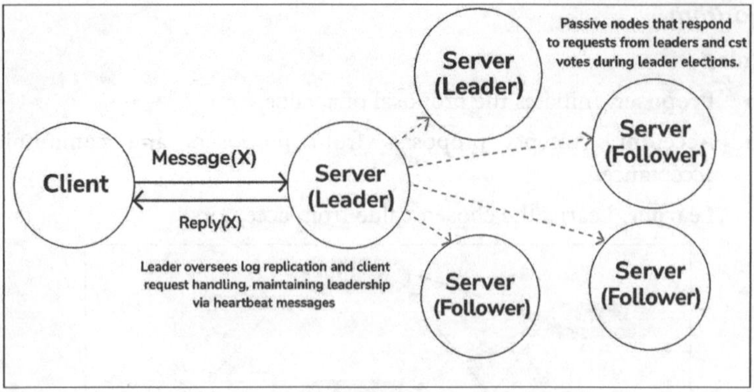

Fig. 2.4

Raft Algorithm

- **Key Concepts:**
  - **Leader Election:** Nodes elect a leader responsible for managing log replication and handling client requests.
  - **Log Replication:** Leader replicates its log entries to followers, ensuring consistency across the cluster.
  - **Safety and Liveness:** Raft guarantees safety (log entries are consistent) and liveness (a leader is elected and log entries are eventually committed) under normal operation.
- **Phases:**
  - **Leader Election:** Nodes participate in leader election based on a term number and leader's heartbeat.
  - **Log Replication:** Leader sends Append Entries messages to followers to replicate log entries, ensuring consistency.
- **Use Cases:**
  - Raft is widely used in modern distributed systems such as key-value stores, consensus-based replicated databases, and systems requiring strong consistency guarantees.

3. Byzantine Fault Tolerance (BFT) Algorithm

Byzantine Fault Tolerance (BFT) algorithms are designed to address the challenges posed by Byzantine faults in distributed systems, where nodes may fail in arbitrary ways, including sending incorrect or conflicting information. These algorithms ensure that the system can continue to operate correctly and reach consensus even when some nodes behave maliciously or fail unexpectedly.

BFT Algorithm

- **Key Concepts:**
  - **Byzantine Faults:** Nodes may behave arbitrarily, including sending conflicting messages or omitting messages.

› **Redundancy and Voting:** BFT algorithms typically require a 2/3 or more agreement among nodes to determine the correct state or decision.

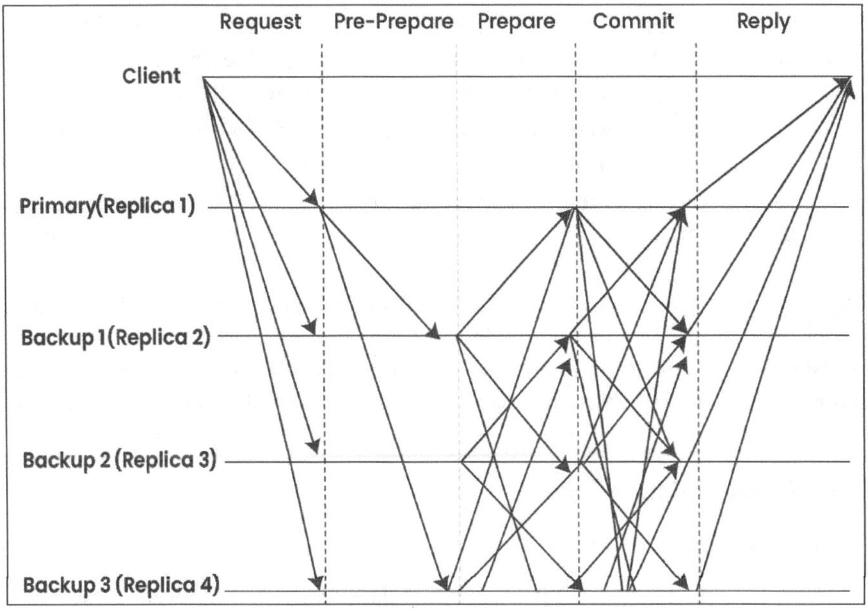

Fig. 2.5

- **Examples:**
  - › **Practical Byzantine Fault Tolerance (PBFT):** Used in systems where safety and liveness are crucial, such as blockchain networks and distributed databases.
  - › **Simplified Byzantine Fault Tolerance (SBFT):** Provides a simpler approach to achieving BFT with reduced complexity compared to PBFT.
- **Use Cases:**
  - › BFT algorithms are essential in environments requiring high fault tolerance and security, where nodes may not be fully trusted or may exhibit malicious behavior.

A practical Byzantine Fault Tolerant system can function on the condition that the maximum number of malicious nodes must not be greater than or equal to one-third of all the nodes in the system. As the number of nodes increase, the system becomes more secure. pBFT consensus rounds are broken into 4 phases.

- The client sends a request to the primary(leader) node.
- The primary(leader) node broadcasts the request to the all the secondary(backup) nodes.
- The nodes(primary and secondaries) perform the service requested and then send back a reply to the client.
- The request is served successfully when the client receives 'm+1' replies from different nodes in the network with the same result, where m is the maximum number of faulty nodes allowed.

4. Challenges and Considerations

- **Network Partitions and Delays:** Algorithms must handle network partitions and communication delays, ensuring that nodes eventually reach consensus.
- **Scalability:** As the number of nodes increases, achieving consensus becomes more challenging due to increased communication overhead.
- **Performance:** Consensus algorithms should be efficient to minimize latency and maximize system throughput.
- **Understanding and Implementation:** Many consensus algorithms, especially BFT variants, are complex and require careful implementation to ensure correctness and security.

In summary, distributed consensus algorithms are crucial for enabling cooperation and coordination among nodes in distributed systems. They ensure that all nodes agree on a consistent state or decision, providing reliability, fault tolerance, and consistency across decentralized networks in various applications from distributed databases to blockchain networks.

2.3.3 Merkle Patricia Tree

What Is Merkle Patricia Trie?

The Merkle Patricia Trie (MPT) is an essential data structure employed in the Ethereum blockchain, combining the features of Merkle trees and Patricia tries. Its principal duty is to serve as a resilient data storage system for overseeing the extensive collection of transactions and receipts on the network.

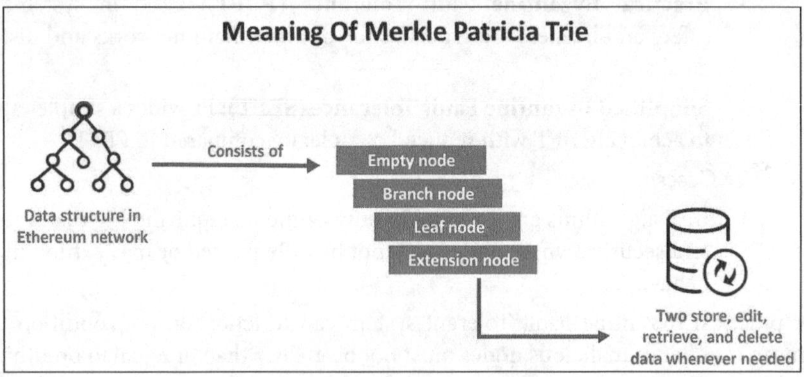

Fig. 2.6

In contrast to Bitcoin, the Merkle Patricia Trie is purpose-built for Ethereum, meeting the special requirements of the network. It stands as a unique and crucial component of Ethereum's architecture, enabling efficient data management capabilities customised to Ethereum's decentralized and smart contract centred ecosystem.

- The Merkle Patricia Trie (MPT) is a crucial database structure that integrates Patricia Tries with Merkle Trees, predominantly utilised in the Ethereum blockchain.
- It has multiple node kinds, such as empty, branch, leaf, and extension nodes, creating a structured data storage system.

- Ethereum utilises three separate tree structures: the transaction tree, the receipt tree, and the state tree. Empty nodes function as backups for branch nodes, while other nodes house keys and pathways.
- This architecture enhances data storage and retrieval within the Ethereum network.

Merkle Patricia Trie Explained

The Merkle Patricia Trie is a database utilised by Ethereum, representing a variant of the Patricia Trie. It provides a systematic method for arranging and preserving data in a hierarchical framework. In this sense, Patricia originates from Practical Algorithm To Retrieve Information Coded In Alphanumeric, whereas Trie pertains to retrieval. A comparable database exists in Bitcoin, although it does not meet Ethereum's specifications. In contrast to Bitcoin's immutable transaction ledger, Ethereum's dynamic characteristics and the establishment of new accounts necessitate adaptability.

Consequently, the MPT was intentionally built for Ethereum. It functions using a key-value mapping framework, utilising keys (transaction IDs) and values (transactions). It functions to store and retrieve data efficiently, although it eliminates actions subsequent to a transaction. The altered MPT in Ethereum consists of many nodes identifiable through hashing. The root node functions as a parent node or cryptographic embodiment of the complete Trie. Moreover, various tree architectures, including transactions, receipts, and state trees, fulfil distinct purposes. The transaction tree governs block inclusion, the receipts tree extracts transaction-related information, and the state tree authenticates balance modifications and account existence inside the network.

Features (Nodes)

In the Ethereum network's MPT, essential components, or nodes, play crucial roles. Every node has a distinct hash value that serves as a key, linking to branches via nibbles to differentiate objects according to their intrinsic values. Let us examine these types of nodes:

1. Null Nodes

These nodes signify empty strings and function as placeholders for absent or deleted values when required. They not only substitute such values but also serve as evidence of the MPT for a particular datum.

2. Branch Nodes

Branch nodes are akin to the branches of a tree, as the name implies. Each branch node comprises 17 items, with one item denoting the value and the other 16 being hexadecimal characters. The final item functions as the key-value pair.

3. Leaf nodes

A node devoid of child nodes is designated as a leaf node (or terminal node). It derives from a branch node and comprises two elements: path and value. For example, if AxBE is a branch node in the MPT, the next leaf nodes would be AxBEF and AxBEC. Every leaf node, such as AxBEF, exhibits AxF as the path and 1000 as the value.

4. Extension nodes

The extension node functions as a shortcut to stored data. It is an enhanced iteration of a branch node. In certain cases, branch nodes possess a singular child node without any following siblings. To optimise the Trie, these branch nodes are consolidated into extension nodes, which encompass a prefix, path, and value associated with the child node. The hash value originates from another node in this situation.

Examples

Let us examine few examples to enhance our understanding of the concept:

Example 1

Assume TICK functions on the Ethereum blockchain network. This network routinely documents millions of transactions, including the establishment of countless accounts to enable these exchanges. These accounts retain critical information regarding keys and account balances, then organised and archived in the MPT for future retrieval. Multiple accounts, including Account #1, #2, and #3, are incorporated into this database. The beginning phase begins with an empty node, which acts as the fundamental element of the Trie. Consequently, all three accounts develop into branch nodes. At this level, it is essential to furnish a Merkle Patricia Trie proof to authenticate the account balances. This proof is derived from the root node and extends to Account #1, incorporating the hashes of the empty node, branch node, and leaf node. When an account holder transfers 20 ETH to another wallet, the Merkle Patricia Trie is updated. Thus, the proof produced subsequently will exhibit these alterations in its condition. This procedure comprehensively gathers all data from the TICK blockchain.

Example 2

In the swiftly advancing realm of cryptocurrencies, June 2023 has introduced significant advancements with the inception of Kakarot zkEVM. This Ethereum Virtual Machine (EVM) implementation, developed in Cairo, is set to significantly transform the Ethereum and StarkWare ecosystems. Kakarot zkEVM delineates an ambitious three-phase program. Phase one emphasises the incorporation of EVM capabilities into Starknet, facilitating application deployment. In the subsequent phase, Kakarot and Madara amalgamate to create L3 zkEVM, augmenting security and decentralisation via proof of validity. The concluding step amalgamates Kakarot and Madara to establish type 1 zkEVM, facilitating L1 consensus proofs and possibly shifting from Pedersen Merkle Patricia Trie (MPT) to Keccak MPT. This strategic advancement enhances efficiency while diminishing computational and storage expenses, indicating a favourable future for a more secure, scalable, and economical blockchain environment.

Importance

MPTs are essential data structures in both blockchains and computer systems. Their importance to network participants might be encapsulated as follows: MPTs effectively retain both transient and enduring data. They employ Patricia attempts for the former and integrate static data into Merkle trees. These structures are proficient in enabling frequent data modifications and updates within nodes. They facilitate data deletion post-operations, guaranteeing the removal of obsolete data nodes as fresh ones are updated.

MPTs provide developers with the benefit of code reusability for protocol updates, functioning as a universal framework for significant upgrades without necessitating the creation of wholly new code from the ground up. MPTs are crucial in minimising data storage needs and related expenses in the recording and maintenance of databases. Their compression methodologies, especially within the Ethereum network, effectively tackle this issue.

2.3.4 Gas Limit

Ethereum Gas is a metric that quantifies the computational effort required to execute specified functions. Every function that executes a position in Ethereum, such as transactions and smart contracts, requires a portion of gas for performance. The blockchain P2P network relies on this power, much to how fuel enables an automobile to operate. Gas denotes the expense incurred to execute a transaction on the Ethereum network.

- Information regarding Ethereum Natural gas
- Petrol prices are expressed in Ethereum's native currency, ETH.
- Petrol prices are expressed in "gwei," a unit of Ethereum, where one "gwei" is equal to 0.000000001 ETH.
- Instead of indicating that the petrol costs 0.000000001 ether, specify that the petrol costs 1 "gwei".
- The term "gwei" denotes "Giga-wei," equivalent to 1,000,000,000 "wei.". "Wei" is named after "Wei Dai," the originator of b-money (the smallest unit of ETH).

GWEI

Gwei is a portmanteau of "giga" and "wei". It is a faction of the blockchain technology Ethereum; this cryptocurrency functions on the Ethereum peer-to- peer network. ETH is a blockchain platform, akin to Bitcoin and Binance, enabling users to conduct transactions related to the purchasing and selling of interests and benefits without the necessity of an intermediary.

Example

For example, Rahul needs to give 1 ETH to Shubham. During the transaction, the gas boundary is 21000 units, and the gas price is 200 gwei.

Total fee costs = Gas units (limit) * Gas price per unit

= 21000 * 200

= 4,200,000 gwei (0.0042 ETH)

- When Rahul dispatched the funds, 1.0042 ETH would be subtracted from Rahul's account.
- Shubham would be credited 1.0000 ETH only as 0.0042 is the fess of Miner.

Now **after upgradation**, increased advantages presented by the difference contain more profitable trade fee computation, typically more rapid trade inclusion, and cancelling the ETH distribution by burning portion of trade fees

- Beginning with the peer-to-peer network upgrade, each block unit has a ground fee, the lowest price per unit of gas for inclusion in this block unit, estimated by the network founded on request.

- Because the ground fee of the trade fee is burnt, users are also hoped to put a tip in their dealings.
- The information pays miners for managing and breeding user trades in blocks and is hoped to be set automatically by most wallets.

Total fee after upgradation = Gas units (limit) * (Base fee + Tip)

For example, Shubham has to pay 1 ETH to Rahul. This process has a gas limit of 21000 units and base fee of 100gwei. Shubham includes tip of 10 gwei.

Total fee after upgradation

= Gas units (limit) * (Base fee + Tip)
= 21000 * (100 + 10)
= 2,310,000 gwei (0.00231 ETH).

- When Shubham sends the funds, 1.00231 ETH will be subtracted from Shubham's account.
- Rahul will be credited 1.0000 ETH and 0.00021 ETH will be received by the miner as the tip.
- A ground fee of 0.0021 ETH is ignited.

Gas Fees

The petrol fees encompass Base, Priority, Max, and calculation fees. Let us examine these terms comprehensively.

1. **Base fees:** Every alliance imposes a ground fee that functions as a fund price. The ground charge is calculated independently of the current alliance and is explicitly determined by the alliances prior to enhancing trade prices for users. Upon excavation of the block, the base charge is rendered void, removing it from regulation. The ground charge is assessed based on directives that juxtapose the length of the preceding block with the designated size. The base charge is intended to increase by a maximum of 12.5% per block if the designated block size is exceeded.
2. **Priority fee:** In addition to the base cost received, the advancement included a priority charge, which serves as a tip to miners to expedite a transaction inside the alliance. Miners can find it financially feasible to drill cleared blocks without tips, as they can secure the precise alliance reward. Typically, a modest gratuity offers miners less motivation to uphold a transaction. For transactions that necessitate preferred execution over other trades inside the same block, a higher tip will be required to surpass competing trades.
3. **Max fee:** Users can specify the maximum amount they are willing to spend to complete transactions on the P2P network. This supplementary circumference is referred to as the maximum fee/Gas. For a trade to be executed, the maximum fee must exceed the sum of the base and priority fees. The trade sender gets reimbursed the difference between the maximum fee and the sum of the base fee and tip.
4. **Calculating fees:** The primary advantage of the upgrading is the improvement of the user's understanding regarding the assessment of trade fees. Providers will automatically establish a recommended transaction charge (base fee plus suggested priority fee) in the wallets that support the upgrade, rather than explicitly instructing users to pay the transaction from a wallet, hence reducing the complexity imposed on consumers.

Importance of Gas Fees

Here are few reasons why petrol fees are significant:

- Petrol fees contribute to the security of the Ethereum peer-to-peer network. By imposing a fee for each analysis conducted on the web grid, it deters malicious actors from spamming the web grid.
- To avoid unforeseen or malicious infinite loops and various computational inefficiencies, it is essential for each transaction to establish a limit on the operational scope of several coding efforts.
- The fundamental classification of accounting is "gas".
- A trade establishes a boundary, and any petrol unit not employed in the trade is substituted (i.e. maximum fee minus (base fee plus tip)).

Why Gas Fees can go High?

The rise in petrol prices is attributable to the prominence of Ethereum. Executing any operation on Ethereum requires using gas, and the gas fee is decided every transaction. Prices encompass metrics, managing or using data, and assimilating different components of "gas" units. As app functionality increases in complexity, the number of tasks a smart contract may do likewise expands, indicating that each transaction introduces more additional space within a set measure block. In instances of strong demand, consumers are required to offer a higher tip to compete with the transactions of others. A higher tip can enhance the likelihood that your transaction will be included in the next block.

Initiative to Reduce Gas Costs

The gains in ETH efficiency are expected to address certain gas cost issues, enabling the medium to handle thousands of trades globally per moment. Second layer scaling aims to substantially improve petrol fees, user experience, and scalability. The latest proof-of-stake (POS) model based on the Beacon Chain is expected to reduce excessive energy use and reliance on technological hardware. This chain resolution enables decentralised ETH P2P networks to enhance network security while minimising petrol usage by imposing economic accountability.

Strategies to Reduce Gas Costs

Methods to reduce petrol expenses for ETH. Users can choose a direction to present the significant status of the user's transaction. Miners intend to execute deals that indicate a higher petrol tip, as they retain the tips customers pay and are inclined to prioritise transactions with lower specified tips. Users interested in monitoring gas costs can send ETH for smaller transactions and utilise several tools listed below: "Etherscan Transaction Gas Price Estimator," "Blocknative ETH Gas Estimator" for assessing both Class 0 inheritance transactions and Class 2 EIP-1559 transactions, "ETH Gas Station" which provides user-directed metrics for Ethereum gas demand, and "Cryptoneur Gas Fees Calculator" for calculating gas prices in local currency for various trades.

Why do Gas Fees Exist?

Petrol prices contribute to the security of the Ethereum network. By imposing a fee for each analysis conducted on the grid, it mitigates the risk of malicious actors inundating the grid with spam. To circumvent unforeseen code, each transaction must provide a constraint on the numerous computing attempts of regulatory performance. The fundamental unit of analysis is "gas". Furthermore, a trade has a constraint; any gas not utilised in a transaction is returned to the user (i.e., max fee minus (base fee plus tip) is returned).

How does Block Size Affect the Base Fees?

The base fee is calculated using a method that correlates the dimensions of the most recent block (the portion of petrol consumed for all transactions) with the intended size. The base price will increase by a maximum of 12.5% per alliance if the specified block size is exceeded.

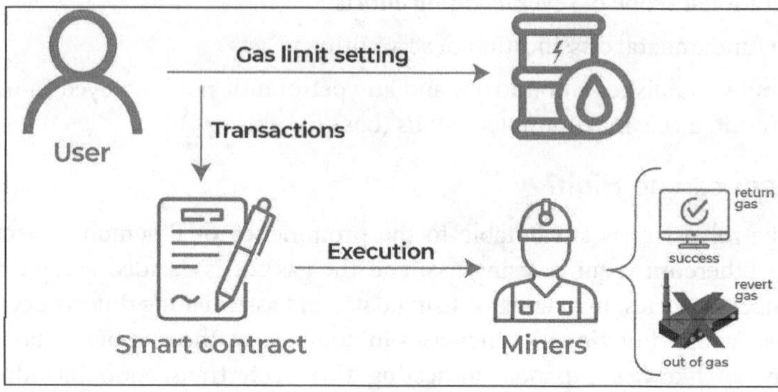

Fig. 2.7

2.3.5 Transactions And Fee

Transaction fees fulfil two critical functions within blockchain networks: they compensate miners or validators for confirming transactions and safeguard the network against spam attacks. The magnitude of transaction fees can vary, influenced by network activity and market dynamics. Elevated fees may impede broader blockchain adoption, whereas excessively low fees could raise security issues.

Why Transaction Fees?

Transaction fees have been a fundamental component of most blockchain systems since their introduction. You are likely to have encountered them while sending, depositing, or withdrawing cryptocurrency. The predominant cryptocurrencies utilise transaction fees for two significant purposes. Primarily, fees diminish the volume of spam on the network. It also renders large-scale spam attacks financially burdensome and costly to execute. Secondly, transaction fees serve as an incentive for users who assist in verifying and validating transactions. Consider it a recompense for assisting the network. Transaction fees on most blockchains are generally affordable, although they can become quite costly depending on network congestion. Your selected fee amount dictates the priority of your transaction for inclusion in the subsequent block. A greater price results in a more expedited confirmation process.

Bitcoin Transaction Fees

Bitcoin, as the inaugural blockchain network, established the benchmark for transaction fees utilised by several cryptocurrencies currently. Satoshi Nakamoto recognised that transaction fees may safeguard the network against extensive spam attacks and promote ethical conduct. Bitcoin miners obtain transaction fees during the confirmation of transactions into a new block. The collection of unverified transactions is referred to as the memory pool (or mempool). Miners will inherently prioritise transactions that offer larger fees, which customers consented to pay when transferring their BTC to another bitcoin wallet. Malicious entities intending to impede the network must thus incur a cost for each transaction. If the fee is set excessively low, miners are likely to disregard their transactions. Establishing them at an appropriate level incurs substantial economic costs. Transaction fees serve as a straightforward yet efficient spam filter.

How Are BTC Transaction Fees Calculated?

Within the Bitcoin network, specific cryptocurrency wallets enable users to manually configure their transaction costs. It is feasible to transmit BTC without incurring fees; but, miners are likely to disregard such transactions, resulting in their non-validation. Contrary to popular belief, Bitcoin fees are determined by the transaction size (in bytes) rather than the amount sent. For instance, consider a transaction size of 400 bytes, with the average transaction price now at 80 satoshis per byte. Consequently, you would need to remit around 32,000 satoshis (equivalent to 0.00032 BTC) to enhance the likelihood of your transaction being incorporated into the subsequent block. During periods of elevated network traffic and increased demand for BTC transactions, the requisite transaction cost for prompt confirmation escalates as other Bitcoin users attempt to execute similar transactions. This may transpire during phases of significant market volatility.

The elevated fees render the utilisation of BTC in everyday transactions problematic. Purchasing a $3 cup of coffee may be impractical if the associated fees significantly exceed that amount. A block can accommodate a limited amount of transactions, with a maximum size of 1MB. Miners append these blocks to the blockchain as expeditiously as feasible; yet, there remains a constraint on their speed. The scalability of bitcoin networks is a pivotal factor in determining network costs. Blockchain engineers are persistently striving to resolve the issue. Prior network enhancements have augmented scalability, including the adoption of SegWit and the Lightning Network.

Ethereum Transaction Fees

Ethereum transaction fees operate differently than those of Bitcoin. The charge considers the needed computational power for transaction processing, referred to as gas. The price of petrol fluctuates and is measured in ether (ETH), the native token of the network. The gas required for a particular transaction may remain constant, although gas prices can fluctuate. The petrol price is directly correlated with network traffic. Paying a greater petrol price will likely lead miners to prioritise your transaction.

How Are Ethereum Transaction Fees Calculated?

The total petrol fee is a charge that encompasses the cost and an incentive for processing your transaction. Additionally, one must take into account the petrol limit, which stipulates the maximum fee incurred for that transaction or operation. The gas cost represents the work necessary, while the gas price denotes the payment for each hour of work. The relationship between these two factors and the gas limit determines the overall charge for an Ethereum transaction or smart contract execution. Let us select a random transaction on Etherscan.io as an illustration. The transaction incurred a cost of 21,000 petrol, with a petrol price of 71 Gwei. The aggregate transaction cost amounted to 1,491,000 Gwei, equivalent to 0.001491 ETH. As Ethereum makes its way towards a Proof of Stake model (see Casper), there is an expectation that gas fees will decrease.

The amount of gas needed to confirm a transaction will be lower as the network will need only a fraction of the computational power to validate transactions.

? Value:	0.284585730935860475 Ether ($503.75)
? Transaction Fee:	0.001491 Ether ($2.64)
? Gas Price:	0.000000071 Ether (71 Gwei)
? Gas Limit:	21.000
? Gas used by Transaction:	21.000 (100%)

But, network traffic can still affect transaction fees as validators prioritize higher-paying transactions.

How are BNB Smart Chain Transaction Fees Calculated?

As mentioned, the BSC fee structure is very similar to the one found on Ethereum. The transaction fees are denoted in Gwei, which is a small denomination of BNB equal to 0.000000001. Users can set their gas prices to prioritize their transactions added to the block. To find out the current and historical average price of gas, BscScan provides a daily average along with the lowest and highest price paid. As of March 2021, the average fee on BSC is around 13 Gwei.

In the example below, the gas price was 10 Gwei. Note that the gas limit was set to 622,732 Gwei, but only 352,755 (52.31%) Gwei was used in this transaction, resulting in a transaction fee of 0.00325755 BNB.

? Value:	1.0441558 BNB ($503.75)
? Transaction Fee:	0.00325755 BNB ($0.92)
? Gas Limit:	622,732
? Gas used by Transaction:	325,755 (52.31%)
? Gas Price:	0.00000001 BNB (10 Gwei)

The BSC fees are usually very low, but if you try to send tokens without BNB in your account, the network will notify you that you have insufficient funds. Make sure you keep some extra BNB in your wallet to pay for your transaction fees.

2.3.6 Anonymity

What Is Blockchain Anonymity?

"Anonymity" is an often debated and sometimes misconstrued characteristic of blockchain technology. This is a crucial element of decentralised systems, focussing on the necessity for privacy and confidentiality in transactions executed on public ledgers. In contrast to conventional financial systems, blockchain networks seek to offer pseudonymity and confidentiality independent of centralised authorities. The notion of anonymity in blockchain pertains to concealing transaction specifics, including sender addresses, recipient addresses, and transaction amounts. Diverse strategies, including cryptographic methods, ring signatures, zero-knowledge proofs (ZKPs), and mixing services, are utilised to augment privacy.

Anonymity in blockchain has become significant due to apprehensions regarding data privacy and the pursuit of financial independence. Privacy-centric cryptocurrencies such as Monero and Zcash have surfaced, highlighting robust anonymity attributes. Comprehending blockchain anonymity is crucial for individuals and organisations manoeuvring through the changing terrain of digital finance.

What Is Pseudonymity?

Despite transactions being publicly documented on the blockchain network, pseudonymity provides an additional layer of secrecy. It resembles the use of a pseudonym, whereby one functions under a fictitious identity, such as a blockchain address, that does not explicitly disclose one's true name. Transactions are associated with this pseudonym, creating a degree of isolation between your online activities and your actual identity. This can be advantageous in circumstances where total anonymity is not essential, however discretion in your operations is desired.

For instance, one may employ a pseudonym to acquire goods on a decentralised marketplace while safeguarding personal information. Nonetheless, it is crucial to recognise that pseudonymity does not equate to absolute anonymity. Anonymity renders one invisible, whereas pseudonymity offers a disguise.

Why Anonymity Matters in Blockchain?

Anonymity is essential for blockchain systems to maintain the fundamental concepts of decentralisation, privacy, security, and financial sovereignty. It grants people authority over their financial information and advances the aspiration for a more inclusive and equitable global financial system. It is an essential prerequisite in blockchain technology for various convincing reasons.

1. Preserves Individual Privacy

Primarily, blockchain was conceived to provide a decentralised and censorship- resistant framework for financial transactions. Anonymity is essential for safeguarding personal privacy and liberty within this context. In the absence of sufficient anonymity, transactions on public blockchains such as Bitcoin might be linked to particular individuals or entities, hence risking the exposure of sensitive financial data.

2. Fosters Inclusivity

Furthermore, anonymity promotes inclusivity and facilitates wider acceptance of blockchain technology. By allowing users to execute transactions without apprehension of monitoring or examination, blockchain becomes more attainable for individuals and enterprises globally, especially in areas with stringent financial restrictions or privacy concerns.

3. Protection Against Identity Theft

A vital consideration is safeguarding against identity theft and fraud. Blockchain anonymity, facilitated by pseudonymous addresses and cryptographic methods, mitigates the risk of personal information being utilised for nefarious ends.

4. Exchange of Cryptocurrency

Moreover, anonymity augments the fungibility of cryptocurrencies. If each coin or token can be tracked to its source, certain units may be regarded as less valuable or compromised, hence undermining the fungibility principle crucial for a viable currency.

Possible Disadvantages of Anonymity

Anonymity on blockchains, whilst providing significant privacy advantages, presents a series of problems.

Let us examine these possible disadvantages:

1. Haven for Illegal Activity

The absence of user identity may foster an environment conducive to illicit operations. Criminals can utilise anonymity for money laundering, terrorism financing, or promoting illicit trade via anonymous transactions. This subverts the fundamental ideas of trust and transparency that blockchain seeks to build.

2. Regulatory Hurdles

Anonymity presents a substantial obstacle for authorities aiming to uphold financial stability and deter criminal activity. The inability to identify users substantially complicates the tracking of suspected transactions and the enforcement of legislation such as anti-money laundering (AML). This challenge may impede the widespread use of blockchain technology.

3. Erosion of Trust

Absolute anonymity can foster suspicion. In anonymous markets, buyers and sellers are unable to authenticate each other's identities, which may result in fraud or scams. This may deter legitimate consumers from engaging in the ecosystem.

4. Challenges with Dispute Resolution

A crucial element of any financial system is equitable and effective dispute resolution. Nonetheless, anonymity complicates the identification and accountability of individuals engaged in fraudulent transactions. The absence of accountability may dissuade users and impede the development of decentralised marketplaces.

Key Techniques for Achieving Anonymity

Anonymity is an essential component of blockchain technology, providing users with privacy and confidentiality in financial transactions. A variety of novel methods are utilised to augment anonymity in decentralised networks:

1. Cryptographic Techniques

Cryptography is essential for ensuring anonymity in blockchain technology. Every user has a distinct public-private key pair. Transactions are authenticated with the sender's private key and validated through their public key, guaranteeing validity while preserving the user's anonymity. Elliptic curve cryptography (ECC) is frequently employed because of its efficacy and security.

2. Ring Signatures

Ring signatures facilitate transaction obfuscation by amalgamating the sender's transaction with others in a 'ring.' This conceals the sender's identity, complicating the tracing of transactions to a particular user inside the group.

3. Stealth Addresses

Stealth addresses augment recipient anonymity by creating distinct, ephemeral addresses for every transaction. When a sender transmits funds to a stealth address, the transaction is recorded on the blockchain while concealing the recipient's true address. This mitigates address reuse and augments transaction privacy.

4. Zero-Knowledge Proofs (ZKPs)

Zero-Knowledge Proofs enable someone to demonstrate possession of specific information (e.g., awareness of a confidential key) without disclosing the information itself. In blockchain technology, Zero-Knowledge Proofs (ZKPs) facilitate the verification of transactions while maintaining the confidentiality of the sender, receiver, and transaction amount. This safeguards privacy while maintaining the integrity of the blockchain.

5. Mixing Services and CoinJoin

Mixing services and protocols such as CoinJoin allow users to amalgamate their transactions with those of others, thereby concealing the connection between input and output addresses. The mixing process complicates the tracking of individual transactions, hence augmenting privacy and anonymity.

6. Privacy Coins

Certain cryptocurrencies are explicitly engineered with integrated privacy functionalities. Monero employs a synthesis of ring signatures, stealth addresses, and secret transactions to ensure robust privacy assurances. Zcash employs zero-knowledge proofs to facilitate selective transparency, permitting users to reveal transaction data solely to authorised entities. These strategies collectively facilitate anonymity in blockchain transactions, enabling users to execute financial transactions securely and confidentially. It is crucial to recognise that attaining total anonymity may necessitate ongoing innovation and enhancement of privacy-enhancing technologies. Blockchain anonymity not only benefits individual users but also addresses broader concerns around financial privacy and data protection. By employing these strategies, blockchain networks aim to maintain decentralisation, security, and user autonomy while reducing dangers related to identity theft, surveillance, and unauthorised data exposure.

2.3.7 Reward

Incentives for miners within the blockchain are crucial methods that encourage individuals to engage in the network by confirming transactions and safeguarding the blockchain. These incentives largely manifest as coinbase rewards and transaction fees, which remunerate miners for their computational endeavours. By harmonising the interests of miners with the integrity of the network, these incentives guarantee the stability and security of blockchain ecosystems.

Types of Blockchain Incentives

Coinbase Transactions: The initial transaction within a block, generated by miners upon successfully mining a new block. Compensates miners with newly created cryptocurrency (e.g., Bitcoin) and may also incorporate transaction fees from additional transactions within the block. The reward amount is fixed and may diminish over time (e.g., due to halving events in Bitcoin).

- **Transaction Fees:** Charges incurred by users to compensate miners for executing their transactions. Establish an alternative revenue source for miners, particularly if block rewards diminish over time. Transaction fees may fluctuate due to network congestion, transaction volume, and the user's readiness to pay for expedited processing.
- **Staking Rewards (Proof of Stake):** Validators receive rewards for their involvement in the consensus mechanism of Proof of Stake (PoS) networks. Urges users to stake their cryptocurrency assets to enhance network security and authenticate transactions. Rewards are generally allocated as supplementary tokens, contingent upon the quantity staked and the staking term. Supplementary Token Incentives: Rewards offered as governance tokens or other native assets for particular activities inside the ecosystem. Incentives offered as governance tokens or other native assets for particular acts inside the ecosystem.
- **Economic Framework of Mining Incentives Regulation of Supply and Inflation:** Mining incentives, chiefly via coinbase rewards, regulate the generation of new coins. Bitcoin's supply is limited to 21 million coins, and the pace of new coin generation diminishes during halving events. This regulated supply aids in controlling inflation, preserving the cryptocurrency's value over time. As the influx of new coins diminishes, scarcity may enhance demand and value.

  The rewards allocated to miners influence the market dynamics of bitcoin value. Elevated mining rewards may result in heightened selling pressure, whilst diminished rewards could stabilise or elevate prices due to reduced supply. An well designed incentive model can enhance investor confidence by guaranteeing the network's security and functionality, hence impacting market perception and value.
- **Long-Term Viability of Mining Incentives:** As block rewards diminish, networks may increasingly depend on transaction fees to motivate miners. This transition necessitates a robust transaction volume to guarantee the economic viability of miners. The sustainability of mining rewards is contingent upon network involvement. If mining ceases to be economical, it may result in diminished security and perhaps heighten susceptibility to attacks.
- **Risk and Reward Equilibrium:** Miners assess the expenditure of resources (e.g., electricity, hardware) in relation to prospective gains. Volatile bitcoin prices and transaction volumes might affect profitability. An equitable economic model guarantees that mining continues to appeal to participants, thus preserving network security and decentralisation.

Challenges and Limitations of Mining Incentives

- **Centralisation Risks:** Mining frequently consolidates into a few number of substantial pools, resulting in centralisation that compromises the decentralised essence of blockchain networks and renders them susceptible to attacks or manipulation.

- **Volatility of Transaction Fees:** As block rewards decrease, miners may rely more on transaction fees for income. Nonetheless, fee volatility might induce instability, complicating miners' ability to forecast their revenues and sustain profitability.
- **Environmental Impact:** The energy-intensive nature of mining, particularly in Proof of Work systems, raises significant environmental concerns. Excessive energy use may result in adverse public opinion and heightened regulatory oversight.
- **Regulatory Concerns:** As governments globally endeavour to regulate cryptocurrencies, modifications in legal frameworks may impact mining operations and the incentives that underpin them, thereby increasing uncertainty for miners and investors.
- **Risks Associated with Network Security:** If mining becomes unprofitable owing to diminishing payouts or elevated operational expenses, miners may withdraw from the network, thereby decreasing total hashing power and heightening susceptibility to attacks, such as 51% attacks.

Conclusion

In conclusion, blockchain incentives are essential for motivating miners to validate transactions and protect networks. These incentives, chiefly via Coinbase rewards and transaction fees, guarantee the survival and integrity of blockchain ecosystems.

Nevertheless, obstacles such as centralisation, environmental issues, and regulatory concerns must be resolved to sustain a balanced and effective incentive framework. A meticulously crafted incentive system is essential for the sustained viability and prosperity of cryptocurrencies.

2.3.8 Chain

The Chaining Process

The chaining process in blockchain refers to how individual blocks are linked together to form a secure and immutable ledger. Here is an overview of the steps involved:

1. **Transaction Initiation:** A user initiates a transaction, which is broadcast to the network of nodes for verification.
2. **Block Creation:** Validated transactions are grouped together into a new block. This block contains essential information, including the transaction data, a timestamp, a nonce (if applicable), and the hash of the previous block.
3. **Hashing:** Each block undergoes a cryptographic hashing process, generating a unique hash that represents the data within the block. This hash is critical for linking the block to its predecessor.
4. **Linking Blocks:** The newly created block includes the hash of the previous block, forming a chain. This linking mechanism ensures that each block is securely tied to the one before it.
5. **Consensus Verification:** The new block is distributed across the network. Nodes validate the block and the transactions it contains, ensuring consensus is reached before adding it to the blockchain.

6. **Block Addition:** Once validated, the new block is added to the existing blockchain, making the data within it a permanent part of the ledger. The chain of blocks continues to grow as new transactions occur.

The Impact of Consensus on Chaining Blocks

Here is an overview of how the consensus impacts the chaining process:

1. **Transaction Validation:** Consensus mechanisms validate transactions before they are added to a block. This prevents invalid transactions from being included in the blockchain, ensuring the integrity of the data.
2. **Block Addition:** After transactions are validated, nodes must reach a consensus to agree on the new block to be added to the blockchain. Different consensus algorithms (e.g., Proof of Work, Proof of Stake) dictate how this agreement is reached.
3. **Security and Trust:** Consensus enhances the security of the blockchain by requiring agreement from a majority of nodes. This decentralization makes it difficult for any single entity to manipulate the chain, thereby fostering trust *among participants.*
4. **Prevention of Forks:** By establishing rules for block addition, consensus mechanisms help prevent forks (divergence in the blockchain). This ensures a single, unified version of the blockchain, which is crucial for maintaining a consistent history.
5. **Performance and Scalability:** Different consensus algorithms affect the performance and scalability of the blockchain. For instance, PoW may be slower due to its computational intensity, while PoS can offer faster transaction times and higher throughput. This, in turn, influences how quickly new blocks are added to the chain.

Applications of Chaining Blocks

Here are some key applications:

1. **Cryptocurrencies:** Chaining blocks is the core mechanism behind cryptocurrencies like Bitcoin and Ethereum, where each transaction is recorded in a secure and immutable ledger. This allows for peer-to-peer digital currency exchanges without the need for intermediaries.
2. **Supply Chain Management:** Blockchain can track the movement of goods in real-time, providing transparency and accountability. Chaining blocks enables all parties in the supply chain to access a single version of the truth, improving traceability and reducing fraud.
3. **Healthcare:** In the healthcare sector, blockchain can securely store patient records, ensuring that they are tamper-proof and accessible only to authorized individuals. Chaining blocks helps maintain the integrity and confidentiality of sensitive health data.
4. **Digital Identity Verification:** Blockchain can provide a secure and decentralized solution for identity management. By chaining blocks that store personal information and verification data, individuals can control their identities and share them with trusted parties without risking data breaches.

5. **Voting Systems:** Blockchain technology can enhance the security and transparency of electoral processes. Chaining blocks can securely record votes, making them tamper-resistant and easily auditable, thus increasing public trust in elections.

Challenges and Limitations

Here are some key challenges and limitations:

1. **Scalability:** As the number of transactions grows, the blockchain can become congested, leading to slower processing times and higher transaction fees. This is particularly evident in public blockchains like Bitcoin and Ethereum, where the number of users can exceed the network's capacity.
2. **Energy Consumption:** Consensus mechanisms like Proof of Work (PoW) require significant computational power and energy to validate transactions and mine new blocks.
3. **Complexity and Usability:** The technical complexity of blockchain technology can be a barrier to entry for non-technical users and businesses. Understanding how to interact with blockchain systems and implement them effectively requires specialized knowledge.
4. **Data Privacy:** While blockchain provides transparency, this can also pose privacy challenges. Public blockchains expose transaction details to all participants, which may not be suitable for sensitive information.
5. **Network Security:** Although blockchain is generally secure, it is not immune to attacks. Issues like the 51% attack, where a group of miners controls the majority of the network's hash rate, can jeopardize the integrity of the blockchain.

Conclusion

In conclusion, Chaining blocks is a foundational concept in blockchain technology that ensures the integrity, security, and immutability of data. By linking blocks through cryptographic hashes, blockchain creates a tamper- proof ledger that facilitates trust and transparency in digital transactions. While this mechanism enables various applications, including cryptocurrencies, supply chain management, and smart contracts, it also faces challenges such as scalability, energy consumption, and regulatory uncertainties. Addressing these challenges is vital for enhancing the effectiveness and adoption of blockchain solutions across diverse industries, paving the way for innovative and secure digital ecosystems.

Intentionally Left Blank!

UNIT 3 CRYPTOCURRENCY AND BLOCKCHAIN TECHNOLOGY

3.1 INTRODUCTION TO CRYPTO AND CRYPTO CURRENCY

A cryptocurrency is not a form of currency applicable in the physical world. It is exclusively applicable for doing transactions in the digital realm. To engage in the buying or selling of cryptocurrency, it must be translated from its digital format to a recognised fiat money utilised in the physical economy. For instance, Dollars, Rupees, etc. Cryptocurrencies lack a central issuing authority, use a decentralised method to document transactions and generate new units.

What is Cryptocurrency?

Cryptocurrency is a digital payment mechanism that operates independently of banks for transaction verification. Cryptocurrency transactions are solely represented as digital entries within an online database. Cryptocurrency fund transfers are documented in a public ledger. In cryptocurrency, "coins" (publicly recognised records of ownership) are created by "miners." Miners are individuals who operate programs on ASIC (Application Specific Integrated Circuit) devices designed specifically to resolve proof-of-work challenges. The labour involved in mining coins confers worth upon them, while their scarcity and demand result in value fluctuations. Cryptocurrencies can be utilised for the purchase of things in a manner analogous to fiat currency. Cryptocurrencies employ encryption to authenticate and safeguard transactions. It lacks a tangible form and is generally not distributed by any central authority. They employ decentralised governance as opposed to central bank digital currency.

Examples of Cryptocurrency

The most renowned cryptocurrencies include:

- **Bitcoin:** Bitcoin is the most universally recognised cryptocurrency. Established in 2009 by Satoshi Nakamoto, it remains the most often traded. It is a decentralised digital money that may be exchanged on a peer-to-peer Bitcoin network.
- **Ether:** Ether is the indigenous coin of the Ethereum blockchain network. Every Ethereum account possesses an ETH balance and is capable of transferring ETH to any other account. The smallest subunit of Ether is referred to as Wei.
- **Litecoin:** Litecoin is a peer-to-peer cryptocurrency that is technically analogous to Bitcoin. It employs a script in its proof-of-work mechanism. It is a modification of Bitcoin designed to facilitate payments.
- **Stablecoins:** Stablecoins are a kind of cryptocurrencies engineered to maintain a consistent value in relation to tangible assets, such as the U.S. Dollar.
- **Solana:** Solana is an Ethereum competitor that prioritises speed and cost- efficiency.

Traditional Currencies vs. Cryptocurrencies

Let's understand the difference between the working of a cryptocurrency and fiat currency like the U.S. Dollar while purchasing goods. There are two things that make cryptocurrency work and fiat currency work differently: Transactions and the Consensus protocol. A block in a Blockchain has the following structure:

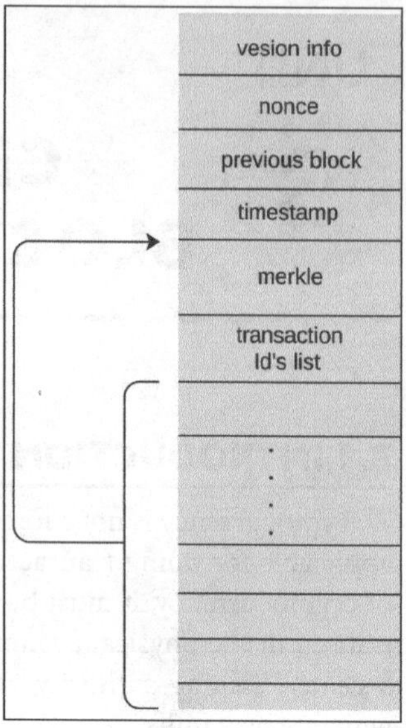

Fig. 3.1

As we can see, a block contains multiple transactions at a time in the transaction's id_list.

1. **Transactions:** The transactions performed in the crypto world are very different than those that of which are performed in the real world. Let's consider that Alice wants to buy a Bicycle.
   - **Real-world:** In the real world Alice can pay in any available currency. The seller will return the change if any to Alice.
   - **Crypto world:** Suppose the bicycle costs 0.6 BTC and Alice has 0.7 BTC in the Bitcoin Wallet. Alice has to consider the whole amount i.e 0.7 BTC
     - **Transaction 1:** Transfer only 0.6 BTC from Bitcoin wallet to the seller's wallet. Now, Alice has already exhausted 0.6 out of 0.7 BTC. The remaining 0.1 BTC has to be transferred back to Alice's wallet. There is no change in BTC being offered by the seller to Alice.
     - **Transaction 2:** Alice offers 0.1 BTC back to herself. So 0.1 BTC is an unspent transaction amount in Alice's wallet.
2. **Consensus protocol:** Consensus decision-making is a group decision- making process in which group members develop, and agree to support a decision in the best interest of the whole. Basically, it states that the longest valid chain in the Blockchain network should exist on every node in the Network.

How Does Cryptocurrency Work?

Cryptocurrencies operate independently of any central authority, functioning outside the banking system through various forms of coinage.

1. **Mining:** Cryptocurrencies are produced by a process known as mining. During this procedure, miners must solve a mathematical challenge using a specialised computer system to receive bitcoins as a reward.
2. **Buying, selling, and storing:** Users can buy cryptocurrencies from central exchanges, brokers, or individual currency owners and sell crypto to them. Cryptocurrencies can be preserved in wallets.
3. **Investment:** Cryptocurrencies are transferable between digital wallets.

Cryptocurrencies provide the following functions:

- Acquisition of commodities and services.
- Exchange them.
- Convert them into currency.

How To Buy Cryptocurrency?

The process of purchasing cryptocurrency consists of three steps:

1. **Choosing a platform:** There are two platforms available to choose from: Traditional Brokers: Online brokers facilitate the buying and selling of cryptocurrencies alongside stocks, bonds, and other assets, but they often provide reduced trading costs and limited cryptocurrency functionalities. Cryptocurrency exchanges: Various types of cryptocurrency exchanges are available, each offering distinct coins, wallet storage options, and other features.
2. **Funding your account:** After choosing the platform, the next step is to fund the account. Most cryptocurrency exchanges permit users to acquire cryptocurrencies using fiat currencies such as the U.S. Dollar or Euro, as well as credit and debit cards; however, this differs by platform. A crucial aspect to consider is the fees encompassing potential deposit and withdrawal transaction fees, in addition to trading fees.
3. **Placing an order:** The order can be placed via exchanges or broker's web or mobile platform.
    - Choose the Purchase option.
    - Select the type of order.
    - Input the quantity of cryptocurrency.
    - Validate the order.
    - A comparable procedure must be adhered to for the sale of cryptocurrency.

Advantages of Cryptocurrencies

- **Private and Secure:** Blockchain technology ensures user anonymity and at the same time the use of cryptography in blockchain makes the network secure for working with cryptocurrencies.
- **Decentralised, Immutable, and Transparent:** The blockchain network operates on the premise of collective ownership, devoid of a singular regulatory authority, with data accessible to all authorised members and resistant to tampering.
- **Inflation Hedge:** Cryptocurrencies serve as a viable investment during inflationary periods due to their finite supply and the restrictions on mining various cryptocurrencies.
- **Faster Settlement:** Payments for most cryptocurrencies settle in seconds or minutes. Bank wire transfers may incur higher fees and often need three to five business days for settlement.
- **Easy Transactions:** Crypto transactions can be done more easily, in a private manner in comparison to bank transactions. Utilising a basic smartphone and a cryptocurrency wallet, individuals can transmit or receive an array of cryptocurrencies.

Disadvantages of Cryptocurrencies

- **Cybersecurity issues:** Cryptocurrencies will be subject to cybersecurity breaches and may fall into the hands of hackers. Addressing this will necessitate ongoing upkeep of security infrastructure.

- **Price Volatility:** Cryptocurrencies exhibit significant price volatility due to their lack of intrinsic worth, with their prices determined by a supply-demand dynamic.
- **Scalability:** Scalability is one of the major concerns with cryptocurrencies. The usage of digital coins and tokens is accelerating; yet, the inherent sluggishness of blockchain technology renders cryptocurrencies susceptible to transaction delays. Cryptocurrencies are incapable of rivalling the transaction volume processed daily by payment giants such as VISA and Mastercard.
- **Less awareness:** Cryptocurrency is still a new concept for the people and the long-term sustainability of cryptocurrencies remains to be seen.

3.1.1 Primitives of Crypto

A cryptographic primitive is a fundamental technique employed to construct cryptographic protocols within a security framework. It serves as the fundamental building pieces for cryptography designers. These components constitute a cryptosystem, which comprises a collection of cryptographic algorithms essential for executing a specific security service, such as encryption functions or one-way hash functions. As fundamental components, these primitives are engineered to perform a specific, well-defined, and highly dependable function.

Developing and validating a cryptographic primitive for reliability is a time-consuming and challenging endeavour, making the design of a new cryptographic primitive tailored to the requirements of an innovative cryptographic system quite uncommon. Cryptographic primitives resemble programming languages in this regard. It is uncommon for a programmer to create a new programming language while developing a new software. Rather, they will utilise an established language, akin to how a cryptography designer employs a pre-existing primitive to circumvent the laborious and error-prone process of developing a novel primitive.

Common Cryptographic Primitives

- **One-way hash function:** A mathematical function that transforms a variable-length input string into a fixed-length binary sequence.
- **Symmetric key cryptography:** An encryption methodology wherein the sender and recipient of a communication possess a singular, shared key utilised for both the encryption and decryption of the message.
- **Public-key cryptography:** Public-key cryptography, or asymmetric cryptography, is a system that employs a pair of keys: a public key and a private key. Any individual may encrypt a message utilising the recipient's public key; however, the encrypted message may solely be decrypted with the recipient's private key.
- **Mix network:** A routing protocol that establishes difficult-to-trace communications. A series of proxy servers, secured with public-key encryption, receive messages from various senders, randomise their order, and subsequently forward them to the next destination.
- **Private information retrieval:** A technique enabling a client to obtain data from a database without the database owner being aware of the precise information accessed.

3.2 BITCOIN

What Is Bitcoin?

Bitcoin is a decentralised digital money that may be purchased, sold, and exchanged directly, without the need of an intermediary such as a bank. Satoshi Nakamoto, the founder of Bitcoin, initially articulated the necessity for "an electronic payment system founded on cryptographic proof rather than reliance on trust." anyone Bitcoin transactions are recorded on a public ledger available to anyone, rendering them challenging to reverse and tough to counterfeit. This is intentional: Fundamental to its decentralised essence, Bitcoins lack governmental or institutional backing, with no guarantees of value beyond the intrinsic proof included inside the system. "Its monetary worth is solely attributed to our collective decision to ascribe value to it—much like gold," states Anton Mozgovoy, co-founder and CEO of the digital financial service firm Holyheld. Since its public introduction in 2009, Bitcoin has experienced a significant increase in value. Previously priced below $150 per coin, as of June 8, 1 BTC is valued at approximately $30,200. Due to its finite quantity of 21 million coins, many anticipate that its price will continue to ascend over time, particularly as an increasing number of institutional investors regard it as a form of digital gold to mitigate market volatility and inflation. At now, around 19 million coins are in circulation.

How Does Bitcoin Work?

Bitcoin is constructed upon a decentralised digital ledger known as a blockchain. Blockchain, as its name suggests, is a connected repository of data composed of units known as blocks, which encapsulate information regarding each transaction, including date and time, total value, buyer and seller, and a unique identifier for each trade. Entries are sequentially linked in chronological sequence, forming a digital chain of blocks.

"Once a block is incorporated into the blockchain, it becomes available for public viewing, serving as a transparent ledger of cryptocurrency transactions," states Stacey Harris, consultant for Pelicoin, a network of cryptocurrency ATMs. Blockchain is decentralised, indicating that it is not governed by a singular entity. Buchi Okoro, CEO and co-founder of the African cryptocurrency exchange Quidax, states, "It resembles a Google Doc that is accessible for collaborative work by anyone." "It is not owned by anyone, yet anyone with a link can contribute to it." As many individuals modify it, your version concurrently receives updates. The notion that anyone can modify the blockchain may appear precarious; nonetheless, it is precisely this characteristic that renders Bitcoin reliable and secure.

For a transaction block to be incorporated into the Bitcoin blockchain, it must receive validation from the majority of Bitcoin holders, and the unique codes utilised to identify users' wallets and transactions must adhere to the appropriate encryption standards. These codes consist of lengthy, arbitrary numerals, rendering them exceedingly challenging to replicate fraudulently. The degree of statistical randomness in blockchain verification codes, essential for each transaction, significantly diminishes the likelihood of fraudulent Bitcoin transactions.

What is the Mechanism of Bitcoin mining?

Bitcoin mining refers to the procedure of incorporating new transactions into the Bitcoin blockchain. The task is arduous. Individuals who opt to mine Bitcoin utilise proof of work, employing computers in a competition to resolve mathematical problems that authenticate transactions. To incentivise miners to continue competing to solve the riddles and sustain the entire system, the Bitcoin protocol rewards miners with 6.25 BTC for each newly created block. The specified quantity of BTC corresponds to around $190,000. Okoro said, "This is the process by which new coins are generated and recent transactions are incorporated into the blockchain."

The typical individual could mine Bitcoin in its early days, but that is no longer feasible. The Bitcoin algorithm is designed to progressively increase the difficulty of its puzzles, necessitating greater computational resources over time. Currently, Bitcoin mining necessitates robust computers and substantial access to inexpensive electricity for success. Bitcoin mining now yields lower returns than previously, exacerbating the difficulty of offsetting increasing computational and energy expenses. "In 2009, when this technology was initially introduced, each stamp awarded a significantly greater quantity of Bitcoin than is currently the case," states Flori Marquez, co-founder of BlockFi, a cryptocurrency asset management firm. The increasing number of transactions results in a diminishing payment for each stamp. By 2140, it is projected that all Bitcoins will have been circulated, resulting in no new coins being generated by mining, hence compelling miners to depend on transaction fees.

How To Use Bitcoin

In the United States, individuals typically utilise Bitcoin as an alternative investment to diversify their portfolios beyond stocks and bonds. Bitcoin can be utilised for transactions; however, several businesses exclusively take the original cryptocurrency. Prominent corporations that accept Bitcoin include Microsoft, PayPal, and Whole Foods, among others. Some local stores or specific websites may accept Bitcoin, but further investigation is required.

A service is available that enables you to link a debit card to your cryptocurrency account, allowing you to utilise Bitcoin similarly to a credit card. This often entails a financial institution promptly changing your Bitcoin into cash. In various nations, especially those with unstable currencies, individuals occasionally utilise bitcoin in lieu of their national money. Bitcoin offers individuals the ability to preserve value independently of government- backed currencies. It provides individuals with a means to mitigate against a worst-case scenario. Individuals in nations such as Venezuela, Argentina, and Zimbabwe, which are significantly indebted, are increasingly adopting Bitcoin.

Utilising Bitcoin as a money rather than an investment in the U.S. necessitates awareness of certain tax considerations.

How to Buy Bitcoin

The majority of individuals acquire Bitcoin through cryptocurrency exchanges. Exchanges facilitate the acquisition, disposition, and retention of cryptocurrencies. Establishing an account resembles the process of starting a broking account; it necessitates identity verification and the provision of a financing source, such as a bank account or debit card. Prominent exchanges comprise Coinbase, Kraken, and Gemini. Bitcoin can also be purchased using an online broker such as Robinhood. No matter the source of your Bitcoin acquisition, a Bitcoin wallet is essential for its storage. This may be referred to as a "hot wallet" or a "cold wallet." A hot wallet, often referred to as an online wallet, is maintained by an exchange or a cloud-based service. Online wallet providers include Exodus, Electrum, and Mycelium.

A cold wallet, also known as a mobile wallet, is an offline device utilised for the storage of Bitcoin that remains disconnected from the Internet. Mobile wallet alternatives comprise Trezor and Ledger. Several crucial considerations with the acquisition of Bitcoin: Although Bitcoin is costly, it is possible to get fractional Bitcoin from certain suppliers. Be mindful of fees, which typically constitute minor percentages of your cryptocurrency transaction amount but can accumulate significantly on low-value purchases. Ultimately, Bitcoin acquisitions are not immediate like numerous other equity transactions. Due to the necessity for miners to authenticate Bitcoin transactions, it may require a minimum of 10 to 20 minutes for your Bitcoin acquisition to reflect in your account.

How to Invest in Bitcoin

Similar to a stock, Bitcoin can be acquired and retained as an investment. It is currently possible to do so in specialised retirement accounts known as Bitcoin IRAs. Regardless of the location you select for your Bitcoin holdings, individuals' investment mindsets differ significantly. Some investors choose a buy-and-hold strategy for the long term, others purchase with the intention of selling following a price surge, while some speculate on a decline in price. In 2020, Bitcoin's price fluctuated significantly, reaching a low of $5,165 and a high of $28,990. "In certain locations, individuals may utilise Bitcoin for transactions; however, it is fundamentally an asset poised for significant appreciation in value over a relatively short period," asserts Marquez. "Why would one sell an asset that is projected to appreciate significantly in value over the next year?" The predominant holders are long-term investors.

Consumers may invest in a Bitcoin mutual fund by purchasing shares of the Greyscale Bitcoin Trust (GBTC). The minimum investment threshold is $50,000. This indicates that the majority of Americans are unable to participate in it. In Canada, diverse Bitcoin investment is increasingly becoming available. In February 2021, the Purpose Bitcoin ETF (BTCC) commenced trading as the inaugural Bitcoin ETF, and the Ontario Securities Commission subsequently sanctioned the Evolve Bitcoin ETF (EBIT). American investors seeking exposure to Bitcoin or similar assets may contemplate blockchain ETFs that invest in cryptocurrency technologies.

An important note: While crypto-based funds may add diversification to crypto holdings and decrease risk slightly, they still carry substantially more risk and charge much higher fees than broad-based index funds with histories of steady returns. Investors seeking consistent wealth accumulation may choose index-based mutual funds and exchange-traded funds (ETFs).

3.2.1 Point of Bitcoin

President-elect Donald Trump has advocated for the establishment of a 'Strategic National Bitcoin Stockpile,' although the objective of this entity remains ambiguous. This week, the price of bitcoin (BTCUSD) reached an unprecedented high, temporarily exceeding $108,000, following President-elect Donald Trump's reiteration of his campaign plan for the government to officially possess a portion of the cryptocurrency. Despite Bitcoin's rapid reversal following this week's Federal Reserve meeting, the concept of a reserve is gaining traction. This has elicited scepticism from economists who question the rationale behind creating a strategic reserve of a volatile speculative asset. Trump initially introduced the concept at a Bitcoin convention in Nashville in July. He stated that the cryptocurrency confiscated by the government during criminal cases would constitute the foundation of a "Strategic National Bitcoin Stockpile," and that his objective would be to never sell it. As reported by BitcoinTreasuries, a platform that monitors cryptocurrency holdings, the United States possesses 198,000 bitcoins valued at $21 billion. The supply of Bitcoin is limited to 21 million, with 19.79 million currently in circulation.

What Are Other Strategic Reserves that the US Holds?

The concept resonates with the Strategic Petroleum Reserve. The reserve was established in 1975 during the oil embargoes against the U.S., which resulted in shortages and disrupted the economy. The United States reserves up to 727 million barrels of oil in subterranean caves for emergency utilisation. The government, akin to a proficient trader, aims to sell oil from the reserve during periods of elevated prices to decrease prices, and subsequently replenish it when prices are low. The proposal to create a corresponding national reserve of bitcoins has gained traction as cryptocurrency investors have increased their sway in Washington. In July, Senator Cynthia Lummis, a Republican from Wyoming, proposed legislation for the government to acquire 1 million bitcoins over five years as a safeguard against economic uncertainty and monetary instability, akin to the gold bullion held by the Federal Reserve.

The Case For a Strategic Bitcoin Reserve

In July, Tyler Cowen, an economics professor at George Mason University and a Bloomberg writer, asserted that the United States purchasing bitcoin would bolster the dollar's status as the world's reserve currency, so reinforcing U.S. dominance in the global financial system. Padhraic Garvey, regional head of research for the Americas at ING, said Investopedia that there are multiple potential justifications for creating a cryptocurrency reserve. By regulating the bitcoin supply, Trump may aim to deter its acquisition by nefarious individuals. He also stated that Trump may want to inhibit other nations from using bitcoin as a substitute for the currency.

The Case Against A Strategic Bitcoin Reserve

However, the concept of a cryptocurrency reserve elicited scepticism from specialists. In contrast to gasoline, bitcoin is not essential for economic operations and cannot be converted into fuel for military vehicles or aircraft during a national crisis. Although government acquisition of bitcoin may assist crypto investors by elevating prices, its advantages to the economy are less apparent. "The purpose of a crypto reserve remains ambiguous, aside from guaranteeing sufficient U.S. influence over it," Garvey stated. The reserve may also include economic hazards. According to Ramaa Vasudevan, an economics professor at Colorado State University, establishing a reserve would obligate the state and taxpayers to support bitcoin, a volatile financial instrument, as stated in an email to Investopedia. "The fund would assure bitcoin speculators that, in the event of a crash, the State will utilise this fund for its rescue," she stated.

3.2.2 Working of Bitcoin

Utilising Bitcoin differs from employing other currencies. You obtain it, retain it, and utilise it. Let us examine the functionality of each of these stages within the context of Bitcoin.

How to Create Bitcoin

The mining process generates new Bitcoins. The Bitcoin developers established a system to generate coins at a predetermined rate until miners extract the total of 21 million designated

Bitcoins. Bitcoin is generated by resolving intricate mathematical problems utilising a mining rig, a high-performance computer capable of producing millions of random strings every second to solve the problem. This procedure authenticates bitcoin transactions and generates fresh Bitcoin as compensation.

Mining rigs can vary from a computer equipped with a high-performance central processing unit to an application-specific integrated circuit designed just for cryptocurrency mining.

How to Earn Bitcoin

There are other methods to acquire Bitcoins apart from mining, including: **Odd jobs:** Some companies offer Bitcoins as a reward for completing tasks, like testing their website or retweeting posts. Occasionally, the work is as simple as responding to an inquiry.

Form of payment

Many major payment apps now allow people to pay each other with Bitcoin and other digital currencies. Upon providing a service or selling a product, you may solicit payment in Bitcoin through CashApp, Venmo, or PayPal.

Online Games

Some online games offer Bitcoin rewards for completing tasks or winning games.

How to Store Bitcoin

Upon acquiring Bitcoin, it must be stored in a digital wallet. Nonetheless, not all digital wallets are same. Digital wallets are categorised into two types: hot wallets and cold wallets.

Hot digital wallet. A hot wallet is internet-connected, providing quick access to funds for transactions and trading. This often occurs on a computer, smartphone, or tablet, but may also take place on a cryptocurrency exchange. You will possess a collection of keys for your hot wallet, which aids in its security. However, if the keys are misplaced, the cryptocurrency will be irretrievable. Cryptocurrency may also be lost due to computer faults, errors, and hacks; thus, it is common to maintain a small quantity of cryptocurrency in a hot wallet. Storing your Bitcoin on an exchange compromises security, as the exchange possesses the keys rather than the user. If the exchange is compromised or suffers a server failure, you may forfeit all your cryptocurrency.

Cold Wallet

A cold wallet is a cryptocurrency wallet that lacks an internet connection, rendering it impervious to hacking and hardware malfunctions. These are generally USB devices that retain your private keys. A paper wallet is another option, representing the most secure form of storage. This wallet can be generated from a cold wallet website, which produces public and private keys that can be printed. The printed keys may be laminated and securely placed in a safety deposit box or safe for protection. In the absence of these printed keys, access to your wallet is impossible.

Where to buy Bitcoin Mining

Bitcoin is not the sole method of acquisition. Bitcoin is available for acquisition on the open market. Here are some locations where it can be purchased. Bitcoin may be acquired on multiple cryptocurrency exchanges with fiat dollars. Create an account and acquire Bitcoin.

- **Investing firms:** Certain investing firms have commenced providing Bitcoin as an alternative. Register to trade Bitcoin and other cryptocurrencies like you would with stocks or bonds.
- **Bitcoin ATMs and retail stores:** Bitcoin can be purchased through Bitcoin ATMs. Utilise your debit or credit card at the ATM to acquire Bitcoin, which will be deposited into your designated digital wallet. Additionally, you may visit a retail establishment that offers Bitcoin for purchase.
- **Banks:** Select banks now support Bitcoin buying and selling. Should your bank provide this option, you may purchase Bitcoin via your online banking platform.

How to Use Bitcoin

Although Bitcoin is not a universally accepted medium of exchange, it can be utilised in other manners beyond from converting it to fiat currency.

- **Debit card:** A Bitcoin debit card allows you to spend crypto anywhere that accepts debit cards. Upon utilisation of the card, the appropriate quantity of Bitcoin is converted to the corresponding local fiat money.
- **Retail stores:** Some online stores, such as Newegg and Overstock, now accept Bitcoin as a payment option. A specific debit card is unnecessary; simply select Bitcoin during checkout.
- **Donation:** Some charities now accept Bitcoin as a donation method. You might qualify for a tax benefit, and the charity incurs no capital gains tax on the Bitcoin it gets.

3.2.3 Bitcoin Predecessor

What Bitcoin Achieves

Bitcoin addresses multiple issues encountered by traditional currencies. The Bitcoin network facilitates peer-to-peer transactions without the necessity of a trusted intermediary. Furthermore, Bitcoin addresses the Byzantine Generals Problem by the utilisation of a Proof-of-Work method and the preservation of its data on a decentralised ledger, enabling consensus among all network participants on a unified state of the ledger.

Bitcoin's Technological Prerequisites

The whitepaper presenting these answers was proposed in 2008, before the inception of Bitcoin in 2009; however, the concepts and technology utilised for its development had been in progress for several decades earlier. The mechanism by which Bitcoin guarantees that only the legitimate owner can utilise their bitcoin, the Elliptic Curve Digital Signature Algorithm, is based on elliptic curve cryptography. Elliptic curve cryptography was introduced by mathematicians in 1985. A vital component of Bitcoin's technology is Proof-of- Work. This technology underpins Bitcoin's mining operations, serving as an essential element of the Bitcoin network's functionality. Proof-of-Work systems evolved incrementally during the 1990s, with significant advancements marked by Wei Dai's b-money in 1998 and Adam Back's Hashcash in 1997.

Bitcoin's Conceptual Prerequisites

Besides technology elements, Bitcoin utilises other pre-existing economic concepts. The concept of an anonymous payment network was first popularised by DigiCash in 1989. In the subsequent decade, this concept underwent multiple iterations, culminating in DigiCash's rebranding as eCash. Both ideas were intended to enable anonymous transfers of existing fiat currencies. Virtual economies, which generated and utilised their own currencies, were established by computer games like RuneScape and World of Warcraft in the early 2000s. The enduring worth of these virtual currencies provided significant evidence regarding the factors that can confer value to a currency. Established in 2006, Liberty Reserve popularised the concept of anonymously facilitating payments beyond the traditional financial system for the global currency market, extending the notion of virtual currencies from video games to a worldwide context. Liberty Reserve was terminated in 2013 due to legal complications.

Bitcoin's Innovations

In addition to utilizing the best parts of past projects, Bitcoin implements innovations that were uniquely its own. Bitcoin's blockchain was the inaugural successful execution of a digital currency that operated independently of a centralised ledger. Satoshi Nakamoto identified this centralisation as a fundamental defect in current electronic payment systems in Bitcoin's whitepaper. Many individuals prematurely disregard e-currency as futile due to the numerous enterprises that have failed since the 1990s. It should be evident that the centralised control of those systems was their downfall. This appears to be our inaugural attempt at a decentralised, non-trust-based system.

The decentralized ledger removes the requirement for a trusted third party to control the currency, instead letting it be governed by every actor in the network. Utilising a decentralised ledger necessitated a resolution to the Byzantine Generals Problem to guarantee that users could concur on a singular state of the ledger, hence preventing duplicate spending and other invalid transactions. Bitcoin utilises a Proof-of-Work approach to address this issue. Through the utilisation of a modified form of reusable Proof-of-Work, Bitcoin achieves consensus independently, without requiring intervention or dispute resolution from a central authority. While prototypes for this notion were introduced in 2004 by Hal Finney, Bitcoin was the inaugural project to effectively realise the idea. Another feature enabling the Bitcoin network to function well without central authority monitoring is Bitcoin's difficulty adjustment. This innovative concept enables the Bitcoin network to autonomously modify the difficulty level of mining an individual block. Difficulty adjustments are implemented according to the rate at which miners generate new blocks. Through the modulation of mining difficulty, Bitcoin can guarantee that new coins are generated at a specified rate, irrespective of the computational power engaged in the network. This automatic adjustment renders the network exceptionally resilient and scalable, alleviating concerns regarding hyperinflation or insufficient network security.

Ultimately, Bitcoin established the principle of blockchain immutability to guarantee that previous transactions on the network remain unalterable. Each new block is added to the conclusion of the current blockchain, thereby reinforcing previous transactions. The sole method to amend a past transaction is rewriting the whole block that encompasses the transaction, along with all following blocks. Furthermore, the malicious actor would thereafter need to generate additional blocks to append to the modified block. This actor must generate new blocks at a rate surpassing that of the whole Bitcoin network to catch up and establish the longest chain.

3.2.4 BITCOIN DECENTRALIZATION

Introduction

One of Bitcoin's indisputable and much emphasised advantages is its decentralisation. The Bitcoin network is frequently asserted to provide unparalleled levels of decentralisation, accessibility, and dispersion compared to other cryptocurrencies. To what extent is Bitcoin truly decentralised? What methods may we employ to assess its decentralisation? Prior to examining these enquiries, it is essential to elucidate the terms of centralisation and decentralisation, as they are frequently conflated. The centralization/decentralization dynamic refers to the extent of authority concentration or spread among system actors. In this context, "authority" denotes the capacity to affect the operation and regulations of the system, regardless of whether the intent is malevolent or benevolent. Consequently, assessing the level of centralisation in a system entails estimating the least number of entities or individuals necessary to modify its operations or regulations. A lower number indicates a higher degree of centralisation. In a pivotal 2017 study, Balaji S. Srinivasan and Leland Lee presented a significant statistic for this purpose: the Nakamoto coefficient.

The Nakamoto coefficient, based on the Lorenz curve utilised in determining the Gini coefficient, specifies the minimal number of people required to undermine or dominate the system. For example, in the prominent case of Bitcoin's hashrate, if we suppose that five mining pools together control over 50% of the overall hashrate, then this quantity would be five. A simple majority of 50% of the hashrate would enough to perpetrate a double spending operation on the blockchain. The crucial threshold may differ for other variables.

Various Aspects of Centralisation

Let us now focus on the fundamental issue highlighted by the authors of the paper: the identification of subsystems essential to the system's functionality. Focussing exclusively on the concentration of hashrate in Bitcoin neglects the comprehensive dynamics of centralisation and decentralisation inside the network and disregards the risk of a 50%+1 attack. In their article, Balaji S. Srinivasan and Leland Lee propose five supplementary quantifiable subsystems of the Bitcoin Network: client platform, code developers, nodes, custodial/exchanges, and ownership.

According to Balaji S. Srinivasan, the six dimensions of centralization within the Bitcoin network are as follows:

- Client centralization
- Ownership centralization
- Node centralization
- Developers centralization
- Custodial/exchanges centralization
- Hashrate centralization

In addition, we might consider adding one last dimension:

- Hardware Centralization

While this list is comprehensive, what's lacking is a qualitative assessment of these dimensions. Which among them are truly pivotal for Bitcoin's network functionality, and which are not? For instance, one could argue that the client or ownership variables aren't as crucial in measuring Bitcoin's decentralization. Currently, Bitcoin Core serves as the de facto standard client. It is important to acknowledge that this program is open-source and was created by Satoshi Nakamoto. Provided it stays open-source, actively maintained, and monitored, its preeminence does not inherently imply susceptibility. It is essential to acknowledge the difference between Bitcoin Core's dominance and a monopoly, as theoretically, alternative operational clients exist—such as Bitcoin Knots, BTCD, Libbitcoin, BitcoinJ, Bitcoin Unlimited, and Gocoin—that can support the Bitcoin protocol.

In practice, however, a limited number of network nodes employ these alternatives, preferring Nakamoto's original design. In this context, Satoshi Nakamoto stated in 2010: "I do not believe that a second, compatible implementation of Bitcoin will ever be advantageous." Qualitative damage assessment rating: 2 out of 5. The second feature mentioned – the distribution of Bitcoin ownership – certainly possesses considerable socio-economic ramifications; yet, it does not directly influence Bitcoin's infrastructure. Due to Bitcoin's dependence on a proof-of-work mechanism, the influence of Bitcoin holders over nodes and the protocol's functioning is virtually nonexistent. The centralisation of sat ownership may become problematic if currency concentration escalates to a degree that undermines the network effect, so affecting its utility as a means of trade and a store of value.

Despite the polarisation of Bitcoin wealth, we are not yet at that juncture; different evaluations indicate that as Bitcoin use rises, the concentration of satoshis progressively diminishes. Qualitative damage evaluation rated from 1 to 5: 3. In contrast, subsystems like as nodes and code are essential for attaining genuine network decentralisation, representing potentially the most crucial elements inside the Bitcoin system. The potential for node takeover and ensuing hard forks or orchestrated malicious activities within the protocol presents considerable and enduring risks to network confidence. The likelihood of such occurrences is already minimal and has consistently diminished over time, considering the increasing number of active or readily activatable nodes (approximately 16,000 and 53,000, respectively, according to the most recent data) and their distribution across various locations, entities, and legal jurisdictions. Qualitative damage evaluation rating: 5

In this scenario, the concentration of Bitcoin Core code developers—referred to as Core developers and maintainers—remains significantly high and arguably increasing from a particular viewpoint: there are relatively few programmers actively engaged in writing and maintaining the client, despite its critical role in the overall technological infrastructure of the Bitcoin network. Currently, an average of 40 to 60 engineers contribute to this work monthly, as indicated by GitHub data. They autonomously and willingly determine the timing and manner of their contributions to the development of Bitcoin Core software on GitHub. Historically, there has been significant turnover within this group of developers, comprising both long-standing contributors from the early iterations of Bitcoin Core and more newer entrants. Numerous historical characters have departed over time, while others have subsequently re-emerged; some function continuously and regularly, and others do so in a limited and occasional fashion. This group lacks a formal structure, as Bitcoin is an open-source project, and it comprises an even smaller number of key developers who influence the community's activities.

GitHub data indicates that from its inception, 30% of the recorded commits to the Bitcoin Core master repository were contributed by merely two people, with nearly 25% (7347 out of a total of 29,822 identified commits) attributed solely to Wladimir van der Laan, the former Lead Maintainer of Bitcoin. Since his resignation in 2022, there has been no singular coordinator overseeing the Bitcoin Core development; yet, his substantial contributions are unequivocally acknowledged. Currently, the Bitcoin Core development is directed by a limited leadership team of senior developers Gennady Stepanov, Michael Ford, Ava Chow, and Gloria Zhao, each responsible for managing a particular component of the client.

One may question whether the limited and decentralised cohort of developers and maintainers currently contributing to the code could represent an Achilles' heel inside Bitcoin's diverse subsystems, so rendering the entire framework susceptible to attack. The extensive, intricate, and significantly valued architecture of the contemporary Bitcoin network depends on the sporadic and predominantly uncompensated efforts of a select group of dedicated supporters and maintainers. It is accurate that individual nodes ultimately determine the acceptance of any new update or version of the Bitcoin Core client via the consensus mechanism. Conversely, one may enquire about the number of nodes that scrutinise the new code for vulnerabilities, detrimental alterations, or defects before to its installation.

What would transpire if, hypothetically, there were incremental infiltrations of saboteurs among the restricted group of Key Core developers and Maintainers, intending to initially establish trust and influence within the community, subsequently compromising the new iterations of the code? They may, for instance, conceal virtual time bombs within them (in the guise of defects or zero-day vulnerabilities). The hypothesis is Machiavellian and intricate to implement, yet feasible, particularly if we account for a gradual, clandestine operation carried out by entities possessing substantial financial, human, and technological resources, along with a robust incentive to destabilise the network, such as the intelligence agency of a formidable nation. What would be the ramifications of a successful operation on Bitcoin? Likely quite grave, if not existential. It could incite disorder among nodes that inadvertently adopted the compromised update, resulting in mandatory hard forks that impact the stability, integrity, and trustworthiness of the Bitcoin network. A technological brute force attack could not achieve what social engineering targeted at undermining consensus could. Estimating the likelihood of a successful attack on the Bitcoin Core code is challenging; however, the limited number of individuals responsible for its development and maintenance, coupled with the general apathy of the broader user community towards their significant contributions (and, importantly, their compensation), renders this subsystem especially susceptible to a meticulously planned assault. Qualitative damage assessment rating: 4 out of 5 The trend towards centralisation in custodial and exchange services is not unequivocal. Although the number of exchanges has increased significantly since the inception of Bitcoin (notably MtGOX), the majority of trading volumes against fiat currencies is still dominated by a limited number of prominent entities (such as Binance, Bybit, Coinbase, OKX, Kraken, Bitfinex, etc.). As of now, three principal firms possess over 55% of the Bitcoin kept in custody by third parties, while Binance dominates fiat-BTC trades, accounting for 30% of total public exchanges. The dangers arising from excessive centralisation in this particular subsystem are less associated with the security of the Bitcoin network itself and more with its convertibility to fiat currencies and the security of those entrusted with custody (i.e., all Bitcoin users relying on their sats and, consequently, their "physical" possession). In the initial scenario, further centralisation (a decrease in the number of exchanges) would make the system more susceptible to organised litigation or cyberattacks intended to disrupt and potentially destroy the connection between fiat currencies and Bitcoin. This adheres to the principle that a reduced number of doors facilitates simpler locking. In the second scenario, within an oligopolistic framework, individuals choosing custodial solutions over self-custody would encounter heightened counterparty risk. This would arise from the reduced bargaining power of users relative to custodial entities, enabling them to impose more onerous economic terms and more restrictive provisions (for instance, concerning access to custodied bitcoins) than would be feasible in a competitive landscape.

Furthermore, with only a limited number of major operators able to manage substantial bitcoin holdings for their clients, the potential for misconduct (such as non-consensual fractional reserve practices), cyberattacks (as wealthier targets are more enticing), and political-regulatory interference (including collusion with governmental entities, overregulation, and bureaucratisation) would be significantly elevated in contrast to a more fragmented and competitive custodial framework. At the extreme of the counterparty risk spectrum exists the potential for a 6102 attack: the extensive confiscation of bitcoins stored on exchanges and custodial wallets inside a certain country through legislative measures. Although this would not immediately affect the operation of the Bitcoin network, it would likely erode public confidence in Bitcoin as a secure payment method and store of value, ultimately endangering its viability as a free, permissionless currency. Qualitative damage evaluation rated from 1 to 5:3. We will not elaborate further on the hash rate/mining subsystem, as the concerns regarding its decentralisation and the potential for 51% assaults have been thoroughly examined by more credible sources. We will simply mention the most prevalent attack scenarios: double spending assault, selective transaction censorship, and empty block attack. The ramifications of such assaults could be severe and must not be underestimated; nonetheless, extensive literature elucidates the limitations of this attack modality and the remedies that node consensus could implement to mitigate or effectively resist it. Nevertheless, it continues to be one of the most fragile and susceptible subsystems, mostly because of its level of centralisation. Currently, two mining pools, Foundry USA and Antpool, dominate over 50% of the hash rate. Qualitative damage assessment rating: 4 out of 5.

Finally, turning to the hardware dimension (originally absent in the work of Balaji S. Srinivasan and Leland), we need to analyze the diversification of mining equipment in terms of manufacturers, models, and their respective market shares of Bitcoin's hashrate. It's undeniable that nowadays the number of hardware manufacturers for mining (ASICs) has significantly increased compared to the past. Major companies in the sector include Bitmain, Whatsminer, Canaan, Zhejiang Ebang Communication, Halong Mining, Helium, Bitfury, Bee Computing, and HIVE Blockchain. However, the total hashrate of miners is currently dominated by a few ASIC models and even fewer manufacturers. According to recent estimates by Coinmetrics, over 70% of the global hashrate is produced by ASICs from a single leading company, Bitmain. Additionally, including just three other manufacturers (Whatsminer, Canaan, and Ebang) accounts for virtually all of the computational power used by the Bitcoin network. Moreover, the overwhelming majority of the hashrate is generated by only seven ASIC models from these aforementioned companies: Antminer S19xp, Antminer S19jpro, Antminer S19, Canaan 1246, Antminer S17, MicroBT m20s, and MicroBT m32.

The risks of such centralization of hardware in terms of models and manufacturers are numerous. With very few large manufacturers, primarily now located in China, they could easily be compelled by governments and lawmakers of the jurisdictions they're subject to, to halt production in their facilities, hand over batches of manufactured hardware, or secretly infiltrate backdoor hardware and trojans into their ASIC models. The consequences would immediately impact the mining subsystem, causing instability and potentially a collapse in the network's hashrate, resulting in significant economic losses for miners using corrupted ASICs or those unable to acquire new ones. A significantly lower and prolonged hashrate would reduce the security of the entire network, as it would increase the chances of a 51% attack, perhaps precisely by the actor who initiated the hardware attack. Here, we see how an attack on one poorly decentralized subsystem can virtually weaken another and thus attack it in a dangerous chain reaction with dangerous consequences for the integrity of the Bitcoin network. Damage qualitative assessment from 1 to 5: 3.

Given this non-exhaustive overview of the various subsystems of Bitcoin and their vulnerabilities, we can endeavor to synthesize the six dimensions into a single table. This table would measure the risk of centralization as a matrix between probability (P) and damage incidence (D, i.e.: the relevance of effects on the network), illustrating the dynamics toward increasing or decreasing centralization.

$$R = P * D$$

SUBSYTEM MASTER TABLE

See the datasets on the following sheets

		subjective value	*subjective value*	*R=P*D*			
Sub system	**Variable**	**Prob. Score (P: 1 to 5)**	**Damage Score (D: 1 to 5)**	**Risk score (R)**	**Effects**	**Trend**	**Data Source**
Nodes	Nodes (by Active/Total Nodes)	1	5	5	*Could lead to network splits, loss of trust, and potential protocol manipulation*	▼	Bitnodes
Mining	Mining	5	4	20	*Enable double spending, transaction censorship, and empty block attacks, affecting network security and trust*	▲	Hashrate Index
Exchanges/ Custodials	Exchanges (by traded volume)	3	3	9	*Risks include legal/cyberattacks disrupting Bitcoin-flot links and increased counterparty risks for users*	▼	Coingecko
	Custodials (by btc stored)	4		12		▲	Arkham
Developers	Developers (by GitHub contributed)	5	4	20	*A successful infiltration could introduce vulnerabilities or malicious code, potentially cousing widespread disruption*	▲	GitHub
Clients	Bitcoin Network Clients (by Protocol Clients)	5	2	10	*Dominance of a single client could pose risks, but alternative clients exist, mitigating the threat level*	=	Bitnodes

Sub system	Variable	Prob. Score (P: 1 to 5)	Damage Score (D: 1 to 5)	Risk score (R)	Effects	Trend	Data Source
Hardwaes	Hardwares	5	3	15	*Centralization among few manufacturers could lead to supply chain risks, backdoors, and a decrease in network security*	▼	Coin Metrics
Ownership	Ownership (by btc addresses)	1	3	3	*High concentration of wealth could affect Bitcoin's utility and trust as a decentralized currency, but trend is improving*	▼	BitInfo-Charts

A probability score (P) is assigned on a scale from 1 to 5 based on an inverse and non-linear function of the number of entities required to reach a given critical centralization threshold. In other words, the greater the number of existing entities required to reach a certain threshold, the lower the probability score. The aforementioned threshold is a percentage (sometimes subjectively defined) of the total estimated number of entities participating in a given subsystem, beyond which the system becomes seriously vulnerable to compromise. In some cases, this threshold is objective, as in the case of the mining dimension, while in others it is more arbitrary, such as in the case of developers or the client; however, in general, it could be understood as the tipping point of centralization.

A damage variable (D) is also assigned a score from 1 to 5. This is attributed in relation to the negative consequences expected from an attack on the specific subsystem on the security, stability, and functionality of the Bitcoin network as a whole. This latter score is obviously subjective and undoubtedly could be subject to criticism and subsequent revisions by more in-depth analyses. Finally, the specific risk score, which summarizes the risk of centralization of each subsystem, is obtained from the product of these two scores.

Geographical and Economic Decentralization

Additional versions of the decentralization/centralization dichotomy can be seen, intersecting with the seven categories already delineated: geographical (jurisdictions) and economic (economic entities). Geographical decentralisation examines the physical and legal locations of nodes, wallets, exchanges/custodians, and miners. Economic decentralisation pertains to the ownership of economic enterprises, such as the proprietorship of mining pools. Who governs the exchanges? The geographical and economic dimensions may appear to intersect first, however they are fundamentally distinct. For example, a Bitcoin ecosystem may consist of numerous independent miners, all situated within the same country and hence exposed to identical political-legal risks. In this context, economic and ownership centralisation would be minimal, however geographical centralisation would be significantly elevated.

Conversely, numerous mining facilities may be distributed worldwide yet governed by the same economic body, thereby essentially constituting a singular point of failure. The identical reasoning might similarly pertain to nodes, hardware, or bitcoin ownership. In a world governed by nation-states and multinational enterprises, overlooking these elements can be detrimental. The sheer quantity of participants in a Bitcoin subsystem provides limited insight into decentralisation if they are predominantly clustered inside a single jurisdiction or subjected to same economic management. Consequently, both the qualitative geographical dimension and the economic component must be incorporated into any effort to assess the extent of decentralisation of the Bitcoin network.

What changes with ETFs?

The recent introduction of Bitcoin ETFs in the US market may significantly influence the decentralisation of the network, especially for the Custodial/Exchanges subsystem. Investing in an ETF considerably streamlines access to bitcoin performance relative to other fiduciary options; nonetheless, this choice substantially increases counterparty risks for investors. Individuals who "invest in bitcoin" via an ETF do not genuinely possess the assets; they are exposed to the counterparty risk associated with the ETF manager and the Custodial/Depository upon which the ETF depends (unless the manager chooses the improbable option of self-custody), in addition to the risk posed by the intermediary/broker through which they obtain the instrument.

In essence, the maxim "Not your keys, not your coins" simplifies to "Not your coins, farewell," particularly in the context of a hypothetical 6102 attack on ETFs. At a macro level, the reasons applicable to custodial and exchange organisations also pertain to passive funds invested in Bitcoin: as institutional and retail investors increasingly utilise these funds as a means of investing in Bitcoin, a greater volume of Bitcoin is assimilated into their holdings. As a result, their coercive influence over users and economic authority over other subsystems of the Bitcoin Network intensify. If a particular Bitcoin ETF were to obtain a substantial, if not preeminent, share of circulating bitcoin over time and systematically utilise its proceeds to subsidise developers of the Bitcoin Core client, it could affect their actions, direct client implementations, and consequently steer the developmental trajectory of the entire network according to its objectives. This scenario illustrates how the centralisation of one aspect, specifically custodians via ETFs, results in the centralisation of a more critical dimension: that of developers already mentioned.

3.2.5 STORE AND USE OF BITCOIN

How to Use Bitcoin Online

Prior to purchasing and utilising bitcoin, it is essential to establish a wallet for its storage. Here is a concise guide to commence utilising Bitcoin:

- **Set Up a Wallet:** Choose a secure Bitcoin wallet for your needs. To receive funds, you require a public key (analogous to an account number) and a private key (like to a password) for transaction authorisation. A variety of hot wallets and cold wallets exist, each presenting distinct advantages and disadvantages for various users.
- **Find Vendors that Accept Bitcoin:** Many online services and products now accept Bitcoin, although some may only accept other cryptocurrencies. Upon identifying a merchant, you may utilise your wallet to transmit Bitcoin directly for goods or services.
- **Send Bitcoin to Other Users:** Bitcoin transfers are similar to traditional bank transfers, though they remain independent of banks. Request the recipient's wallet address, then execute a straight transfer of funds to their wallet.

How to Store Bitcoin Safely

Securing your funds is paramount when utilising Bitcoin. Below are essential wallet types and optimal procedures for secure Bitcoin storage:

- **Hot Wallets:** These are digital wallets that are internet-connected, including mobile or web applications. Hot wallets facilitate frequent transactions but are more susceptible to cyber risks.
- **Cold wallets:** Cold wallets, like as hardware wallets, serve as offline storage options, optimal for long-term asset retention. These wallets are offline, rendering them less susceptible to potential hackers. Although they offer enhanced security, they may be less convenient for rapid transactions.
- **Seed Phrases and Private Keys:** Upon establishing a wallet, you often receive a seed phrase—a recovery phrase that allows you to restore your cash in the event of losing access to your wallet. It is imperative to safeguard both your seed phrase and private key in an offline and secure manner. The public key may be disseminated to facilitate Bitcoin reception, whereas the private key must be kept confidential to safeguard your assets.

Why You Should Use Bitcoin

Numerous factors motivate individuals to utilise Bitcoin, with the following being among the most prominent advantages:

- **Privacy and Decentralisation:** Bitcoin's autonomy from central banks and financial institutions enables users to conduct private, pseudonymous transactions. This attribute renders it an attractive option for individuals seeking to safeguard their financial privacy.
- **Global Payment Solution:** Bitcoin enables customers to execute transactions internationally without concern for exchange fees. A little transaction charge will be required on cryptocurrency exchanges, eliminating the necessity to convert fiat currencies such as dollars to euros.
- **Wider Acceptance:** Bitcoin is becoming embraced by a rising number of companies and internet platforms. Bitcoin's utility continues to broaden, whether utilised for gambling on platforms such as Stake.com or for routine transactions.

Bitcoin: The Future of Finance

Bitcoin provides a decentralised and secure means of executing transactions that prioritises user autonomy, confidentiality, and a streamlined financial procedure. With the increasing utilisation and acceptance of Bitcoin, acquiring knowledge on its secure usage and storage has become paramount. Adhering to these recommended practices will safeguard your assets and enable you to reap the advantages of this transformative digital currency.

3.2.6 Bitcoin Mining

What Is Bitcoin Mining?

Bitcoin is a digital currency that employs a process known as mining to secure its network and authenticate transactions. Bitcoin mining constitutes a network- wide contest to provide a cryptographic solution that fulfils designated requirements. Upon reaching a valid solution, the miner(s) who initially achieved it are awarded a reward consisting of bitcoin and transaction fees for their efforts. The reward mechanism persists until the total supply of 21 million Bitcoins is in circulation. Upon reaching that amount, the mining process is anticipated to terminate, and Bitcoin miners will receive compensation through fees for their efforts.

How Does Bitcoin Mining Work?

This is a concise illustration of the mining process. Suppose you request friends to estimate a number between 1 and 100. Your friends need not ascertain the precise number; they merely must be the first to propose a number that is less than or equal to your number. If you consider the number 19 and a friend suggests 21, another proposes 55, and yet another indicates 83, they are disqualified as their guesses exceed 19. However, they are permitted to make additional guesses, which are 16, 41, and 67. The individual who predicted 16 is the victor, as they were the first to select a number less than or equal to 19. The number you selected, 19, signifies the target hash generated by the Bitcoin network for a block, while the random selections made by your friends represent the attempts of the miners. Bitcoin mining is the same thing but at a much larger scale. It uses cryptography, encryption, distributed computing, and technology to verify and secure transactions. Here are the main ideas behind mining that make it work.

The Hash

At the heart of Bitcoin mining is the hash. The hash is a 64-digit hexadecimal number that is the result of sending the information contained in a block through the SHA256 hashing algorithm. This part of the process takes little time to complete—in fact, you can generate a hash in under a second, pasting some content into an online SHA256 hash generator. This is the encryption method used by Bitcoin to create a block hash. However, decrypting that hash back to the content you pasted is the difficult part: a 64-digit hash can take centuries to decode with modern hardware.

For example, here's a hash for the previous paragraph run through a hash generator: a54f83a5db7371eeefa2287a0ede750ac623e49a8ba29f248eb785fe0a678559

If you change one value in that content, like switching one "t" to an "a," the hash changes. Here is the same paragraph, but the first word is misspelled as "Aa" instead of "At": fbfa33ff980d1492b3a9275a1eb945d89bd6b699ca19c3c470021b8f253654af This is the number called the block hash, which is used in the next block's header as part of the information run through encryption. Each block uses the previous block's hash, which acts to chain them together. This is where the term "blockchain" came from.

Target Hash

The target hash, used to determine mining difficulty, is the number miners are trying to solve for. This number is a hash generated by the network. So, a block hash might look like this (block 786,729): 00000000000000000005a849c28eb24b8a5e04fcecc1ccb3eb2998e4730a456e The target hash looked like this: 0x175c739

This number is a compacted representation of the difficulty target: 0...000005c73900000...0

So, miners needed to generate a number equal to or less than the above number.

Mining

Bitcoin mining requires the mining program to generate a hash and append another number to it called the nonce, or "number used once." When a miner begins, it always starts this number at zero. The nonce changes by one every attempt—first, it's 0, then 1, 2, 3, and so on. If the hash and nonce generated by the miner are more than the target hash set by the network, the attempt fails, and the miner tries again. Once the nonce reaches about 4.5 billion, it rolls over like an odometer, using another counter called the extra nonce from another field. Every miner on the network does this until a hash and nonce combination is created that is less than or equal to the target hash. The first to reach that target has their proposed block added to the chain, receives the reward and fees, and a new block is opened. Once that block fills up with information (about one megabyte), it is closed, encrypted, and mined. The Bitcoin network is made up of thousands of devices that mine 24 hours per day. Because the mining reward goes to the first to solve the problem, they are all competing. This competition led miners to create pools to gain an advantage over other miners because they needed more computational power to increase their chances of winning.

Proof-of-Work

The mining method, referred to as proof-of-work (PoW), involves the effort required to produce the successful hash, which serves as evidence that the miner has authenticated the transactions within the block, hence the designation proof- of-work. Proof-of-Work (PoW) is occasionally referred to as a consensus method; nevertheless, it constitutes merely a component of the consensus process. Consensus is attained once the miner incorporates the block into the blockchain, followed by validation from the remainder of the network through hash verification. This process demands minimal energy and processing resources, as each mining node does this task concurrently while mining the most recent block. As additional blocks are incorporated, the network validates them.

Confirmation

Every block encompasses the hash of the preceding block; hence, when the hash of the subsequent block is formed, the hash of the prior block is incorporated. Note that every alteration of a single character will result in a change to the hash, thereby altering the hashes of all subsequent blocks. Upon mining and closing a block, it remains unconfirmed. The block is not deemed confirmed until five further blocks have been added, resulting in a total of six validations. It is feasible to modify information within a block prior to achieving six validations; however, this scenario is exceedingly improbable, as the individual or entity seeking to implement the alteration must own a majority of the nodes to exert influence over the network.

Rewards

The incentive for correctly validating a block is Bitcoin. In 2009, one would obtain 50 bitcoin for mining a block. The block reward is reduced by half every 210,000 blocks (about every four years), resulting in a decrease to 25 in 2013, followed by 12.5, and then 6.25. During Bitcoin's most recent halving event in April 2024, the reward was adjusted to 3.125. Transaction fees provide as an additional incentive for Bitcoin miners to engage in the process. Besides rewards, miners also obtain fees from transactions included in that block. Upon Bitcoin attaining its predetermined cap of 21 million, anticipated around 2140, miners would get compensation through transaction fees paid by network users. These fees guarantee that miners retain the motivation to mine and sustain the blockchain network. The premise is that competition for these fees will ensure they remain low following the completion of halving events.

Difficulty

Mining difficulty refers to the amount of effort required to produce a value lower than the goal hash. Mining difficulty adjusts every 2,016 blocks, roughly every fortnight. The subsequent difficulty level is contingent upon the efficiency of miners in the prior cycle and the number of miners engaged. The Bitcoin network fluctuates the hash rate, which denotes the computational power required for mining the cryptocurrency. An increase in the number of miners vying for a solution correlates with an escalation in problem difficulty.

When processing capacity is removed from the blockchain network, the difficulty level decreases to facilitate mining. This is implemented to maintain block times at an average of approximately 10 minutes. On December 4, 2024, the mining difficulty level was 103.919 trillion. The probability of a computer generating a hash below the target is 1 in 103.919 trillion. In context, you are approximately 355,644 times more likely to win the Powerball Grand Prize with one lottery ticket than to accurately calculate the correct hash on a single attempt.

History of Bitcoin Mining

Two factors have influenced the evolution and structure of Bitcoin mining as it exists now. The bespoke fabrication of Bitcoin mining rigs initially contributed to the centralisation of the network. Bitcoin mining is fundamentally a sequential process of trial and error, where the likelihood of obtaining the correct solution prior to another miner is predominantly determined by the hashing speed of your devices. Initially, Bitcoin mining was predominantly conducted on desktop computers equipped with standard CPUs. Nonetheless, they started to experience prolonged delays in identifying the solution on the blockchain network as the algorithm's complexity escalated over time. Estimates suggest that using CPUs would have required "several hundred thousand years on average" to discover a valid block at the difficulty level of early 2015.

GPU Mining

Over time, miners recognised that graphics processing units (GPUs), or graphics cards, were more efficient and expedient for mining purposes. However, they expended much energy and were not engineered for intensive mining operations. Ultimately, manufacturers were had to restrict their mining activities due to the surge in demand for GPUs, which resulted in exorbitant costs and diminished availability for other customers.

ASIC Mining

Numerous miners already utilise bespoke mining devices known as Application-Specific Integrated Circuit (ASIC) miners, which are outfitted with specialised chips to enhance the speed and efficiency of Bitcoin mining. Their cost ranges from several hundred to tens of thousands of dollars. Currently, Bitcoin mining is highly competitive, necessitating the use of the latest ASICs for profitability. However, even with the latest equipment available, a single unit is seldom sufficient to compete against mining pools and substantial Bitcoin mining enterprises. These mining operations resemble huge data centres populated with mining-specific machines. The computational capacity they possess is astonishing—hundreds of trillions per second.

Issues With Bitcoin Mining

With odds of one in 103 trillion, increasing difficulty levels, and a vast network of people validating transactions, a block of transactions is confirmed around every 10 minutes. However, it is essential to recognise that 10 minutes constitutes a target rather than a mandate.

Speed

The Bitcoin network presently processes between three and six transactions per second, with transactions recorded in the blockchain around every 10 minutes. In contrast, Visa asserts its capability to execute around 65,000 transactions per second. Second-layer solutions and enhancements to the Bitcoin blockchain have sought to mitigate speed limitations; nonetheless, contemporary financial networks and alternative blockchains significantly surpass the transaction capacity of the Bitcoin network.

Scalability

The primary concern within the Bitcoin protocol is scalability—the blockchain's capacity to manage increased workloads efficiently. While Bitcoin miners largely concur that a solution for scalability is necessary, there is a lack of consensus on the appropriate method to do it. Bitcoin has undergone modifications through updates and the incorporation of off-chain solutions, however it continues to face scaling challenges. In the context of modifications, blockchain is primarily influenced by three key factors: decentralisation, security, and scalability. With contemporary technology, no alteration can occur without impacting another element. Altering the Bitcoin blockchain for enhanced scalability will likely compromise security and promote centralisation.

Energy Use

In an era where all activities must assess and mitigate their environmental impacts, the exorbitant energy consumption of Bitcoin mining has garnered scrutiny and condemnation. The competitive proof-of-work mechanism of Bitcoin is responsible for its high energy consumption. Estimates indicate that the blockchain mining process consumes electricity comparable to that of certain small nations. Throughout the majority of Bitcoin's brief history, its mining process has consistently been energy-intensive.

In the ten years following its inception, Bitcoin mining was predominantly situated in China, a nation that depends on fossil fuels, particularly coal, for the majority of its electrical generation. However, governmental crackdowns in China compelled miners to relocate their operations. Research conducted by the University of Cambridge indicates that the preponderance of Bitcoin mining activities is currently concentrated in the United States.

Approximately 38% of global Bitcoin mining occurs in the U.S., with over 62% concentrated in four states: Georgia (30.76%), Texas (11.22%), Kentucky (10.93%), and New York (9.77%). Four states account for about 23% of global Bitcoin mining energy consumption and, theoretically, its hashing capacity. Hashing power refers to the speed at which a computer, miner, or network can produce solutions (hashes) to the cryptographic challenge. As of December 2024, the Bitcoin network exhibited an average hashrate above 796 exahashes per second. That equates to 796 x 10^18, or 796 followed by 18 zeros, hashes per second.

3.3 ETHEREUM

Ethereum functions as a decentralised computing network. It enables developers to construct and execute apps on its blockchain through the utilisation of smart contracts. Blockchain technology garnered global attention with the emergence of Bitcoin in 2009. Bitcoin is a cryptocurrency that operates on blockchain technology and is the most popular and highest-ranked cryptocurrency. Ethereum was launched in 2015. Within two years of its launch, it was regarded as the second-best blockchain network, with Bitcoin holding the first position. The Ethereum network garnered more global attention following China's declaration that it is the premier blockchain network ever developed.

What is Ethereum?

Ethereum is a blockchain network that features an integrated Turing-complete programming language, enabling the development of diverse decentralised applications (commonly referred to as Dapps). The Ethereum network operates using its native cryptocurrency, known as 'ether'. The Ethereum network is renowned for facilitating the execution of smart contracts. Smart contracts can be regarded as 'cryptographic bank vaults' that hold specific values. These cryptographic vaults can only be accessed when specific criteria are fulfilled. In contrast to Bitcoin, Ethereum is a versatile network applicable across multiple sectors. Ethereum is frequently referred to as Blockchain 2.0 due to its demonstration of blockchain technology's potential beyond the financial sector. The consensus mechanism employed in Ethereum is Proof of Stake (PoS), which is more energy-efficient compared to the Proof of Work (PoW) mechanism utilised by the Bitcoin network. Proof of Stake is contingent upon the quantity of stake possessed by a node.

History of Ethereum

- **2013:** Ethereum was first described in Vitalik Buterin's white paper in 2013 with the goal of developing decentralized applications.
- **2014:** In 2014, EVM was specified in a paper by Gavin Wood, and the formal development of the software also began.
- **2015:** In 2015, Ethereum created its genesis block marking the official launch of the platform.
- **2018:** In 2018, Ethereum took second place in Bitcoin in terms of market capitalization.
- **2021:** In 2021, a major network upgrade named London included Ethereum improvement proposal 1559 and introduced a mechanism for reducing transaction fee volatility.
- **2022:** In 2022, Ethereum has shifted from PoW(Proof-of-Work) to PoS(Proof-of-State) consensus mechanism, which is also known as Ethereum Merge. It has reduced Ethereum's energy consumption by ~ 99.95%.

Features of Ethereum

1. **Smart contracts:** Ethereum allows the creation and deployment of smart contracts. Smart contracts are created mainly using a programming language called solidity. Solidity is an Object Oriented Programming language that is comparatively easy to learn.

2. **Ethereum Virtual Machine (EVM):** It is designed to operate as a runtime environment for compiling and deploying Ethereum-based smart contracts.
3. **Ether:** Ether is the cryptocurrency of the Ethereum network. It is the only acceptable form of payment for transaction fees on the Ethereum network.
4. **Decentralized applications (Daaps):** Dapp has its backend code running on a decentralized peer-to-peer network. It can have a frontend and user interface written in any language to make calls and query data from its backend. They operate on Ethereum and perform the same function irrespective of the environment in which they get executed.
5. **Decentralized autonomous organizations (DAOs):** It is a decentralized organization that works in a democratic and decentralized fashion. DAO relies on smart contracts for decision-making or decentralized voting systems within the organization.

Type of Ethereum Accounts

Ethereum comprises two categories of accounts: Externally Owned Accounts (EOA) and Contract Accounts.

The following explanations are provided below:

- **Externally Owned Account (EOA):** Externally owned accounts are governed by private keys. Every Externally Owned Account (EOA) possesses a public- private key pair. Users can transmit messages by generating and endorsing transactions.
- **Contract Account:** Contract accounts are governed by contract codes. The codes are retained with the account. Every contract account possesses an associated ether balance. The contract code of these accounts activates if a transaction from an externally owned account (EOA) or a message from another contract is received. Upon activation of the contract code, it enables the reading and writing of messages to local storage, the transmission of messages, and the creation of contracts.

How Does Ethereum Work?

Ethereum implements an execution environment called Ethereum Virtual Machine (EVM). When a transaction triggers a smart contract all the nodes of the network will execute every instruction. All the nodes will run The EVM as part of the block verification, where the nodes will go through the transactions listed in the block and runs the code as triggered by the transaction in the EVM. All the nodes on the network must perform the same calculations for keeping their ledgers in sync.

Every transaction must include:

- Gas limit.
- Transaction Fee that the sender is willing to pay for the transaction.

If the total amount of gas needed to process the transaction is less than or equal to the gas limit then the transaction will be processed and if the total amount of the gas needed is more than the gas limit then the transaction will not be processed the fees are still lost. Thus it is safe to send transactions with the gas limit above the estimate to increase the chances of getting it processed.

Real-World Applications of Ethereum

- **Voting:** Voting systems are adopting Ethereum. The results of polls are publicly accessible, establishing a transparent and equitable system, hence eradicating electoral malpractices.
- **Agreements:** Ethereum smart contracts facilitate the maintenance and execution of agreements and contracts without any modifications. Ethereum facilitates the creation of smart contracts and the digital documentation of transactions derived from them.
- **Banking systems:** Due to the decentralized nature of the Ethereum blockchain it becomes challenging for hackers to gain unauthorized access to the network. It enhances payment security on the Ethereum network, prompting banks to utilise Ethereum as a medium for transactions.
- **Shipping:** Ethereum offers a tracking system that facilitates cargo monitoring and mitigates the risk of products being lost.
- **Crowdfunding:** Utilising Ethereum smart contracts in blockchain-based crowdfunding platforms enhances confidence and information symmetry. It generates numerous opportunities for entrepreneurs by securing capital to develop their own digital currencies.
- **Domain names:** Ethereum name service allows crypto users to buy and manage their own domain names on Ethereum, thus simplifying decentralized transactions without putting users to remember long, machine-readable addresses.

Advantages of Ethereum

- **Accessibility:** The decentralised nature of the Ethereum network ensures continuous availability without downtime. Even if one node fails, other computing nodes remain accessible.
- **Privacy:** Users are not required to input personal credentials when utilising the network for exchanges, hence enabling them to maintain anonymity.
- **Security:** Ethereum is engineered to be impervious to hacking, as attackers must gain control of the majority of network nodes to compromise the system. **Less ambiguity:** The smart contracts that are used as a basis for trade and agreement on Ethereum ensure stronger contracts that differ from the normal traditional contracts which require follow-through and interpretation.
- **Rapid deployment:** On Ethereum decentralized networks, enterprises can easily deploy and manage private blockchain networks instead of coding blockchain implementation from scratch.
- **Network capacity:** The Ethereum network can accommodate hundreds of nodes and millions of users.
- **Data coordination:** The decentralised architecture of Ethereum optimally distributes information, eliminating the need for network users to depend on a central authority for system management and transaction mediation.

Disadvantage of Ethereum

- **The complexity of the programming language:** Acquiring proficiency in Solidity for developing smart contracts on Ethereum can be arduous, primarily due to the lack of accessible introductory courses. Investing in Ethereum is precarious due to the extreme volatility of Ether's price, which can lead to substantial profits or considerable losses.

- **Low transaction rate:** Bitcoin has an average transaction rate of 7TPS and Ethereum has an average speed of 15 TPS which is almost double that of bitcoin but it is still not enough.

3.3.1 Ethereum Ecosystem

The Ethereum blockchain ecosystem consists of numerous essential components. The Ethereum blockchain is fundamentally based on a decentralised peer-to-peer network. Moreover, an Ethereum client, commonly Geth, operates on the nodes and connects to the peer-to-peer Ethereum network, enabling the download and local retention of the blockchain. This client offers a range of functionalities, including mining and account management. The local blockchain copy is consistently synchronized with the network. Another essential element is the **web3.js** library, which enables interaction with the **Geth** client through the **Remote Procedure Call (RPC)** interface.

Components of Ethereum Ecosystem

The components of Ethereum Ecosystem are given as follows:

- Keys and Addresses
- Accounts
- Transactions
- Messages
- Ether Cryptocurrency/Tokens
- The EVM

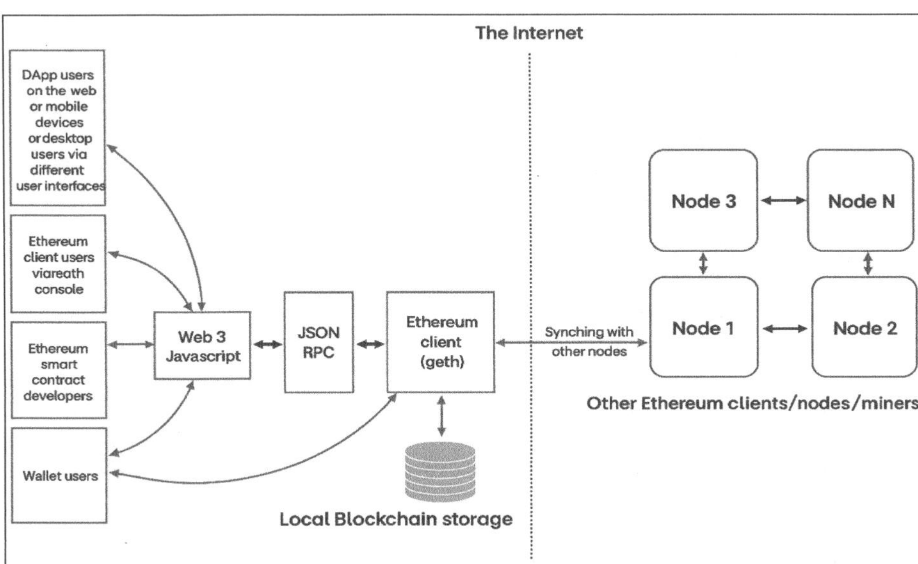

Fig. 3.2

1. Keys and Addresses

In the Ethereum blockchain, keys and addresses signify ownership and enable the transfer of ether. These keys consist of pairs, including a private key and a public key. The private key is generated randomly and kept confidential, whereas the public key is derived from the private key. Addresses, consisting of 20-byte codes, are derived from public keys and serve to identify accounts.

How to Generate Keys and Addresses?

The process for generating keys and deriving addresses is as follows: First, a private key is randomly chosen (a 256-bit positive integer) in accordance with the elliptic curve secp256k1 specifications. Subsequently, the public key is derived from the private key using the Elliptic Curve Digital Signature Algorithm (ECDSA) recovery function. Lastly, an address is generated from the public key, specifically from the last 160 bits of the Keccak hash of the public key.

Accounts of the Ethereum Ecosystem

Accounts function as essential elements of the Ethereum blockchain. They comprise pairs of private and public keys. Users employ accounts to interact with the blockchain via transactions. Before a transaction is submitted to the network through a node, it is digitally signed by the corresponding account. Ethereum's state, as a transaction-driven state machine, is created or altered through account interactions and transaction executions.

State Transition of the Ethereum Ecosystem

Every account in the Ethereum network has a state that, when combined, represents the network's overall condition. The Ethereum network's state is updated with the addition of each new block. The actions performed on and between these accounts represent state transitions. The Ethereum state transition function facilitates this shift, operating as follows:

- The transaction's validity is verified through assessments of syntax, signature authenticity, and nonce.
- The transaction fee is established, and the sender's address is verified using the signature.
- The sender's account balance is confirmed and modified accordingly, with the nonce incremented.
- Adequate ETH must be supplied to cover transaction fees, which are computed per byte and escalate exponentially with the amount of the transaction. This phase entails the actual transfer of value from the sender's account to the recipient's account.
- If the designated destination account is not yet established, it is created automatically.

In cases of transaction failure due to inadequate balance or gas, all state changes are reversed, save for the fee, which is paid to the miners. Ultimately, any residual fee is refunded to the sender as change, and the fee is allocated among the miners proportionately. At this juncture, the function produces the resultant state, which is concurrently documented on the blockchain.

Types of Accounts

There are two categories of accounts within the Ethereum Ecosystem:

- Externally Owned Accounts (EOAs)
- Contract Accounts (CAs)

Externally Owned Accounts function similarly to Bitcoin accounts, being governed by a private key. In contrast, Contract Accounts are distinguished by their association with executable code in addition to a private key. The key features and properties of both types of accounts are given in the following section:

EOAs

The key features of Externally Owned Accounts are given as follows:

- They possess a state.
- They are linked to a human user, which is why they are referred to as user accounts.
- EOAs maintain an ether balance.
- They have the ability to send transactions.
- They do not contain any associated code.
- Control is exercised through private keys.
- EOAs are unable to initiate a call message.
- Accounts feature a key-value store.
- EOAs are capable of initiating transaction messages.

CAs

The key features of Contract Accounts are given as follows:

- They possess a state.
- They are not inherently linked to any user or entity on the blockchain.
- CAs maintain an ether balance.
- They include associated code that is stored in memory or on the blockchain. They have access to storage.
- They can be triggered to execute code in response to transactions or messages from other contracts.
- CAs can preserve their permanent states and can invoke other contracts.
- CAs are unable to initiate transaction messages.
- CAs can initiate a call message.
- CAs feature a key-value store.
- The addresses of CAs are generated upon deployment, and this address is utilized to identify their location on the blockchain.

Transactions of Ethereum Ecosystem

In the Ethereum Ecosystem, a transaction is defined as a data packet that is digitally signed with a private key, containing specific instructions that, upon execution, lead to either a message call or the establishment of a contract.

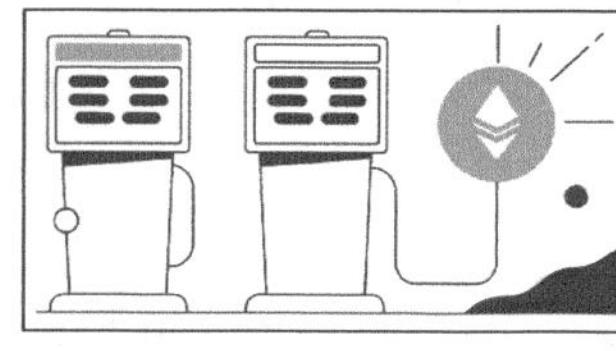

Fig. 3.3

Transactions can be classified into two main categories based on their results.

Message Call Transactions

These transactions enable the communication of messages between various contract accounts (CAs) without establishing new accounts.

2. Contract Creation Transactions

These transactions result in the formation of a new contract account. The successful completion of this transaction results in the establishment of an account linked to a certain code.

Key Terms in Transactions

Both transactions comprise various standard fields, which are outlined as follows.

Nonce

The nonce is a sequential number that increments by one with each transaction initiated by the sender. It must align with the aggregate number of transactions transmitted and functions as a distinctive identifier for the transaction.

Gas Price

The gas price field denotes the quantity of Wei required to execute the transaction. This charge is imposed per unit of gas for all computational costs associated with the execution of the transaction.

Gas limit

The gas limit parameter indicates the maximum quantity of gas permitted for executing the transaction.

To

The To field denotes the address of the transaction's recipient, represented as a 20-byte value. Value.

Value

The Value field denotes the entire quantity of Wei to be transmitted to the receiver. In the context of a contract account (CA), this denotes the balance that the contract will uphold.

Signature

The signature consists of three elements: V, R, and S. These numbers denote the digital signature (R, S) and other information that facilitates the recovery of the public key (V).

Init

The Init field is solely employed in transactions intended for contract generation, specifically in contract creation transactions. It signifies a byte array of indeterminate length that delineates the EVM code to be utilised in the account initialisation procedure.

Data

In a message call transaction, the Data field supplants Init and encompasses the input data for the intent call. This field possesses limitless capacity and is organised as a byte array.

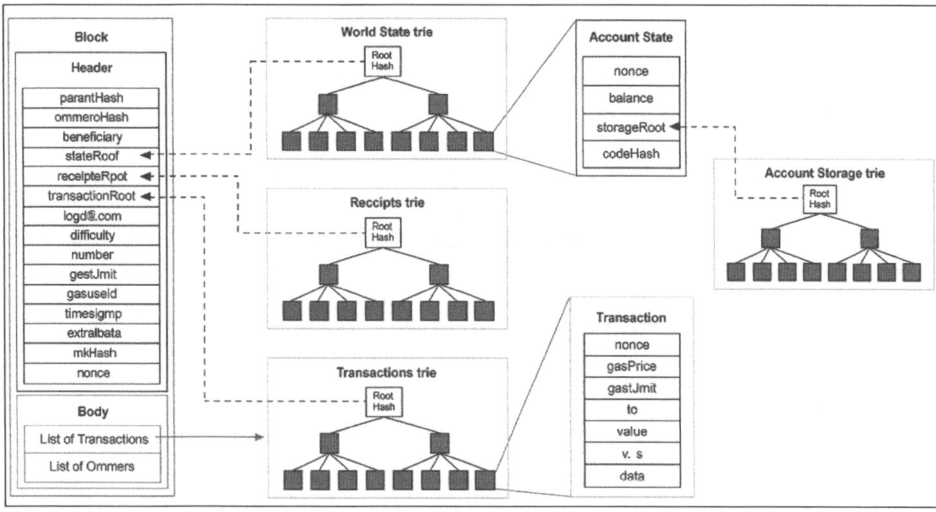

Fig. 3.4

Messages of Ethereum Ecosystem

The yellow paper defines Messages as the data and values sent between two accounts. A message is fundamentally a data packet that transmits both information and a value, specifically the quantity of ether involved. Messages can be conveyed via a smart contract, functioning as an autonomous entity, or triggered by an external actor, referred to as an Externally Owned Account (EOA), through a digitally signed transaction. Contracts possess the power to transmit messages to other contracts. Messages live exclusively inside the execution context and are not retained. Although messages exhibit similarities to transactions, the principal difference resides in their source: messages are produced by contracts, while transactions emanate from external entities within the Ethereum ecosystem (EOAs).

Components of a Message

A message is composed of several key elements:

- The individual or entity sending the message
- The individual or entity receiving the message
- The quantity of Wei to be transferred along with the message directed to the contract address
- An optional data field, which serves as input for the contract
- The maximum gas limit (**startgas**) that may be utilized

Messages are created when the **CALL or DELEGATECALL** opcodes are executed by the contract operating within the EVM.

Ethereum Tokens (ETH/ETC)

Ethereum possesses a native cryptocurrency referred to as ether (ETH). A hard fork was initiated to rectify the problem following the previously discussed hack of the Decentralised Autonomous Organisation (DAO). Consequently, there are two separate Ethereum blockchains: Ethereum Classic, denoted by the currency ETC, and the hard-forked variant,

ETH, which persists in its development. Ethereum Classic (ETC) has fostered a dedicated community of advocates who are diligently engaged in its development, preserving it as the original, unaltered iteration of Ethereum. Ether is produced by miners as compensation for their computing efforts in protecting the network via transaction and block validation. In the Ethereum blockchain, ether functions as the currency for executing contracts on the Ethereum Virtual Machine (EVM). Furthermore, ether is employed to acquire gas, which serves as the essential fuel for executing computations on the Ethereum blockchain. The subsequent table presents the denominations of various units together with their corresponding values.

Unit	Alternative name	Wei value	Number of weis
Wei	Wei	**1 Wei**	**1**
KWei	Babbage	**1e3 Wei**	**1,000**
MWei	Lovelace	**1e6 Wei**	**1,000,000**
GW	Shannon	**1e9 Wei**	**1,000,000,000**
microether	Szabo	**1e12 Wei**	**1,000,000,000,000**
millieither	Finncy	**1e15 Wei**	**1,000,000,000,000,000**
ether	ether	**1e18 Wei**	**1,000,000,000,000,000,000**

3.4 CASE STUDY: BITCOIN CASH

This repository contains an in-depth study and analysis of Bitcoin, showcasing its unique value proposition as a decentralized digital currency. The project explores Bitcoin's creation, blockchain technology, monetary policy, and comparison with traditional fiat currencies. Additionally, it highlights real- world use cases, institutional adoption, and Bitcoin's potential as a financial asset. Here is link for the full presentation.

Purpose

The primary goals of this study are:

- To explain **why Bitcoin is valuable** and its transformative potential for the financial system.
- To compare Bitcoin with fiat currencies in resilience, scarcity, inflation resistance, and transparency.
- To analyze **blockchain technology** and its role in ensuring security, trust, and decentralization.
- To present **real-world use cases** and adoption trends.

Tools and Methodology

Tools Used:

- **Keynote**: For crafting professional and visually appealing slides.
- **Python (Matplotlib, Pandas)**: For designing custom charts, performing data analysis, and creating timelines.
- **Excel**: For initial data organization and exploratory analysis.
- **Canva**: For additional graphic design and layout enhancements.

- **Google Slides**: For collaborative editing and final presentation adjustments.
- **GitHub**: For version control and sharing the project.
- **Figma**: For advanced design mockups and visual alignment.
- **Power BI**: For interactive data visualization and insights presentation.
- **SQL**: For querying and managing data to extract valuable insights.

Data Sources

- **PrimaryResearch**: Bitcoin's whitepaper and blockchain documentation.
- **Secondary Sources**: Data and reports from platforms like CoinMarketCap and Statista.
- **Market Trends**: Publicly available insights on financial trends and institutional adoption.

Methodology

1. **Conceptualization**: Defining the project's goals, structure, and presentation style.
2. **Data Analysis**: Analyzing Bitcoin's historical price trends, halving events, and ROI comparisons with gold and the S&P 500.
3. **Visualization**: Creating engaging visuals, such as:
    - Bitcoin creation timeline.
    - ROI and inflation resistance comparisons.
    - Real-world adoption case studies.

Project Highlights

Bitcoin Creation Timeline

Fig. 3.5: *Process of Creation*

- A chronological overview of Bitcoin's creation and milestones:
    - **2008**: Introduction by Satoshi Nakamoto.
    - **October 31, 2008**: Publication of Bitcoin's whitepaper.
    - **January 3, 2009**: Genesis Block mined.
    - **January 12, 2009**: First Bitcoin transaction.

Blockchain Technology

The Blockchain

- **Definition:** A blockchain is a distributed ledger that records transactions in a secure, transparent and immutable way.
- **Structure:** The blockchain is a chain of block, where each block containing, transactions, cryptography, and timestamp.

Key Features

- **Decentralization:** It operates across a global network of computers instead of being managed by a central authority.
- **Transparency:** Anyone can view the Bitcoin blockchain, making transactions publicly accessible.
- **Immutability:** Once a block is added to the chain, it cannot be altered without consensus from the network.
- **Security:** It uses cryptographic techniques to secure data and validate transactions.
- Explains the blockchain's structure, emphasizing key features:
  - **Decentralization**: Operates without a central authority.
  - **Transparency**: Publicly accessible transaction records.
  - **Security**: Cryptographic techniques ensure data integrity and validation.

Bitcoin vs Fiat Currency

Criteria	Bitcoin	Fiat Currency
Control	Decentralized	Centralized (Government/Banks)
Supply	Limited (21 Million)	Unlimited (Can Be Printed)
Transparency	Public, Blockchain-Based	Private, Bank Records
Transaction Fees	Generally Lower	Higher (3rd Party Involved)
Inflation Resistance	Resistant Due To Its Supply	Prone To Inflation

- Highlights differences between Bitcoin vs Fiat.

Bitcoin's Monetary Policy

- Unlike fiats currencies that can be printed endlessly, Bitcoin has a hard cap of 21 million coins.
- This limit is programmed into Bitcoin's code and cannot be changed without global consensus, ensuring scarcity.
- They are called Halving Events, which are programmed to happen every four years.
- Describes Bitcoin's hard cap of 21 million coins.
- Explains halving events and their impact on scarcity and value.

Real-Life Use Cases of Bitcoin

- **Cross-Border Payments:** Allows for instant low-cost global payments.

  A migrant worker sending money home can save up to 90% in fees using Bitcoin instead of services like Western Union.

  Enables low-cost, instant global transactions.

- **Store of Value:** Bitcoin is often referred to as "digital gold" due to its scarcity and deflationary nature. In regions experiencing hyperinflation, Bitcoin provides a stable alternative for preserving wealth.

  In Venezuela, Bitcoin adoption has surged as citizens seek refuge from the country's 400% annual inflation rate.

  Serves as "digital gold" in regions experiencing hyperinflation.

- **Markets Adoptions:** Bitcoin's appeal has grown among institutions, with companies integrating it into their treasury strategies to hedge against inflation and diversify their assets.

  Companies, Banks, Countries are urging the need to create a bitcoin reserve, as rumours starts appearing in late December 2024.

  Increasing integration into financial strategies by companies and countries.

Key Insights

1. **Bitcoin Outperforms Fiat**:

   The scores (0-10) represent a qualitative comparison between Bitcoin and fiat currencies across three critical dimensions Inflation Resistance. Censorship Resistance, and Decentralization.

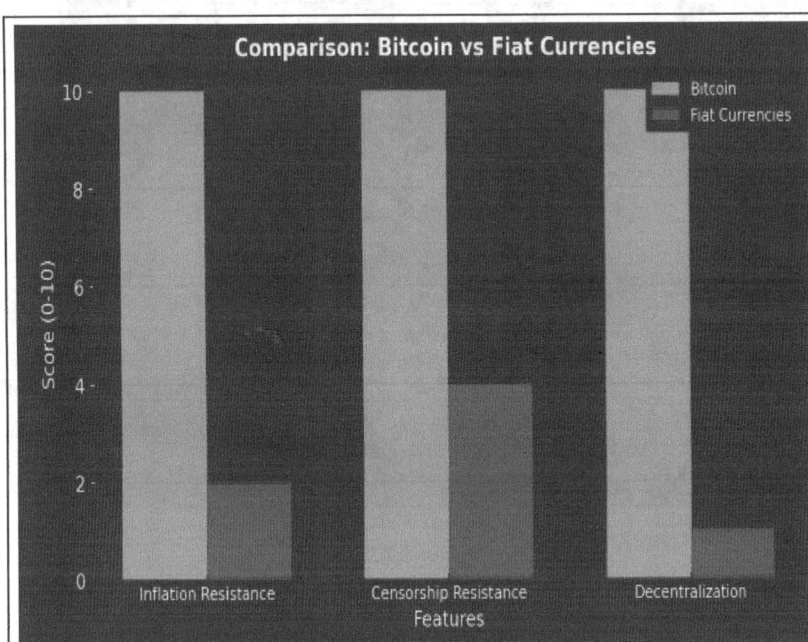

Fig. 3.6

- Bitcoin is unparalleled in inflation resistance because its supply is capped. Fiat currencies lose value over time due to inflation.
- In countries with authoritarian governments, Bitcoin empowers citizens by ensuring their money can't be frozen.
- While fiat currencies work well in stable economies, their centralization makes them vulnerable to misuse.
- Resistant to inflation due to its fixed supply.
- Transparent and decentralized, empowering individuals.

2. **Growing Adoption**:
   - Large companies like Tesla. MicroStrategy, and financial firms like BlackRock and Fidelity have invested in Bitcoin, increasing its legitimacy as a financial asset.
   - Bitcoin is becoming more accessible through user-friendly apps like Cash App. Strike, and platforms like Binance and Coinbase, which allow easy Bitcoin purchases.
   - Countries are starting to create clearer regulations around Bitcoin, which reduces uncertainty and encourages investment.

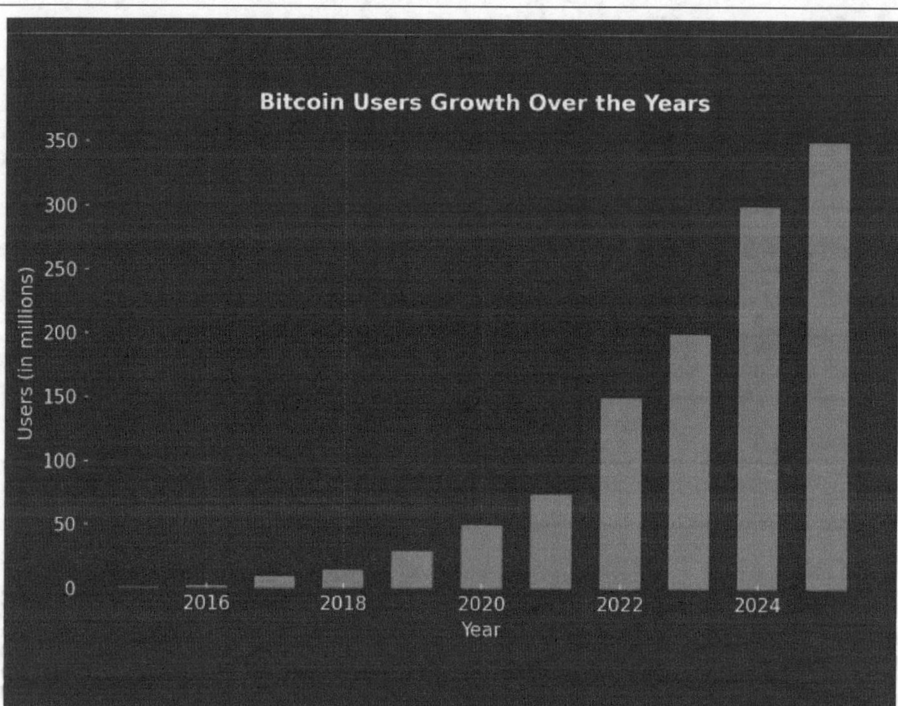

Fig. 3.7

- Institutions like BlackRock and Fidelity validate Bitcoin as a financial asset.
- Regulatory clarity encourages further investment.

3. **Future Potential:**
    - As younger generations become the primary wealth holders, Bitcoin adoption will grow exponentially.
    - By 2030, Millennials and Gen Z could control up to 80% of the Bitcoin market, making it a comerstone of future investment portfolios.

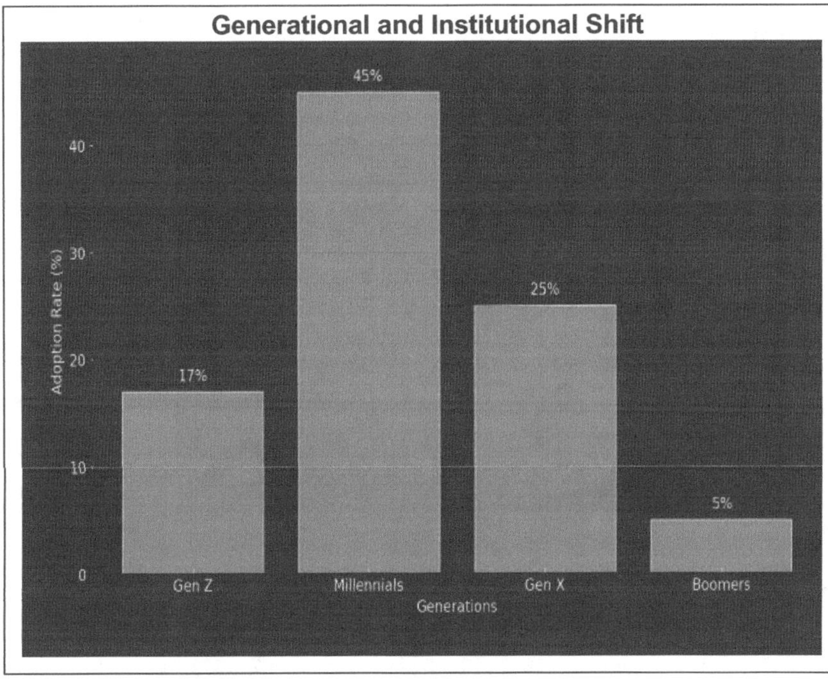

Fig. 3.8

- Bitcoin's technological advancements (e.g., Lightning Network) make it scalable for daily use.
- Millennials and Gen Z are driving exponential adoption.

Code Examples

Python: Data Analysis and Visualization

Below is an example of how Python was used to analyze Bitcoin's historical price data and visualize ROI comparisons.

```
import matplotlib.pyplot as plt

# Data for investment ROI (2011-2021)

investments = [‘Bitcoin’, ‘Gold’, ‘S&P 500’, ‘Silver’, ‘Nasdaq-100’]

roi_values = [12000, 200, 350, 150, 500]        # ROI percentages for each investment

colors = [‘orange’, ‘yellow’, ‘green’, ‘silver’, ‘blue’] # Create a pie chart

plt.figure(figsize=(8, 8))
```

```
plt.pie(roi_values, labels=investments, colors=colors, autopct='%1.1f%%', startangle=140)
plt.title('Proportional ROI Contribution of Major Investments (2011-2021)') plt.show()
```

RESULT

What is ROI?

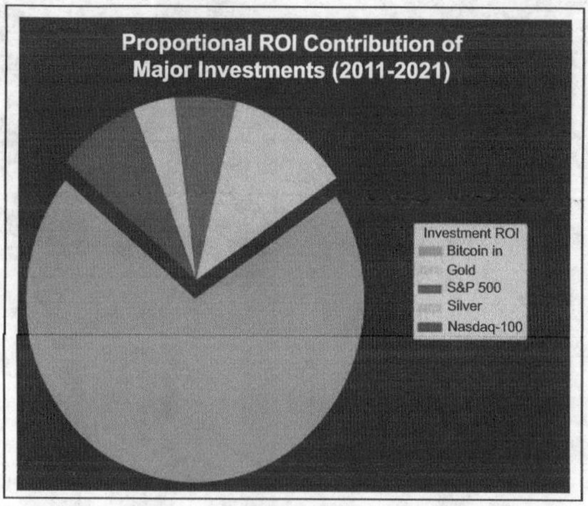

Fig. 3.9

```
import matplotlib.pyplot as plt import numpy as np
# Simulated data for demonstration years = np.arange(2010, 2025)
usd_purchasing_power = 100 * (0.95 ** (years - 2010)) # Declining by 5% each year
btc_purchasing_power = 10 ** (years - 2010) # Exponential growth fig, ax1 = plt.subplots(figsize=(12, 6))
# Plot USD Purchasing Power
ax1.plot(years, usd_purchasing_power, label='U.S. Dollar Purchasing Power', color='cyan', linewidth=2)
ax1.set_xlabel('Year')
ax1.set_ylabel('U.S. Dollar Purchasing Power', color='cyan') ax1.tick_params(axis='y', labelcolor='cyan')
# Create a secondary y-axis for Bitcoin Purchasing Power ax2 = ax1.twinx()
ax2.plot(years, btc_purchasing_power, label='Bitcoin Purchasing Power', color='orange', linewidth=2)
ax2.set_ylabel('Bitcoin Purchasing Power (Log Scale)', color='orange') ax2.tick_params(axis='y', labelcolor='orange')
ax2.set_yscale('log') # Use log scale for Bitcoin's exponential growth # Add title and legend
plt.title('Bitcoin vs U.S. Dollar: Inflation Resistance Comparison', fontsize=14) fig.legend(loc='upper center', bbox_to_anchor=(0.5, -0.1), ncol=2, fontsize=10) # Adjust layout and show the plot
plt.tight_layout() plt.show()
```

RESULT

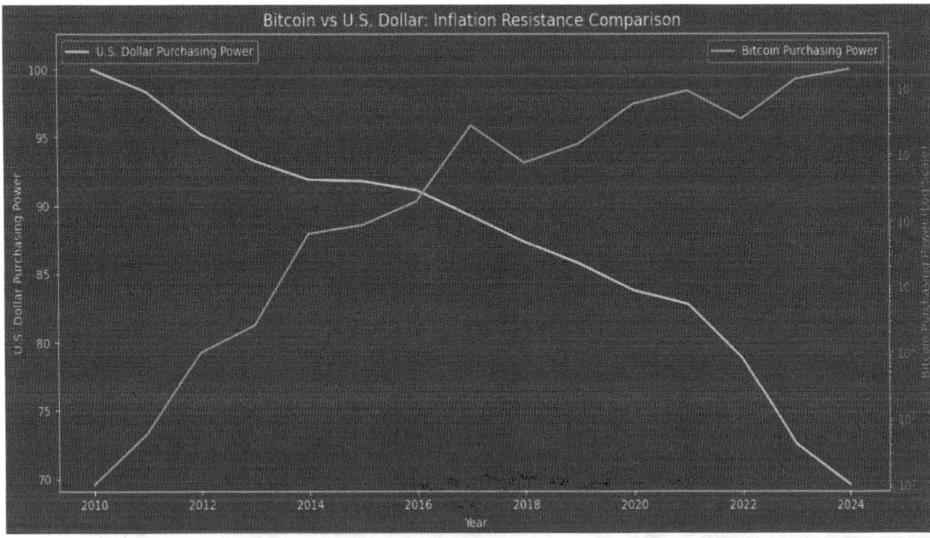

Fig. 3.10

```
import matplotlib.pyplot as plt import numpy as np

# Data for halving years, prices before and after halving halving_years = [2012, 2016, 2020, 2024]

price_before_halving = [12, 650, 8800, 30000] # Example prices in USD

price_after_halving = [120, 2550, 58000, 107000] # Example prices in USD # Create the bar chart

fig, ax = plt.subplots(figsize=(10, 6)) bar_width = 0.35

x_positions = np.arange(len(halving_years)) # Bars for prices before and after halving

bars_before = ax.bar(x_positions - bar_width / 2, price_before_halving, bar_width, label='Price Before Halving', color='orange')

bars_after = ax.bar(x_positions + bar_width / 2, price_after_halving, bar_width, label='Price 1 Year After Halving', color='green')

# Add labels, title, and legend ax.set_xlabel('Halving Year') ax.set_ylabel('Price (USD)')

ax.set_title('Bitcoin Prices Before and After Halving Events')

ax.set_xticks(x_positions) ax.set_xticklabels(halving_years) ax.legend()

# Add value labels on the bars def add_labels(bars):

for bar in bars:

height = bar.get_height()

ax.text(bar.get_x() + bar.get_width() / 2, height + 5000, f'${height:,.0f}', ha='center', va='bottom', fontsize=10)

add_labels(bars_before) add_labels(bars_after)

# Adjust layout and show the plot plt.tight_layout()

plt.show()
```

RESULT

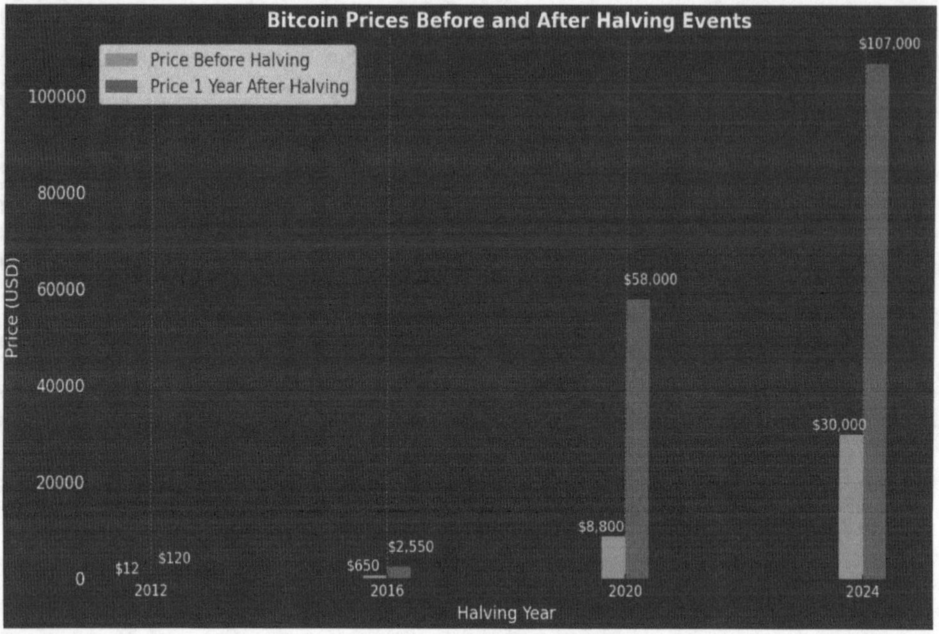

Fig. 3.11

SQL: Querying and Managing Data

The following SQL query was used to extract insights about Bitcoin transaction volumes:

```
Select
    DATE_FORMAT(transaction_date, '%Y-%m') AS month,
    Count(transaction_id) AS total_transactions
From
    bitcoin_transactions
GROUP BY
    month;
SELECT
    DATE_FORMAT(transaction_date, '%Y-%m') AS month,
    AVG(transaction_amount) AS avg_transaction_value
From
    bitcoin_transactions
GROUP BY
    month
ORDER BY
    month;
```

These examples showcase how Python and SQL were leveraged for data processing and visualization.

UNIT

4

ETHEREUM AND SOLIDITY

4.1 ALTERNATIVE APPROACHES TO MINING AND CONSENSUS

Mining is a crucial element of blockchain technology, underpinning decentralisation, security, and consensus within the network. We will examine the complexities of block mining in Web3, focussing on its function, methods, incentives, and the foundational code. Upon concluding this course, you will possess a comprehensive understanding of the operational mechanics of mining within the Web3 environment.

Consensus Algorithms in Web3

Web3 utilises diverse consensus algorithms, each possessing distinct advantages and drawbacks. The two principal consensus techniques employed in Web3 networks are Proof of Work (PoW) and Proof of Stake (PoS).

Proof of Work (PoW)

Proof of Work is the consensus algorithm originally introduced by Bitcoin. It necessitates miners to resolve computationally demanding mathematical problems to authenticate transactions and generate new blocks. This procedure entails identifying a nonce value that, when amalgamated with the block data, generates a hash exhibiting a predetermined quantity of leading zeros. The challenge of locating a valid nonce is dynamically modified to ensure a uniform block generation interval. Miners vie to discover the solution, and the first miner to resolve the problem disseminates the new block to the network. Proof of Work (PoW) ensures security by necessitating significant processing power to alter the blockchain's history.

Proof of Stake (PoS)

Proof of Stake is a consensus algorithm that is predicated on the principle of staking. In Proof of Stake, validators are selected to generate new blocks according to the quantity of bitcoin they own and are prepared to "stake" as collateral. Validators are chosen at random, considering their stake, and are tasked with validating transactions and proposing new blocks. In contrast to Proof of Work, Proof of Stake does not necessitate miners to resolve computationally intensive challenges. It implements a probability-based mechanism that compensates validators according to the quantity of coins they possess and the duration for which they are prepared to secure those coins.

Other Consensus Algorithms

In addition to Proof of Work (PoW) and Proof of Stake (PoS), the Web3 ecosystem encompasses various alternative consensus algorithms, including Delegated Proof of Stake

(DPoS) and Practical Byzantine Fault Tolerance (PBFT), among others. These algorithms provide varying degrees of decentralisation, security, and scalability, addressing certain use cases and network demands.

Anatomy of a Block

To understand the mining process, it is crucial to grasp the components that constitute a block in the blockchain.

Block Header

The block header encompasses essential metadata regarding the block, comprising the hash of the preceding block, a date, a nonce, and the Merkle root of the transactions contained within the block. Miners alter the nonce value to discover a valid block hash that satisfies the network's mining difficulty criteria.

Transactions

A block comprises a collection of transactions that denote the activities and information recorded on the blockchain. These transactions may encompass the transfer of digital assets, the execution of smart contracts, or any other processes facilitated by the blockchain network.

Merkle Tree

The Merkle tree, also known as a hash tree, is a data structure employed to efficiently store and validate the integrity of transactions within a block. It arranges transactions into pairs, hashes them, and subsequently hashes the resultant hashes until a singular root hash, referred to as the Merkle root, is achieved. The root hash is contained within the block header, facilitating quick verification of transaction inclusion in the block.

Nonce and Mining Difficulty

The nonce is an essential component of the block header utilised in the Proof of Work consensus mechanism. Miners modify the nonce value through an iterative process to discover a valid block hash that meets the network's mining difficulty requirements. The mining difficulty dictates the computing work necessary to discover an appropriate hash, hence controlling the pace of block generation.

Mining Process

Now let's explore the step-by-step process of mining a block in Web3.

Block Validation

Prior to mining a new block, miners authenticate the transactions they obtain from the network. This entails validating the legitimacy of the transactions, confirming that the senders possess adequate funds, and guaranteeing compliance with the consensus protocols and smart contract logic.

Block Creation

Upon validation of the transactions, miners commence the assembly of a new block by incorporating a collection of transactions into the block's data structure. They also revise the block header, including the hash of the preceding block, timestamp, Merkle root of transactions, and a nonce. Miners systematically adjust the nonce value and compute the block header hash until they obtain a hash that satisfies the network's mining difficulty requirements. The procedure necessitates considerable computer power and unpredictability, as miners must experiment with various nonce numbers to identify the correct hash.

Mining Rewards

Upon successfully identifying a valid block hash, a miner disseminates the new block to the network. In exchange for their endeavours, miners obtain mining incentives, usually in the form of native cryptocurrency tokens. The rewards motivate miners to engage in the mining process, provide processing power, and uphold the security and integrity of the blockchain network.

Advanced Mining Techniques

In addition to the basic mining process, several advanced techniques and considerations enhance the efficiency and effectiveness of mining in Web3.

Mining Pools

Mining pools are cooperative assemblages of miners who aggregate their computational resources to enhance their probability of successfully mining a block and receiving rewards. By consolidating resources, miners may collaboratively resolve mining riddles with more frequency, leading to a more stable income stream. Mining pools often allocate payouts according to the hash power contributed by each miner.

ASIC Resistance

Application-Specific Integrated Circuits (ASICs) are specialised hardware components engineered for cryptocurrency mining. They provide markedly superior processing power relative to general-purpose CPUs or GPUs. To uphold decentralisation and avert the centralisation of mining power, certain blockchain networks endeavour to be ASIC-resistant. They utilise algorithms that are more computationally demanding or memory-intensive, rendering it less beneficial for ASICs to achieve a substantial superiority over other mining technology.

Mining in Web3

Implementing Proof of Work in Solidity

Below is an example of a basic Proof of Work implementation in Solidity: contract PoW {

```
contract PoW {
uint public nonce; bytes32 public target;
constructor(uint _difficulty) {
target = bytes32(2 ** (256 - _difficulty));
target = bytes32(2 ** (256 - _difficulty));
}
function mine(uint _blockNumber, bytes32 _blockData) public returns (bool) {
bytes32 hash = calculateHash(_blockNumber, _blockData, nonce); if (hash < target) {
```

```
// Valid hash found, new block mined
// Perform necessary block validation and storage nonce = 0; // Reset
nonce for the next block return true;
}
 return false;
}
function calculateHash(uint _blockNumber, bytes32 _blockData, uint
_nonce) public pure returns (bytes32) {
return keccak256(abi.encodePacked(_blockNumber, _blockData,
_nonce));
}
}
```

In this instance, the PoW contract establishes mining difficulty via the target value, which dictates the requisite number of leading zeros in the hash for the block to be deemed genuine. The mine function iterates through nonce values, computing the hash via the calculate Hash function. A legitimate block has been mined if the hash is below the goal.

Using Web3.js to Interact with Miners

To interact with miners in a Web3 application, you can utilize the Web3.js library. Here's an example of how to submit a mining request to a local mining node:

```
const Web3 = require('web3');
const web3 = new Web3('http://localhost:8545'); // Connect to a local
Ethereum node
const blockNumber = 1234;
const blockData = '0xabcdef...'; // Replace with actual block data web3.
eth.getCoinbase((error, coinbase) => {
if (error) { console.error(error); return;
}
const powContract = new web3.eth.Contract(abi, contractAddress);
// Replace with actual contract ABI and address powContract.methods.
mine(blockNumber, blockData).send({ from: coinbase
})
.on('transactionHash', (hash) => { console.log('Mining request
submitted:', hash);
})
.on('receipt', (receipt) => {
console.log('Block mined:', receipt.blockNumber);
})
.on('error', (error) => { console.error('Mining error:', error);
});
});
```

In this example, we use the web3.eth.Contract function to create an instance of the contract, providing the ABI and contract address. We then call the mine function on the contract instance, passing the block number and data as arguments. The mining request is submitted from the coinbase account, and we listen for transaction events such as transactionHash and receipt to track the mining process.

Conclusion

The mining of blocks in Web3 is a sophisticated and essential process that guarantees the decentralised and safe functioning of blockchain networks. This thorough guide has equipped you with an in-depth understanding of mining in Web3, including the role of mining, various consensus algorithms, the components of a block, and advanced techniques. Mining in Web3 provides options for reward acquisition, enhancement of network security, and engagement in the governance of decentralised networks. As you immerse yourself further in Web3 development, persist in seeking supplementary resources, conducting research, and engaging in experimentation to enhance your comprehension and proficiency in mining and blockchain technology.

4.2 BITCOIN AND ANONYMITY

Anonymity vs. Privacy

First off, it is useful to draw a basic distinction between anonymity and privacy in the context of financial transactions. We will call a transaction "anonymous" if no one knows who you are. We will call a transaction "private" if what you purchased, and for what amount, are unknown. Let us construct a basic matrix and identify several types of financial transactions within it:

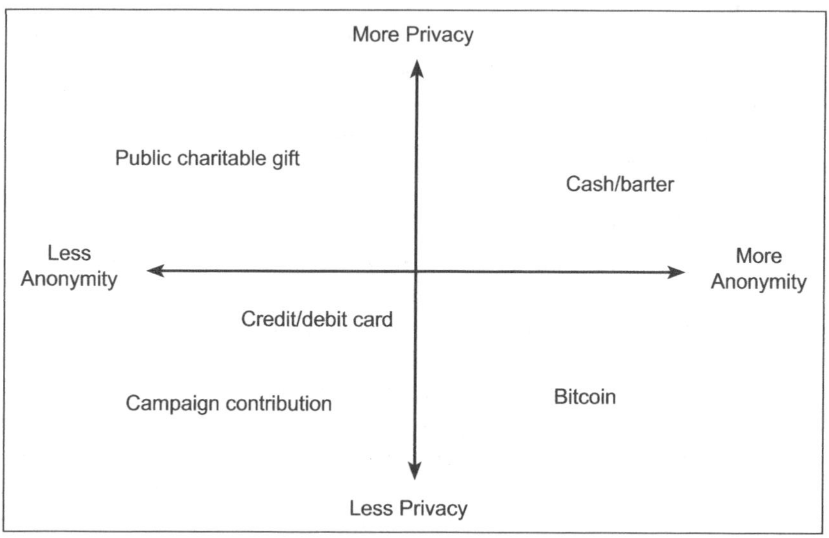

Fig. 4.1

Cash and barter represent the most fundamentally private and anonymous methods of transaction. In the opposite corner are transactions which are neither anonymous nor private. This include, for instance, campaign contributions above a specified threshold. We may also include in this quadrant credit card transactions: although not public knowledge like a campaign contribution, your identity is nevertheless connected to every purchase you make, and this information is available to the merchant, credit card network, issuing bank, and— if subpoenaed— law enforcement. Some financial transactions are confidential yet not anonymous; for instance, the donor wall at the local art museum, which displays the names of contributors without revealing the donation amounts. Bitcoin, by contrast, is anonymous but not private: identities are not recorded in the bitcoin protocol itself, but every transaction made with bitcoin is viewable on the distributed electronic public ledger known as the blockchain.

The anonymity given by bitcoin is at once a source of attraction and a barrier for financial regulation. As the adoption of the currency accelerates and it faces examination by legal and financial frameworks, especially concerning adherence to relevant anti-money laundering (AML) regulations and know- your-customer (KYC) protocols, its actual degree of anonymity will be scrutinised more rigorously. For many users of bitcoin, who access the currency through one of the popular online wallet or exchange services, their participation at the outset entails linking their personal identity to their bitcoin holdings. For these users, Bitcoin is essentially as non-anonymous as a bank account; nevertheless, this erosion of anonymity occurs at the initial point of entry into the currency and is not an inherent characteristic of the Bitcoin protocol itself.

For people who seek to take use of bitcoin's innate anonymity, they must find an alternate entry point, such as acquiring bitcoin via a private transaction, as remuneration for products or services supplied, or as a reward for mining. Subsequent bitcoin transactions may remain anonymous, as real-world identities are not documented on the blockchain ledger; the sole identifying information recorded consists of bitcoin addresses, with corresponding private keys retained by the owners as evidence of ownership. Maintaining one's anonymity from this point on, however, is in no way guaranteed: even if one succeeds to acquire bitcoins without giving up personal information, one's real- world identity can still be found in the course of trading bitcoin inside the network. Let's look at how this can happen. Generally, deanonymization techniques adopt one of two complementary strategies, concerning the public nature of the transaction ledger and the potential for revealing the IP addresses of the computers initiating the transactions.

Anonymity and the Transaction Ledger

A bitcoin holder can control an unlimited number of addresses. All bitcoins can be consolidated into a single address or distributed across numerous addresses, potentially numbering in the thousands. Best practices suggest, though do not mandate, that each address be utilised solely once; any residual funds following a transaction should be transferred to a new address rather than retained in the previous one. This multiplicity of addresses designedly obscures which ones are owned by a single individual at a single point in time, and makes it impossible to follow the flow of cash controlled by that individual over time. It is possible, however, to leverage the perfect transparency of the transaction ledger to reveal spending patterns in the blockchain that allow bitcoin addresses to be bundled by user. This pertains to the realm of transaction graph analysis.

Transaction Graph Analysis

Transaction graph analysis employs various techniques and informed conjectures to associate approximately 57 million transactions occurring among 62 million addresses with a subset of unique bitcoin holders. It then allows transactional relationships between these bitcoin holders to be mapped. One basic technique in transaction graph analysis involves transactions with more than one input address. These inputs are, by definition, governed by a singular individual; consequently, if either address is found elsewhere on the blockchain, the corresponding transactions can likewise be associated with that individual. A secondary technique leverages the aforementioned "good practice": if precisely one of the output addresses in a transaction has not previously appeared in the blockchain, it is a reliable assumption that this new address serves as the change address. A third technique looks at the numerical precision of the amounts involved in a transaction. For example, in a transaction generating two outputs corresponding to two new bitcoin addresses, where one of the outputs is, say, 3 BTC and the other is 2.12791 BTC, then it is a very good bet that the first number corresponds to the recipient and the second number to the change. What is the chance, after all, that the alteration should happen to end up in such a beautiful figure? The address originating the transaction can thus be connected to the change address with a high degree of certainty. The same analysis can be repeated after converting to major currencies such as USD to find "whole numbers" that might otherwise be hidden in bitcoin-denominated transactions and that enable sender to be distinguished from receiver.

Address deanonymization using these methods can be thwarted by sending bitcoins through so-called mixers or tumblers, which take a set of bitcoins and returns another set of the same value (minus a processing fee) with different addresses and transaction histories, thus effectively "laundering" the coins. But these services come with serious caveats. Users must hand over control of their bitcoins and trust the service to return them. Transaction graph analysis can identify use of a mixing service and flag the user as potentially suspicious. Mixers do not work well for very large sums, unless others with similarly large sums happen to be mixing their bitcoins at the same time. Some mixing services do not work as advertised and can be reverse-engineered. Legally operating services are required to maintain comprehensive records of the currency mixing process, which may thereafter be subject to hacking or subpoena. And the new bitcoins obtained might itself be polluted by criminal activities.

Seeding the Transaction Graph

Transaction graph analysis solely exposes the trace of individual agency within the blockchain; it does not disclose any actual real-world identities. For this it is necessary to refer to information not contained in the blockchain. A vast quantity of information relating bitcoin addresses to their names is available publicly. Businesses accepting bitcoin may post a QR code near a cash register or on a website. Individuals may disclose their bitcoin addresses via platforms like blockchain.info/tags, which discloses the proprietors of several addresses. Numerous additional addresses can be extracted from public email forums when individuals incorporate personal bitcoin addresses in the signature lines of their posts. This partial knowledge of identities can be combined with the transaction graph to deanonymize a swath of the transaction ledger. Retroactive geolocation is one potential consequence of this deanonymization.

Suppose a café accepts bitcoin and uses a fixed address for their over-the- counter transactions. If you are a patron of that place, and your bitcoin addresses become associated with your identity, then someone can easily bring forth from the blockchain a partial record of your personal whereabouts over time. Conversely, if an individual sought to associate your identity with your bitcoin address, and you inadvertently disclosed that you dined at the same café that day. Someone can look up the address used by the café, find the subset of transactions on that address taking place over the lunch hour, and filter the results by price to exclude transactions involving just a hot drink. Additional details regarding your lunch selection, an examination of the café's menu, and the likelihood of achieving a successful match are significantly enhanced.

Comprehensive understanding of the transaction ledger implies that any subsequently uncovered information can be retroactively integrated, facilitating the continuous assembly of the identity puzzle at any moment. A single disclosure of identity, even years in the future, and every transaction on that address and those connected to it is compromised.

IP Address Anonymity

A complementary source of potentially deanonymizing information is available to every computer that participates in the decentralized transaction network by hosting a bitcoin node. This information comprises the IP addresses of computers that broadcast new bitcoin transactions. At the time of writing there are around 6,500 nodes accepting inbound connections from other nodes, and perhaps ten times that number which don't accept requests for connections. The former maintain connections to several dozen peers on average, while the latter typically have eight peers. Both types of nodes produce transactions. Transaction dissemination through the node network initiates with the computer that first transmits the event to its peers, who subsequently relay the event to their peers in an information cascade that typically reaches every node in the network within seconds.

The fundamental observation that can be leveraged is that, if one can establish a connection to a majority of nodes, potentially by managing a coordinated sub- network of nodes distributed across multiple devices, the initial node to transmit a transaction is, on average, the originator of that transaction. The risk increases if multiple transactions are relayed from the same IP address. While a tiny random delay is baked into the transaction propagation protocol to assist preserve the anonymity of the original sender, with the correct approaches enough signal is available through the noise to make a definitive identification in many circumstances. And while use of a TOR router offers some measure of protection against IP address discovery, it exposes the user to other potential attacks.

An example of this kind of IP address deanonymization made public is blockchain.info, which discloses the IP address of the first node to report a transaction to its servers. The information is only as reliable as the web site's node connectivity: with a declared 800–900 connected nodes at the time of writing, it is probably not enough to reliably pinpoint the originating IP in all cases. So… How anonymous is bitcoin today? Average users should be aware that it is certainly less anonymous than cash. Meanwhile, dedicated users willing to go through extraordinary lengths can find ways to acquire and use bitcoin anonymously, but the open nature of the transaction ledger and other unknowns leave open the possibility that identities and activities once considered perfectly secure may be revealed at some point down the road. What about the future? As bitcoin adoption continues to increase, it is not out of the question that a technology arms race could arise between anonymizers and deanonymizers: on the one hand, increasingly sophisticated data mining schemes will be developed, possibly combining transaction graph analysis with IP address discovery, to trace the movement of funds in the blockchain between individuals and across borders.

On the other, improved approaches will be designed to better disguise individual identify and behaviour. Here there are many unknowns. Will the core bitcoin code be updated to further safeguard anonymity or to assist regulation? Will bitcoin mixing services become pervasive and secure? Will transaction graph analysis reach a degree of complexity where most user activities can be easily traced? Will an alternate digital currency or side chain evolve which tilts the balance for or against anonymity? All we can say with sure is that bitcoin is still in its infancy and that present ideas and tools in the domain of anonymity are still immature. We have seen only the opening moves; the endgame has yet to be played.

4.3 OVERVIEW OF ALTCOINS

Introduction

The cryptocurrency market has expanded significantly since the introduction of Bitcoin in 2009, resulting in the emergence of thousands of other cryptocurrencies, referred to as altcoins. These altcoins have diversified the blockchain ecosystem by providing distinct capabilities, use cases, and investment prospects. Although Bitcoin is the most prominent cryptocurrency, altcoins such as Ethereum, Cardano, and Binance Coin have garnered attention for their unique attributes and potential to transform sectors. Altcoins encompass smart contract platforms, utility tokens, privacy-centric coins, and stablecoins. Comprehending their objectives, efficacy, and hazards is crucial for investors and devotees traversing this evolving domain. This book offers a comprehensive analysis of altcoins, including their categories, benefits, difficulties, and future prospects, supplemented by real-world examples and case studies.

What Are Altcoins?

Definition

Altcoins, short for "alternative coins," refer to all cryptocurrencies other than Bitcoin. These coins often aim to improve upon Bitcoin's limitations or address specific use cases within the blockchain ecosystem.

Key Characteristics

- **Diversity:** Altcoins includeutility tokens, governance tokens, stablecoins, and more.
- **Innovation:** Many altcoins introduce new technologies, such as smart contracts or enhanced scalability.
- **Market Share:** Altcoins collectively account for a significant portion of the cryptocurrency market, with Ethereum leading the pack.

Types of Altcoins

1. Utility Tokens

Purpose: Facilitate access to services within a blockchain ecosystem.

Examples

Ethereum (ETH): Powers smart contracts and dApps on the Ethereum network. Chainlink (LINK): Provides decentralized oracle services.

2. Stablecoins

Purpose: Maintain price stability by pegging their value to fiat currencies or assets.

Examples

Tether (USDT): Pegged to the US dollar.

- **DAI:** A decentralized stablecoin backed by collateralized crypto assets.

3. Governance Tokens

- **Purpose:** Enable holders to participate in protocol decision-making.

Examples

- **Uniswap (UNI):** Grants voting rights on the Uniswap platform.
- **Aave (AAVE):** Allows governance over the Aave protocol.

4. Privacy Coins

- **Purpose:** Enhance transaction anonymity.

Examples

- **Monero (XMR):** Uses stealth addresses for privacy.
- **Zcash (ZEC):** Offers shielded transactions.

5. Meme Coins

- **Purpose:** Often created as jokes but gain value through community support.

Examples

- **Dogecoin (DOGE):** Initially a parody, now widely recognized.
- **Shiba Inu (SHIB):** A rival to Dogecoin with strong community backing.

Benefits of Altcoins

1. Diversification

- **Investment Options:** A wide range of coins catering to various use cases. Risk Management: Reduces reliance on Bitcoin's performance.

2. Technological Innovation

- **Scalability:** Altcoins like Solana offer faster transaction speeds.
- **Smart Contracts:** Ethereum pioneered programmable blockchain capabilities.

3. Accessibility

- **Lower Entry Barriers:** Some altcoins are more affordable than Bitcoin. Broader Use Cases: Serve niches like gaming, DeFi, and supply chain management.

Challenges of Altcoins Market Volatility

- **Price Fluctuations:** Altcoins often experience significant price swings. Speculative Nature: Many coins lack intrinsic value, driven by hype.

Regulatory Risks

- **Uncertain Frameworks:** Governments are still defining cryptocurrency regulations.
- Legal Challenges: Some altcoins face scrutiny for potential securities violations.

Security Concerns

- **Smart Contract Vulnerabilities:** Exploits can lead to significant losses. Scams: Rug pulls and fraudulent projects are prevalent in the altcoin space.

Real-World Case Studies

Ethereum: The Smart Contract Pioneer

- **Overview:** Introduced in 2015, Ethereum revolutionized blockchain with smart contracts.
- **Achievements:** Hosts over 70% of decentralized applications (dApps). Market Impact: Second-largest cryptocurrency by market cap.

Binance Coin: Utility in the Binance Ecosystem

- **Overview:** Launched in 2017, BNB powers the Binance exchange. Use Cases: Transaction fee discounts, staking, and token burns. Success: Reached a market cap exceeding $50 billion.

Dogecoin: From Meme to Mainstream

- **Overview:** Created in 2013 as a joke, Dogecoin gained massive popularity through community support.
- **Highlights:** Backed by celebrities like Elon Musk, it reached a market cap of

$88 billion in 2021.

Future of Altcoins

Trends

- **Interoperability:** Projects like Polkadot aim to connect multiple blockchains. DeFi Growth: Altcoins play a critical role in decentralized finance. Sustainability: Shift towards energy-efficient consensus mechanisms like Proof of Stake (PoS).

Challenges

- **Overcrowded Market:** Over 20,000 altcoins exist, many with limited utility.
- **Scalability Issues:** Ensuring transaction speed without compromising decentralization.

Platforms like ImmediateX provide tools and insights for traders to capitalize on the evolving altcoin market.

Pros and Cons of Altcoins

Pros

- **Diverse Use Cases:** Serve niches that Bitcoin cannot address.
- **High Growth Potential:** Many altcoins offer significant returns.
- **Technological Advancement:** Drive blockchain innovation.

Cons

- **High Risk:** Prone to volatility and scams.
- **Regulatory Uncertainty:** Lack of clear legal frameworks.
- **Liquidity Issues:** Smaller altcoins may face low trading volumes.

4.4 OVERVIEW OF ETHEREUM

Ethereum is regarded by many as the second most prominent cryptocurrency, surpassed solely by Bitcoin. The Motley Fool reports that the Enterprise Ethereum Alliance (EEA) includes prominent founding members such as Microsoft, Intel, and JPMorgan Chase. CNBC states that "the adoption of Ethereum by the corporate sector may ultimately render it larger than its initial competitor." This signifies the necessity to familiarise oneself with the Ethereum platform, encompassing its characteristics and uses, as well as the distinctions that set Ethereum apart from Bitcoin.

What is Ethereum?

Ethereum is a blockchain-based computing platform that allows developers to create and implement decentralised applications, which operate without a centralised authority. A decentralised application can be developed in which the participants serve as the decision-making authority.

Ethereum Features

Ether: This is Ethereum's cryptocurrency.

- **Smart contracts:** Ethereum facilitates the creation and implementation of it.
- **Ethereum Virtual Machisne:** Ethereum provides the underlying technology—the architecture and the software—that understands smart contracts and allows you to interact with it.
- **Decentralized applications (Dapps):** A decentralized application is called a Dapp (also spelled DAPP, App, or DApp) for short. Ethereum enables the development of integrated apps, referred to as decentralised applications.
- **Decentralised autonomous organisations (DAOs):** Ethereum facilitates the establishment of these entities for democratic governance.

These are the fundamental characteristics of Ethereum. Prior to delving into the Ethereum tutorial, let us examine each of these characteristics in greater depth.

1. Ether

Ether (ETH) is the cryptocurrency of Ethereum. It is the energy that powers the network. It is utilised to compensate for computational resources and transaction costs for any transaction conducted on the Ethereum network. Similar to Bitcoin, Ether functions as a peer-to-peer currency. In addition to facilitating transactions, ether is utilised to purchase gas, which compensates for the computational costs associated with any transaction conducted on the Ethereum network. Furthermore, to launch a contract on Ethereum, you will require gas, which must be compensated in ether. Gas is the execution price incurred by a user for executing a transaction on the Ethereum network. Ether can be employed for developing decentralised applications, creating smart contracts, and facilitating standard peer-to-peer transactions.

2. Smart Contracts

Smart contracts are transforming the functionality of standard contracts, thus necessitating the use of the tutorial for more familiarity. A smart contract is a basic computer program that enables the transfer of any asset between two entities. It may encompass currency, equities, real estate, or any other digital asset intended for exchange. Any participant on the Ethereum network is capable of generating these contracts. The contract basically comprises the terms and conditions mutually agreed upon by the parties.

The principal characteristic of the smart contract is its irrevocability upon execution, ensuring that every transaction conducted inside its framework is permanently recorded—rendering it immutable. Even if you amend the smart contract in the future, the transactions associated with the original contract will remain unaltered; they cannot be modified. The verification procedure for smart contracts is conducted by anonymous participants within the network, eliminating the necessity for a centralised authority, which renders the execution of every smart contract on Ethereum a decentralised operation. The transfer of any asset or currency occurs transparently and reliably, with the identities of both parties safeguarded on the Ethereum network. Upon successful completion of the transaction, the accounts of both the sender and receiver are updated correspondingly, thereby fostering confidence between the parties involved.

Smart Contracts Vs. Traditional Contract Systems

In traditional contract systems, one signs an agreement and thereafter entrusts a third party with its execution. The issue is that data manipulation is feasible in this type of operation. The agreement is encoded within a computer using smart contracts. The outcome is not validated by a centralised authority; it is corroborated by the participants inside the Ethereum blockchain network. Upon execution of a contract, the transaction is recorded and immutable, hence eliminating the possibility of data tampering or alteration. Consider an instance where an individual called Zack has contracted an amount of $500 to another individual named Elsa for the development of his company's website.

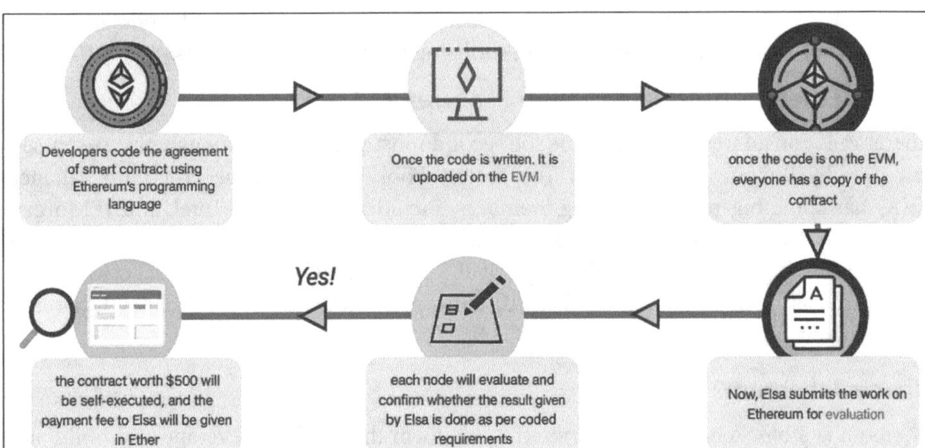

Fig. 4.2

The developers encode the smart contract agreement utilising Ethereum's programming language. The smart contract encompasses all the prerequisites for constructing the website. Upon completion of the code, it is uploaded and deployed on the Ethereum Virtual Machine (EVM). The EVM is a runtime compiler for executing smart contracts. Upon deployment of the code on the EVM, every network member possesses a copy of the contract. Upon Elsa's submission of the work on Ethereum for assessment, each node inside the Ethereum network will analyse and verify if the outcome provided by Elsa adheres to the coding specifications. Upon approval and verification of the result, the contract valued at $500 will execute autonomously, and payment will be rendered to Elsa in ether. Zack's account will be automatically deducted, while Elsa will receive a credit of $500 in ether.

3. Ethereum Virtual Machine

The EVM, as previously stated in this Ethereum tutorial, functions as a runtime environment for the compilation and deployment of Ethereum-based smart contracts. The EVM is the engine that comprehends the language of smart contracts, which are authored in Solidity for Ethereum. The EVM functions within a sandbox environment, allowing for the deployment of a standalone setting that serves as a testing and development platform. You may subsequently test your smart contract an arbitrary number of times, check its integrity, and upon achieving satisfaction with its performance and functionality, deploy it to the Ethereum mainnet. Any programming language used in smart contracts is compiled into bytecode comprehensible to the EVM. This bytecode is interpretable and executable by the EVM. Solidity is among the most prevalent languages for developing smart contracts. After writing your smart contract in Solidity, it is transformed into bytecode and deployed on the EVM, thereby ensuring protection against cyberattacks.

How Does EVM Work?

Assume individual A intends to remit 10 ethers to individual B. The transaction will be transmitted to the EVM via a smart contract for a fund transfer from A to B. To authenticate the transaction, the Ethereum network will execute the proof-of-work consensus mechanism. The miner nodes on Ethereum will authenticate this transaction—verifying the existence of identity A and if A possesses the requisite amount for transfer. Upon confirmation of the transaction, ether will be deducted from A's wallet and deposited to B's wallet, while miners will impose a fee for validating the transaction and will receive a reward. All nodes inside the Ethereum network execute smart contracts utilising their individual EVMs.

What is Ethereum? Explained With Features and Applications

Ethereum is considered by many to be the second most popular cryptocurrency, surpassed now only by Bitcoin. According to The Motley Fool, the Enterprise Ethereum Alliance (EEA) has some big-name founding members, including Microsoft, Intel, and JPMorgan Chase. "The adoption of Ethereum by the corporate world," says CNBC, "means it could eventually be bigger than its early stage rival." That means it's time to get to know the Ethereum platform, including its features and applications, and what makes Ethereum different from Bitcoin.

What is Ethereum?

Ethereum is a blockchain-based computing platform that enables developers to build and deploy decentralized applications—meaning not run by a centralized authority. You can create a decentralized application for which the participants of that particular application are the decision-making authority.

Ethereum Features

- **Ether:** This is Ethereum's cryptocurrency.
- **Smart contracts:** Ethereum allows the development and deployment of these types of contracts.

- **Ethereum Virtual Machine:** Ethereum provides the underlying technology—the architecture and the software—that understands smart contracts and allows you to interact with it.
- **Decentralized applications (Dapps):** A decentralized application is called a Dapp (also spelled DAPP, App, or DApp) for short. Ethereum allows you to create consolidated applications, called decentralized applications.
- **Decentralized autonomous organizations (DAOs):** Ethereum allows you to create these for democratic decision-making.

These are Ethereum's essential features:

1. Ether

Ether (ETH) is Ethereum's cryptocurrency. It is the fuel that runs the network. It is used to pay for the computational resources and the transaction fees for any transaction executed on the Ethereum network. Like Bitcoins, ether is a peer- to-peer currency. Apart from being used to pay for transactions, ether is also used to buy gas, which is used to pay for the computation of any transaction made on the Ethereum network. Also, if you want to deploy a contract on Ethereum, you will need gas, and you would have to pay for that gas in ether. So gas is the execution fee paid by a user for running a transaction in Ethereum. Ether can be utilized for building decentralized applications, building smart contracts, and making regular peer-to-peer payments.

2. Smart Contracts

Smart contracts are revolutionizing how traditional contracts work, which is why you need to use the tutorial to become more familiar with them. A smart contract is a simple computer program that facilitates the exchange of any asset between two parties. It could be money, shares, property, or any other digital asset that you want to exchange. Anyone on the Ethereum network can create these contracts. The contract consists primarily of the terms and conditions mutually agreed on between the parties (peers). The smart contract's primary feature is that once it is executed, it cannot be altered, and any transaction done on top of a smart contract is registered permanently—it is immutable. So even if you modify the smart contract in the future, the transactions correlated with the original contract will not get altered; you cannot edit them.

The verification process for the smart contracts is carried out by anonymous parties in the network without the need for a centralized authority, and that's what makes any smart contract execution on Ethereum a decentralized execution. The transfer of any asset or currency is done in a transparent and trustworthy manner, and the identities of the two entities are secure on the Ethereum network. Once the transaction is successfully done, the accounts of the sender and receiver are updated accordingly, and in this way, it generates trust between the parties.

Smart Contracts Vs. Traditional Contract Systems

In conventional contract systems, you sign an agreement, then you trust and hire a third party for its execution. The problem is that in this type of process, data tampering is possible. With smart contracts, the agreement is coded in a program. A centralized authority does not verify the result; it is confirmed by the participants on the Ethereum blockchain-based network. Once a contract is executed, the transaction is registered and cannot be altered or tampered, so it removes the risk of any data manipulation or alteration. Let's take an example in which someone named Zack has given a contract of $500 to someone named Elsa for developing his company's website.

The developers code the agreement of the smart contract using Ethereum's programming language. The smart contract has all the conditions (requirements) for building the website. Once the code is written, it is uploaded and deployed on the Ethereum Virtual Machine (EVM). EVM is a runtime compiler to execute a smart contract. Once the code is deployed on the EVM, every participant on the network has a copy of the contract. When Elsa submits the work on Ethereum for evaluation, each node on the Ethereum network will evaluate and confirm whether the result given by Elsa has been done as per the coding requirements. Once the result is approved and verified, the contract worth $500 will be self-executed, and the payment will be paid to Elsa in ether.

Zack's account will be automatically debited, and Elsa will be credited with $500 in ether. The Ethereum tutorial video includes a demo on the deployment of an Ethereum smart contract.

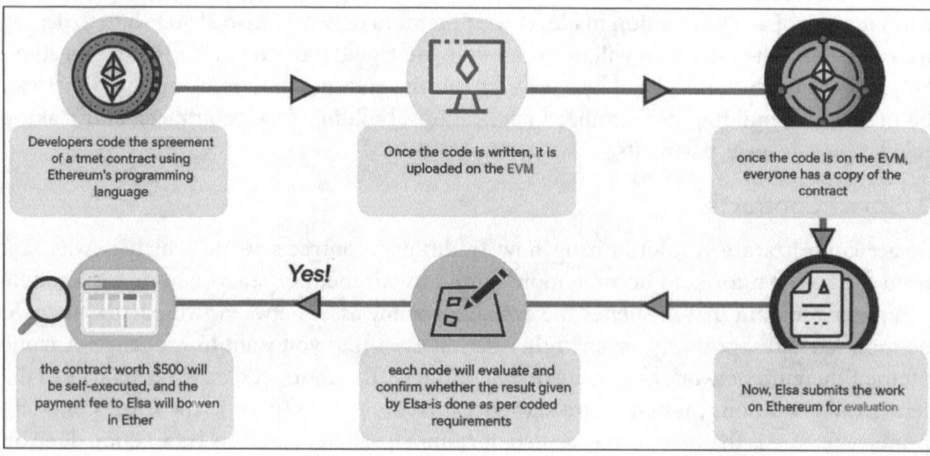

Fig. 4.3

3. Ethereum Virtual Machine

EVM, as mentioned above in this Ethereum tutorial, is designed to operate as a runtime environment for compiling and deploying Ethereum-based smart contracts. EVM is the engine that understands the language of smart contracts, which are written in the Solidity language for Ethereum. EVM is operated in a sandbox environment—basically, you can deploy your stand-alone environment, which can act as a testing and development environment.

You can then test your smart contract (use it) "n" number of times, verify it, and once you are satisfied with the performance and the functionality of the smart contract, you can deploy it on the Ethereum main network. Any programming language in the smart contract is compiled into the bytecode, which the EVM understands. This bytecode can be read and executed using the EVM. Solidity is one of the most popular languages for writing a smart contract. Once you write your smart contract in Solidity, that contract gets converted into the bytecode and gets deployed on the EVM, thereby guaranteeing security from cyberattacks.

(a) How Does EVM Work?

Suppose person A wants to pay person B 10 ethers. The transaction will be sent to the EVM using a smart contract for a fund transfer from A to B. To validate the transaction; the Ethereum network will perform the proof-of-work consensus algorithm. The miner nodes on Ethereum will validate this transaction—whether the identity of A exists or not, and if A has the requested amount to transfer. Once the transaction is confirmed, the ether will be debited from A's wallet and will be credited to B's wallet, and during this process, the miners will charge a fee to validate this transaction and will earn a reward.

All the nodes on the Ethereum network execute smart contracts using their respective EVMs.

(b) Proof of Work

Every node in the Ethereum network has:

- The entire history of all the transactions—the entire chain
- The history of the smart contract, which is the address at which the smart contract is deployed, along with the transactions associated with the smart contract
- The handle to the current state of the smart contract

The objective of miners on the Ethereum network is to authenticate the blocks. Miners utilise their processing power and resources to obtain the correct hash value for each transaction block by adjusting the nonce. The miners will alter the nonce and process it through a hashing method; in Ethereum, this is the Ethash Algorithm.

This generates a hash value that must be inferior than the established target according to the proof-of-work consensus. If the resulting hash value is inferior to the goal value, the block is deemed validated, and the miner receives a reward. Upon solving the proof of work, the outcome is disseminated and communicated to all other nodes to update their ledgers. Upon acceptance of the hashed block as valid by other nodes, the block is included into the Ethereum main blockchain, resulting in the miner receiving a reward, currently set at three ethers. Additionally, the miner receives the transaction fees accrued from validating the block.

(c) Proof of Stake

A mechanism known as proof of stake is currently being developed in Ethereum. It serves as an alternative to proof of work, designed to reduce the expenditure of costly resources associated with mining through proof of work. In proof of stake, the miner, serving as the validator, can authenticate transactions according to the quantity of cryptocurrency they possess prior to initiating the mining process. Consequently, the miner's prior accumulation of cryptocurrency coins enhances the likelihood of successfully mining the block. Currently, proof of stake is not as prevalent as proof of work.

(d) Gas

Similar to the necessity of fuel for operating a vehicle, petrol is required to execute applications on the Ethereum network. To execute any transaction on the Ethereum network, a user must remit a payment in ethers, referred to as gas, to facilitate the transaction. In the Ethereum network, gas is a metric that quantifies the computational resources used to execute a smart contract or transaction. To execute a transaction that updates the blockchain, one must expend gas, which is priced in ethers. In Ethereum, transaction fees are determined by a specific formula (refer to the screenshot below). Each transaction incurs petrol fees and an associated petrol price. The transaction costs are calculated by multiplying the petrol required for execution by the petrol price. Gas limit" denotes the quantity of gas utilised for computation and the corresponding amount of ether a user must remit for that gas.

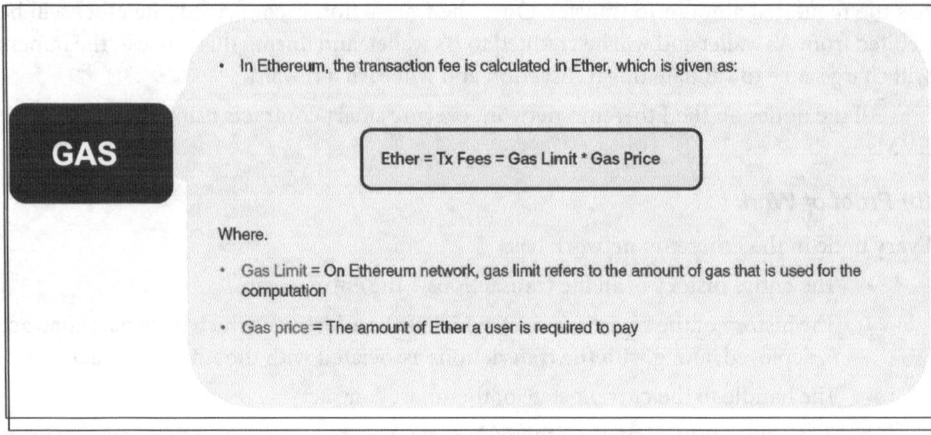

Fig. 4.4

Below is a screenshot from the Ethereum network showing the transaction cost. You can see for this particular transaction, the gas limit was 21,000, the gas used by the transaction was 21,000, and the gas price was 21 Gwei, which is the lowest denomination of ether. So, 21 Gwei * 21,000 gave the actual transaction fees: 0.000441 ethers, or about 21 cents as of today. As mentioned, the transaction fee goes to the miner, who has validated the transaction. To comprehend the petrol restriction and price, let us examine an illustration involving a vehicle. Assume your car achieves a fuel efficiency of 10 km per litre, with petrol priced at $1 per litre.

According to these standards, operating a vehicle for 50 kilometres would require five litres of petrol, valued at $5. Likewise, to execute an operation or run code on Ethereum, one must acquire a specific quantity of petrol, analogous to petrol, which has a per-unit cost referred to as petrol price. If the user provides less than the amount of gas to run an operation, then the process will fail, and the user will be given the message "out of gas." And Gwei, as noted above, is the lowest denomination of ether used for measuring a unit of a gas price.

How is Ethereum Mining Different from Bitcoin Mining?

	Bitcoin	Ethereum
Hashing Algorithm	SHA-256	Ethash
Time taken to mine a block	An average of 10 minutes	An average of 12-15 seconds
Reward	12.5 BTC	3 ETH
USD - 04/10/2019	1 Bitcoin = 5249.03	1 Ether = 180.89

4. Decentralized Applications (Dapps)

Let's compare decentralized applications with traditional applications. When you log in to Twitter, for example, a web application gets displayed that is rendered using HTML. The page will call an API to access your data (your information), which is centrally hosted. It's a simple process: your front end executes the backend API, and the API goes and fetches your data from a centralized database.

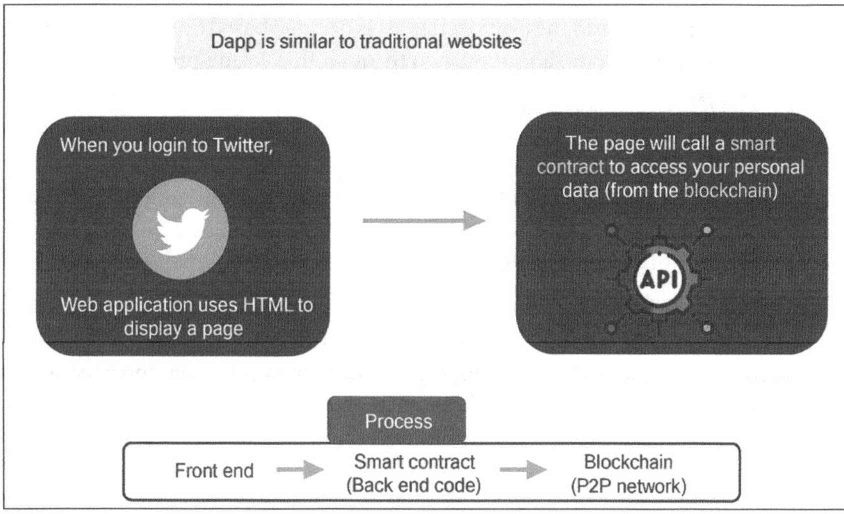

Fig. 4.5

If we transform this application into a decentralized application when you log in, the same web application gets rendered, but it calls a smart contract-based API to fetch the information from the blockchain network. So, the API is replaced by a smart contract interface, and the smart contract will bring the data from the blockchain network, which is its back end. That blockchain network is not a centralized database; it's a decentralized network in which the participants of the network (the miners) validate (verify) all the transactions that are happening using the smart contract on the blockchain network. So, any transaction or action happening on a Twitter-type application that has now been transformed will be a decentralized transaction. A Dapp consists of a backing code that runs on a distributed peer-to-peer network. It is a software designed to work in the Ethereum network without being controlled by a centralized system, as mentioned, and that is the primary difference: it provides direct interaction between the end-users and the decentralized application providers.

An application qualifies as a Dapp when it is open-source (its code is on Github), and it uses a public blockchain-based token to run its applications. A token acts as fuel for the decentralized application to run. Dapp allows the back end code and data to be decentralized, and that is the primary architecture of any Dapp.

5. Decentralized Autonomous Organizations (DAOs)

A DAO is a digital organization that operates without hierarchical management; it works in a decentralized and democratic fashion. So basically, a DAO is an organization in which the decision-making is not in the hands of a centralized authority but preferably in the hands of certain designated authorities or a group or designated people as a part of an authority. It exists on a blockchain network, where it is governed by the protocols embedded in a smart contract, and thereby, DAOs rely on smart contracts for decision-making—or, we can say, decentralized voting systems—within the organization. So, before any organizational decision can be made, it must go through the voting system, which runs on a decentralized application. Here's how it works. People add funds through the DAO because the DAO requires funding in order to execute and make decisions. Based on that, each member is given a token that represents that person's percentage of shares in the DAO. Those tokens are used to vote in the DAO, and the proposal status is decided based on the maximum votes. Every decision within the organization must go through this voting process.

Real-World Applications of Ethereum

- **Voting Systems**

  As we've seen with DAO, voting systems are adopting Ethereum. The results of polls are publicly available, ensuring a transparent and fair democratic process by eliminating voting malpractices.

- **Banking Systems**

  Ethereum is getting adopted widely in banking systems because with Ethereum's decentralized system; it is challenging for hackers to gain unauthorized access. It also allows payments on an Ethereum-based network, so banks are also using Ethereum as a channel to make remittances and payments.

- **Shipping**

  Deploying Ethereum in shipping helps with the tracking of cargo and prevents goods from being misplaced or counterfeited. Ethereum provides the provenance and tracking framework for any asset required in a typical supply chain.

- **Agreements**

  With Ethereum smart contracts, agreements can be maintained and executed without any alteration. So in an industry that has fragmented participants, is subject to disputes, and requires digital contracts to be present, Ethereum can be used as a technology for developing smart contracts and for digitally recording the agreements and the transactions based on them.

Conclusion

Head over to our "Ethereum Explained" Ethereum tutorial video to see an in- depth demo on how to deploy an Ethereum smart contract locally, including installing Ganache and Node in a Windows environment. And if you want to take your career to the next level, what are you waiting for? Sign up for Simplilearn's Blockchain Basics course or Professional Certificate Program in Blockchain. Remember that blockchain is the underlying technology not just for Ethereum but for Bitcoin and other cryptocurrencies. And according to ZipRecruiter, the average salary for a blockchain developer is a little over $154,000 a year and some salaries are as high as $242,000!

4.4.1 Programming Smart Contracts on Ethereum

A great aspect about Ethereum is that smart contracts can be programmed using relatively developer-friendly languages. If you're experienced with Python or any curly-bracket language(opens in a new tab), you can find a language with familiar syntax.

The two most active and maintained languages are:

- Solidity
- Vyper

Remix IDE provides a comprehensive development environment for creating and testing contracts in both Solidity and Vyper. More experienced developers also might want to use Yul, an intermediate language for the Ethereum Virtual Machine, or Yul+, an extension to Yul.

1. Solidity

- Object-oriented, high-level language for implementing smart contracts.
- Curly-bracket language that has been most profoundly influenced by C++.
- Statically typed (the type of a variable is known at compile time).
- **Supports:**
    - Inheritance (you can extend other contracts).
    - Libraries (you can create reusable code that you can call from different contracts – like static functions in a static class in other object oriented programming languages).
    - Complex user-defined types.

Example Contract

```
// SPDX-License-Identifier: GPL-3.0 pragma solidity >= 0.7.0;
contract Coin {
// The keyword "public" makes variables
// accessible from other contracts address public minter;
mapping (address => uint) public balances;
// Events allow clients to react to specific
// contract changes you declare
event Sent(address from, address to, uint amount);
// Constructor code is only run when the contract
// is created constructor() {
minter = msg.sender;
}
// Sends an amount of newly created coins to an address
// Can only be called by the contract creator
function mint(address receiver, uint amount) public { require(msg.sender
== minter);
require(amount < 1e60); balances[receiver] += amount;
}
// Sends an amount of existing coins
// from any caller to an address
function send(address receiver, uint amount) public { require(amount
<= balances[msg.sender], "Insufficient balance."); balances[msg.sender] -=
amount;
balances[receiver] += amount;
emit Sent(msg.sender, receiver, amount);
```

```
}
}
```

This example should give you a sense of what Solidity contract syntax is like.

2. Vyper

- Pythonic programming language
- Strong typing
- Small and understandable compiler code
- Efficient bytecode generation
- Deliberately has less features than Solidity with the aim of making contracts more secure and easier to audit. Vyper does not support:
    - Modifiers
    - Inheritance
    - Example
    - Inline assembly
    - Function overloading
    - Operator overloading
    - Recursive calling
    - Infinite-length loops
    - Binary fixed points

Example

```
Open Auction
Auction params
Beneficiary receives money from the highest bidder beneficiary: public(address)
auctionStart: public(uint256) auctionEnd: public(uint256) # Current state of auction
highestBidder: public(address) highestBid: public(uint256)
# Set to true at the end, disallows any change ended: public(bool)
# Keep track of refunded bids so we can follow the withdraw pattern pendingReturns: public(HashMap[address, uint256])
# Create a simple auction with `_bidding_time` # seconds bidding time on behalf of the
# beneficiary address `_beneficiary`. @external
def ___init___(_beneficiary: address, _bidding_time: uint256): self.beneficiary = _beneficiary
self.auctionStart = block.timestamp
self.auctionEnd = self.auctionStart + _bidding_time # Bid on the auction with the value sent
# together with this transaction.
# The value will only be refunded if the # auction is not won.
@external @payable def bid():
# Check if bidding period is over.
assert block.timestamp < self.auctionEnd # Check if bid is high enough
```

```
    assert msg.value > self.highestBid
    # Track the refund for the previous high bidder self.pendingReturns[self.
highestBidder] += self.highestBid # Track new high bid
    self.highestBidder = msg.sender self.highestBid = msg.value
    # Withdraw a previously refunded bid. The withdraw pattern is # used here
to avoid a security issue. If refunds were directly
    # sent as part of bid(), a malicious bidding contract could block # those
refunds and thus block new higher bids from coming in. @external
    def withdraw():
    pending_amount: uint256 = self.pendingReturns[msg.sender] self.
pendingReturns[msg.sender] = 0
    send(msg.sender, pending_amount)
    # End the auction and send the highest bid # to the beneficiary.
    @external
    def endAuction():
    # It is a good guideline to structure functions that interact
    # with other contracts (i.e. they call functions or send ether) # into
three phases:
    # 1. checking conditions
    # 2. performing actions (potentially changing conditions) # 3. interacting
with other contracts
    # If these phases are mixed up, the other contract could call # back into
the current contract and modify the state or cause # effects (ether payout)
to be performed multiple times.
    # If functions called internally include interaction with external #
contracts, they also have to be considered interaction with
    # external contracts. # 1. Conditions
    # Check if auction endtime has been reached assert block.timestamp >=
self.auctionEnd
    # Check if this function has already been called assert not self.ended
    # 2. Effects self.ended = True # 3. Interaction
    send(self.beneficiary, self.highestBid)
```

This example should give you a sense of what Vyper contract syntax is like.

YUL AND YUL+

If you're new to Ethereum and haven't done any coding with smart contract languages yet, we recommend getting started with Solidity or Vyper. Only look into Yul or Yul+ once you're familiar with smart contract security best practices and the specifics of working with the EVM.

Yul

- Intermediate language for Ethereum. Supports the EVM and Ewasm(opens in a new tab), an Ethereum flavored WebAssembly, and is designed to be a usable common denominator of both platforms. Good target for high-level optimisation stages that can benefit both EVM and Ewasm platforms equally.

Yul+

- A low-level, highly efficient extension to Yul.
- Initially designed for an optimistic rollup contract.

- Yul+ can be looked at as an experimental upgrade proposal to Yul, adding new features to it.

Example contract

The following simple example implements a power function. It can be compiled using solc --strict-assembly --bin input.yul. The example should be stored in the input.yul file.

```
{
function power(base, exponent) -> result
{
switch exponent
case 0 { result := 1 }
case 1 { result := base }
default
{
result := power(mul(base, base), div(exponent, 2))
if mod(exponent, 2) { result := mul(base, result) }
}
}
    let res := power(calldataload(0), calldataload(32))
    mstore(0, res)
return(0, 32)
}
```

FE

- Statically typed language for the Ethereum Virtual Machine (EVM).
- Inspired by Python and Rust.
- Aims to be easy to learn -- even for developers who are new to the Ethereum ecosystem.
- Fe development is still in its early stages, the language had its alpha release in January 2021.

Example contract

The following is a simple contract implemented in Fe.

```
type BookMsg = bytes[100]
contract GuestBook:
pub guest_book: map<address, BookMsg>
event Signed:
book_msg: BookMsg
pub def sign(book_msg: BookMsg):
self.guest_book[msg.sender] = book_msg
emit Signed(book_msg=book_msg)
```

```
14. pub def get_msg(addr: address) -> BookMsg:
15. return self.guest_book[addr].to_mem()
```

How to Choose

As with any other programming language, it's mostly about choosing the right tool for the right job as well as personal preferences. Here are a few things to consider if you haven't tried any of the languages yet:

What is Great About Solidity?

- If you are a beginner, there are many tutorials and learning tools out there. See more about that in the Learn by Coding section.
- Good developer tooling available.
- Solidity has a big developer community, which means you'll most likely find answers to your questions quite quickly.

What is Great About Vyper?

- Great way to get started for Python devs that want to write smart contracts.
- Vyper has a smaller number of features which makes it great for quick prototyping of ideas.
- Vyper aims to be easy to audit and maximally human-readable.

What is great about Yul and Yul+?

- Simplistic And Functional Low-Level Language.
- Allows to get much closer to raw EVM, which can help to optimize the gas usage of your contracts.

4.4.2 Solidity Language

What is Solidity Programming?

Solidity is a programming language utilised for developing smart contracts that operate on the Ethereum blockchain. Smart Contracts are autonomous agreements capable of completing diverse functions, including financial transfers, voting, and data management. Solidity is engineered for compatibility with the Ethereum Virtual Machine (EVM), the execution environment for Smart Contracts. Solidity possesses a syntax akin to those of C++, Python, and JavaScript. It is a statically typed language, necessitating the explicit declaration of variable and function types. Solidity additionally accommodates object-oriented characteristics, like inheritance, interfaces, and libraries.

Elements of Solidity Programming

Some of the essential elements of Solidity are:

(a) **Variables:** Variables are used to store data in Smart Contracts. They can be either state variables or local variables. State variables are stored permanently in the Blockchain, while local variables are only available within a function. Variables can have different data types, like integers, strings, arrays, mappings, etc.

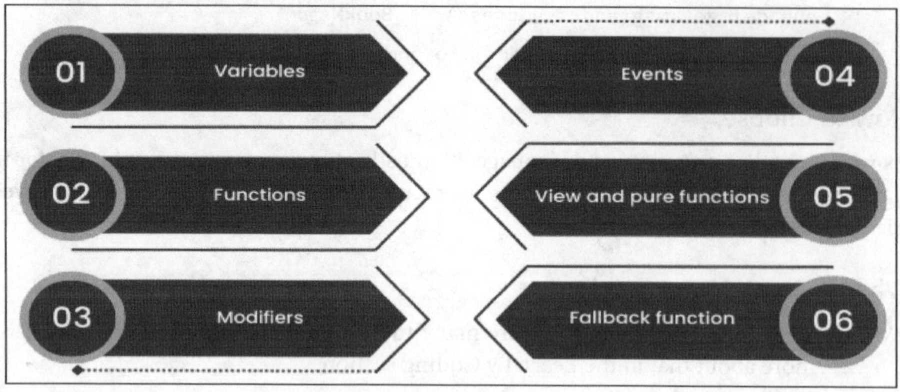

Fig. 4.6

(b) **Functions:** Functions are used to define the logic and behaviour of Smart Contracts. They can have parameters, return values, modifiers, and visibility specifiers. Functions can also emit events, which are used to notify external parties about the changes in the contract state.

(c) **Modifiers:** Modifiers are used to modify the behaviour of functions. They can check certain conditions before executing a function or modify the inputs or outputs of a function. For example, the 'payable' modifier allows a function to receive ether from external callers.

(d) **Events:** Events are used to log information about the contract activity. They can have parameters that store data in the event logs. Events can be emitted by functions or by using the 'emit' keyword. External parties can subscribe to events and react to them accordingly.

(e) **View and Pure Functions:** View and pure functions are special types of functions that do not modify the contract state. View functions can read the contract state but not write to it. Pure functions do not access the contract state at all. They only depend on their inputs and outputs. 'View' and 'pure' functions are marked with the view and pure keywords, respectively.

(f) **Fallback Function:** The fallback function is known as a special function that is executed when a contract receives ether or when no other function matches the call. It has no name and no parameters. It must be marked with the 'fallback' keyword and the 'external' visibility specifier.

Evolution of Solidity Programming

Solidity is an emerging programming language that has swiftly become integral to blockchain development. It is the principal language utilised on the Ethereum platform and other private blockchains such as Monax, which functions on the Hyperledger Burrow blockchain employing Tendermint for consensus. Furthermore, SWIFT has created a proof of concept on Burrow that employs Solidity, demonstrating its growing impact inside the blockchain ecosystem.

What are EVM and Smart Contracts?

In the realm of Blockchain and Decentralised Applications, two fundamental concepts are prominent: the Ethereum Virtual Machine (EVM) and Smart Contracts. Comprehending these notions is crucial for anybody seeking to investigate how blockchain technology facilitates secure, automated transactions and Decentralised Applications.

Ethereum Virtual Machine (EVM)

The Ethereum Virtual Machine (EVM) serves as a runtime environment for the execution of Ethereum smart contracts. It guarantees the secure execution of untrusted programs by utilising a global network of public nodes. The EVM is engineered to thwart Denial-of-Service attacks, guaranteeing that programs are segregated from one another's state while facilitating secure communication without disruption.

Smart Contracts

Smart Contracts are advanced program codes encoded into EVM and subsequently put on the Ethereum blockchain for execution. They enable secure, trustless transactions devoid of third-party intermediaries, guaranteeing that transactions are traceable and irrevocable. Prevalent programming languages utilised for the development of Smart Contracts encompass Serpent, Solidity, Mutan, and LLL.

Data Types of Solidity Programming

In Solidity, data types play a crucial role in defining the kind of data that can be stored and manipulated within Smart Contracts. Understanding these data types is essential for writing efficient and secure smart contracts on the Ethereum blockchain.

1. Value Types

These are the simplest data types that store data directly. Common value types include:

(a) **Boolean:** Represents true or false. Used for conditional statements.

(b) **Integer:** Solidity supports signed (int) and unsigned (uint) integers of varying sizes, from 8 to 256 bits, with uint256 being the most common. Signed integers can represent both positive and negative values, while unsigned integers represent only non-negative values.

(c) **Address:** Holds Ethereum addresses, crucial for identifying accounts and contracts on the blockchain. It supports methods like balance to check the Ether balance of an address.

(d) **Bytes:** Solidity has fixed-size byte arrays (bytesl to bytes32) and dynamic- size byte arrays (bytes), useful for handling raw data.

(e) **Enum:** Enables the creation of user-defined data types with a limited set of possible values, improving code readability.

2. Reference Types

These types do not store data directly but reference locations where data is stored. Common reference types include:

(a) **Arrays:** Can be fixed or dynamic, holding multiple elements of the same type. Arrays are essential for managing lists of data.

(b) **Structs:** Custom-defined data types that group multiple variables, often used to model more complex data structures.

(c) **Mapping:** A key-value store used to associate keys with corresponding values, useful for creating relationships between data elements.

3. Special Types

(a) **Function Types:** Used to define variables that can hold functions, enabling function pointers or callbacks.

4.5 CRYPTOCURRENCIES & THE REAL WORLD

Much attention in cryptocurrency is directed towards the price and volatility of each coin, with few individuals comprehending its underlying purposes.

Bitcoin (BTC)

Digital Gold serves as a reservoir of wealth and a safeguard against inflation. This is due to the finite number of BTC, capped at 21 million, that will ever be mined. Its supply cannot be artificially boosted like fiat currencies (Dollar, Pound, Euro, etc.) that may be merely printed. In many DeFi (Decentralised Finance) platforms, Bitcoin serves as collateral to secure loans in cryptocurrency, allowing users to borrow against its value. We shall elucidate DeFi in greater depth subsequently.

In numerous poor economies, such as El Salvador, Bitcoin serves as an effective means for communities to obtain banking services. In numerous locations, economies remain predominantly cash-based, and individuals are often unable to afford transportation to banks for registration; nonetheless, the prevalence of mobile phone ownership is on the rise. Consequently, utilising digital wallets for Bitcoin transfers, independent of conventional banking systems, may offer a feasible alternative for individuals lacking bank accounts to engage in financial activities and establish a store of value.

Ethereum (ETH) Smart contracts, Essentially, smart contracts are designed to autonomously perform and finalise activities, such as payment transactions, in a digital format. This is fundamental to Ethereum's success and its primary application. It allows developers to construct intricate apps utilising Ethereum's infrastructure. Decentralised Finance applications, The predominant category of smart contracts on Ethereum's platform consists of Decentralised Finance apps. DeFi enables users to perform many banking functions—such as earning interest, borrowing, lending, purchasing insurance, trading derivatives, and exchanging assets—more swiftly and without the necessity of documentation or intermediaries. Similar to cryptocurrency in general, DeFi is global, peer-to- peer (indicating direct transactions between individuals without a centralised intermediary), and accessible to everyone. NFTs represent a burgeoning application of Ethereum utilised as a medium of exchange for NFTs. The majority of NFT pricing are expressed in ETH. NFTs, for those unfamiliar, are essentially digital artworks whose authenticity is verified using blockchain technology. Consider it analogous to the Twitter blue verification badge for exclusive digital artwork.

Cardano (ADA)

The Cardano coin functions as a store of value and facilitates smart contracts, enabling value transfer akin to the use of cash. ADA shares similarities with other cryptocurrencies like Ethereum and Bitcoin, although it possesses additional functionalities. A fundamental principle of Cardano is its Proof of Stake (PoS) blockchain architecture, wherein ADA is staked to validate transactions on the blockchain. This is where Cardano cryptocurrency proves advantageous. Individuals that delegate their ADA to the blockchain receive additional Cardano cryptocurrency as a reward for their participation. This staking mechanism enhances security across the network. The application of ADA in voting is also present.

In Cardano, unlike other blockchain projects, protocol modifications are determined by token holders rather than miners. Consequently, when a new modification or advancement is suggested for the Cardano blockchain, Cardano cryptocurrency holders utilise their ADA to cast votes on these proposals.

Consequently, all cryptocurrency holders has a voice in its evolution. ADA can also be utilised to fuel the smart contract platform on the Cardano blockchain. Developers employ ADA to construct smart contracts and applications that operate on the secure, decentralised Cardano blockchain. Executing smart contracts incurs lower transaction fees compared to Ethereum.

Tether (USDT)

- **Stablecoin:** Secured by US dollars, with a value consistently pegged to approximately £1 per 1 USDT. Utilising Tether as an intermediary, numerous individuals transfer funds between cryptocurrencies, so circumventing the costs typically incurred during exchanges or conversions to fiat currencies.
- **Yield Generation:** Certain Tether users retain their cash in Tether due to its capacity to provide a superior yield or interest rate compared to traditional banking institutions.

Binance Coin (BNB)

Binance Coin is the cryptocurrency issued by the Binance exchange, denoted by the symbol BNB. BNB was originally founded on the Ethereum network but is currently the native currency of Binance's proprietary blockchain, the Binance Chain. Every quarter, Binance allocates one-fifth of its revenues to repurchase and irrevocably eliminate, or "burn," Binance tokens in its treasury.

Binance was established in 2017 as a utility token for reduced trading fees, but its applications have broadened to encompass many purposes, including transaction fee payments (on the Binance Chain), travel reservations, entertainment, online services, and financial services.

Ripple (XRP)

Expeditious and economical cross-border transactions. The principal application of XRP is designed for the transfer of various currencies, commodities, or assets, like gold and oil, via the Ripple network. Whenever a financial institution, such as a bank, utilises the network for transfer and settlement, a nominal fee in XRP is deducted. Cross-border payments between banks and organisations currently operate on a system known as SWIFT. A method established in 1973. Ripple and its cryptocurrency XRP could fundamentally supplant this with a more expeditious and cost-effective solution.

Solana (SOL)

Platform for Smart Contracts. Similar to Ethereum and Cardano, developers creating applications on the Solana blockchain utilise SOL tokens to cover processing and transaction fees on a daily basis. A substantial quantity of NFTs is also accessible on the Solana blockchain.

Polkadot (DOT)

Interoperability – Enable diverse blockchains to communicate and exchange data and functionalities among themselves. This is advantageous for developers creating new blockchains, since they can utilise components of features from other chains without the necessity of developing them anew each time. Unlimited Supply – In contrast to the majority of other cryptocurrencies, DOT possesses an unrestricted supply. This is intended to motivate the network and adapt dynamically based on user involvement rates.

Dogecoin (DOGE)

A meme coin initially developed as a jest or satire of the cryptocurrency realm. Now, however, has attained significant popularity and is even seen as a viable option for payments in the real world. This has yet to gain widespread acceptance, however.

USDC (USD Coin)

A stablecoin, backed by US dollars, is fixed to maintain a value of around £1 per 1 USDT. Less popular and less utilised by the market compared to Tether.

4.5.1 Data Feeds

What is Cryptofeed?

Cryptofeed is an open-source Python module designed for the collecting of cryptocurrency market data. It offers a consolidated interface for gathering real- time and historical trading data, order book updates, and other critical financial information from many exchanges.

Installation Steps

1. Setting Up Your Environment

Prior to installing Cryptofeed, ensure that Python version 3.7 or later is present in your system. The current version of Python can be obtained from the official Python website or via a package manager specific to your operating system.

2. Creating a Virtual Environment

Establishing a virtual environment is an effective method for maintaining the organisation of your Python requirements.

```
python3 -m venv myenv source myenv/bin/activate
```

Here, myenv is the name of the virtual environment. You've now activated it.

3. Installing Cryptofeed

With your virtual environment active, proceed to install Cryptofeed using pip: pip install cryptofeed

This will download and install Cryptofeed along with its dependencies.

Setting Up Market Feeds

1. Basic Example of Live Data Feed

Once you have Cryptofeed installed, you can start gathering live data. Here's a quick example to get live trade data from the Coinbase exchange:

```
from cryptofeed import FeedHandler
from cryptofeed.exchanges import Coinbase from cryptofeed.defines import
TRADES
async def trade(feed, pair, order_id, timestamp, side, amount, price):
print(f"Exchange: {feed}, Pair: {pair}, Side: {side}, Amount: {amount},
Price: {price}")
fh = FeedHandler()
fh.add_feed(Coinbase(channels=[TRADES], pairs=['BTC-USD'],
callbacks={TRADES: trade}))
fh.run()
```

This script collects live trade data for the BTC-USD pair on Coinbase and prints it to the console.

2. Fetching Historical Data

Cryptofeed also allows you to access historical data, though it requires using integrations with other libraries such as Arctic:

```
from cryptofeed.backends.arctic import ArcticREST from cryptofeed import
Cryptofeed
arbic_inst = ArcticREST()
cf = Cryptofeed({'arctic': arbic_inst})
data = arbic_inst.historical(exchange='BINANCE', base='BTC', quote
='USD', start='2021-01-01', end='2021-01-31', timeframe='1m')
```

Ensure you have the necessary database, API access set up to retrieve such data.

Conclusion

With Cryptofeed, the complex task of accessing and managing multi-exchange data becomes significantly simpler. Whether you want live feeds or historical data, this tool provides the functionality and flexibility needed for effective market data handling. Following the steps outlined here, you've set up both real- time and historical data feeds, ready to integrate into your financial applications and analyses.

4.5.2 Applications of Cryptocurrencies and Blockchains

Applications of Blockchain

1. Bitcoin

The principal application of Blockchain is in Cryptocurrencies like Bitcoin. Bitcoin is a decentralized digital money introduced by Santoshi Nakamoto.

2. Banking

Nowadays, Blockchain is also replacing the existing, or we can say overtaking the current Banking system. With the help of Blockchain, we may move the fund from one person to another in a second because the transaction's validation will take place through Blockchain and cryptography. It's a potential that Blockchain will cut down 19.8 Billion Dollars which is going for middleman cost/year. Because of the Blockchain, the hacking of accounts will become impossible. Applications of Blockchain also eliminate the problem of double-spending.

3. Payment and Transfers

Because of Blockchain, just the wallet system has grown up so swiftly, and by using it, we can make the payment and money transfers very quickly; we don't need to enter the public key. We need to scan a unique QR code and pay soon. The amount done using Blockchain will be highly secure with no transfer fees. For blockchain transfer, no bank account is needed.

4. Healthcare

Healthcare is also a domain where Blockchain technology has been employed for storing the details of the patients. This technology assures that anyone accessing this Blockchain can access patients' data. This database will be highly secure and for examining the data connected to the patient-doctor has to log in there with the public key and details, and he may check the patients' data.

5. Law Enforcement

The law enforcement department is now implementing Blockchain technology applications. To establish a Common Database encompassing criminals, their offences, and their biometric information. Due to its tight security, no one may alter it without appropriate authorisation.

6. Voting

Blockchain can be utilised in the forthcoming election or voting process because to its immutable and transformative characteristics. Voting will be rendered more secure and infallible through the implementation of Blockchain technology.

7. Internet of Things (IoT)

Blockchain is now utilised by the Internet of Things (IoT). This guarantees that data transferred to or between devices will be safe and encrypted without interference.

8. Online Music

The online music industry is expanding due to the implementation of Blockchain technology. Companies are placing their music on a blockchain, allowing universal access but preventing alterations. Customers can purchase a specific song and subsequently download it directly from the blockchain.

9. Real Estate

The real estate sector is influenced by Blockchain technology, and in the future, transactions involving property will occur via Blockchain.

10. Digital IDs

Blockchain is currently utilised by several companies for digital identification. These digital identities will be governed by the owner's private keys and will also assist in mitigating dissemination of excessive personal information online.

Applications of Cryptocurrencies

Cryptocurrencies are currently the most accessible investments for individual investors. In addition to stocks, mutual funds, and other investment options, investors may now buy, sell, and trade cryptocurrencies through various broking firms. Most individuals understand cryptocurrency trading as a means of generating passive income, while a minority regard it as an alternative investment compared to traditional investment methods. Cryptocurrencies are becoming popular, attracting a growing number of investors to the market. Consequently, cryptocurrency platforms have created applications. Besides facilitating the buying and selling of virtual currencies, these cryptocurrency applications serve multiple additional purposes. These cryptocurrency applications are frequently mobile and desktop programs that are favoured by individual traders, user communities, and other participants.

Pionex

Pionex is an excellent choice for investors seeking automated trading solutions in cryptocurrency applications. This cross-platform application features 16 complimentary integrated trading bots that facilitate automated trading. Pionex is one of the most secure cryptocurrency platforms, having established a robust reputation in the industry. The tool aggregates liquidity near ticket prices from exchanges such as Huobi and Binance.

Webull

Webull may be one of the premier cryptocurrency programs for those on a limited budget or those intending to invest a modest sum. Significantly, you may establish a Webull account without a minimum deposit, and you can transact in cryptocurrencies for as little as $1 per transaction. This allows you to acquire the fundamentals of bitcoin trading with minimal cost. Webull offers all its markets exclusively on a spread-only basis regarding fees and charges. We found that bitcoin transactions exhibited a minimum spread of 1%, which is not especially competitive. There are two methods available for funding your Webull account: ACH transfer or bank wire transfer.

Coinbase

Coinbase is a viable alternative and is perhaps one of the premier bitcoin programs for beginners. Upon downloading the program onto your device, you will promptly observe the user-friendly nature of the interface. Consequently, if you have no prior experience in purchasing or trading cryptocurrencies, the Coinbase app may be appropriate for you. The primary issue with this beginner- friendly trading platform is the substantial fees imposed for convenience. For example, Coinbase's fundamental trading fees, excluding the spread, are 1.49 percent per transaction. A substantial fee of 3.99 percent will be applied when purchasing cryptocurrencies using the app using a debit or credit card.

Binance

Binance is a premier cryptocurrency program that provides essential functionalities for sending, receiving, staking, and investing in cryptocurrencies. More than 500 coins and tokens are accessible for trade pairings using the service. Consider Binance if you are a trader seeking a cryptocurrency platform with numerous low-cost markets. This renowned trading program facilitates tens of billions of dollars in trading activity daily. With fees of merely 0.10 percent every transaction, you may encounter exceptionally tight spreads across numerous cryptocurrency pairs. Your location influences the options and expenses associated with funding your account. For example, US consumers enjoy a favourable deal since debit/credit card deposits incur only a 0.5 percent fee. Users from other nations may incur fees of up to 4% for the same transaction. The Binance app is available for free download on iOS and Android handsets.

Gemini

Gemini may be the optimal bitcoin application for seasoned traders that consistently deposit significant amounts in their transactions. This premier cryptocurrency platform possesses a license from the New York State Department of Financial Services and is subject to stringent regulation in the United States. By installing this bitcoin software on your mobile device, you will gain access to many institutional-grade insurance policies and security protocols. The application accommodates a limited selection of cryptocurrency assets, and the costs are relatively high. For trades beyond $200, a standard fee of 1.49 percent will be applied every transaction.

Aqru

Aqru distinguishes itself from other cryptocurrency programs by not concentrating on trading services. Aqru is one of the premier sites for earning interest with cryptocurrencies. Investors who deposit their Bitcoin or Ethereum tokens into the Aqru app will receive a substantial annual percentage yield of 7%. Users are not obligated to accept any minimum redemption period imposed by the program, allowing them to withdraw their digital tokens at their discretion without incurring any penalties.

CoinSmart

Customers can utilise credit cards, SEPA, wire transfers, e-transfers, and direct cryptocurrency deposits to acquire bitcoin using CoinSmart. Users may also engage in trading on the spot market. Derivatives markets are excluded from it. The exchange supports a limited amount of advanced orders and manages around 20 coins. It is primarily utilised for converting virtual currency into real money and for acquiring virtual currency with cash.

UNIT 5

CRYPTOCURRENCY REGULATION AND BLOCKCHAIN APPLICATIONS

5.1 CRYPTOCURRENCY REGULATION

Cryptocurrency regulations are intricate and can differ markedly by jurisdiction. This ecosystem is changing, and numerous governments have yet to implement crypto-specific legislation. This handbook elucidates essential cryptocurrency legislation globally. We address regulations concerning cryptocurrency ownership, tax reporting, anti-money laundering, and more topics.

What Are Crypto Regulations?

Cryptocurrency regulations are the statutes and guidelines established by governments to govern the utilisation, exchange, and ownership of cryptocurrency. They address critical domains such as taxation, anti-money laundering, and investor protection. Due to the nascent and developing nature of cryptocurrency, various governments have divergent regulations. However, the objective remains unchanged: to ensure that cryptocurrency operations are secure and transparent for all participants. In numerous jurisdictions, cryptocurrency legislation remain under development. Certain nations impose stringent regulations, categorising cryptocurrency as conventional financial assets. This entails obligations like as remitting taxes on cryptocurrency profits and adhering to stringent identification protocols while utilising exchanges.

Other nations adopt a more lenient approach, fostering innovation while gradually implementing regulations to mitigate problems like as fraud and market manipulation. Formulating adequate rules might be arduous due to the operation of cryptocurrency beyond conventional financial systems. This indicates that legislation is ever evolving as governments endeavour to adapt to the rapidly advancing cryptocurrency sector. For individuals engaged in cryptocurrency, it is essential to remain informed about the most recent regulations in your jurisdiction to maintain compliance.

Types of Crypto Regulations

Diverse regulatory frameworks significantly contribute to maintaining order within the cryptocurrency sector. These regulations guarantee that cryptocurrency activities are executed securely, lawfully, and equitably. This is an overview of the primary categories of cryptocurrency rules that one should be aware of.

- **Regulations on Trading and Exchanges:** These regulations dictate the trading of cryptocurrencies and the functioning of exchanges. The regulations encompass provisions for registration, licensing, client verification (KYC), and adherence to anti-money laundering (AML) legislation.

- **Tax Regulations:** This category pertains to the taxation of bitcoin transactions. It encompasses capital gains taxes on profits derived from trading or selling cryptocurrency, as well as income taxes on incomes from activities such as mining or staking.
- **Anti-Money Laundering (AML) and Counter-Terrorism Financing (CTF) Regulations:** These restrictions seek to prohibit the utilisation of cryptocurrency for illicit activity. They mandate exchanges and other service providers to oversee transactions, authenticate consumers, and report anomalous behaviour.
- **Consumer Protection Regulations:** These regulations aim to safeguard investors against fraud and other unethical actions. They encompass stipulations for risk disclosures, management of consumer funds, and transparency in cryptocurrency initiatives.
- **Data Privacy and Security Regulations:** These regulations ensure the protection of personal data and the security of crypto assets. They necessitate platforms to enforce robust security protocols and adhere to data privacy regulations such as GDPR.
- **Cross-Border Regulations:** Given that cryptocurrency functions on a global scale, these regulations oversee the transfer of crypto assets internationally. They encompass adherence to international AML/CTF rules and legislation pertaining to international transactions.

Who Regulates Crypto?

Although cryptocurrency is a global and borderless asset class, regulation is established on a national basis. Furthermore, several nations possess multiple regulatory bodies tasked with supervising the industry. In the United States, the SEC regulates securities associated with cryptocurrency. This encompasses Bitcoin ETFs, Coinbase shares, and other cryptocurrency initiatives it considers to be offering unregistered securities. The IRS, however, governs cryptocurrency taxes regulations. The CFTC supervises cryptocurrency-related commodity markets, including Bitcoin futures. Furthermore, FinCEN regulates cryptocurrency-related money laundering and terrorism financing activities. This multi-agency strategy for cryptocurrency is seen in other significant economies, such as the United Kingdom and the European Union. All that being said, very few countries have installed crypto-specific legislation. In most cases, existing legislation is applied to crypto assets. This is especially the case when it comes to taxation and financial crime laws. This can make it challenging for stakeholders, as some regulations are open to interpretation.

Benefits of Regulating Crypto

Worldwide, cryptocurrency regulation remains nascent. Let us examine several advantages of controlling this rapidly expanding business.

Consumer Protections

Regulations must be installed to protect consumers from unethical crypto practices. The FTX bankruptcy, for instance, led to the loss of billions of dollars in consumer funds. Moreover, scams associated with ICOs remain widespread. Importantly, judicious regulation may safeguard consumers without obstructing the industry. Exchanges may be mandated to maintain minimum reserves.

Legitimize the Industry

Establishing a regulatory framework for cryptocurrencies will enhance the legitimacy of the business. Individuals yet to engage in this market would possess increased confidence in the acquisition and disposition of cryptocurrency assets. Currently, cryptocurrencies are regarded as unregulated financial instruments. This indicates that conventional securities safeguards do not apply to cryptocurrency projects. Ultimately, regulation will stimulate a new influx of money, benefiting the business collectively.

Financial Crime Prevention

Financial criminality constitutes a significant concern within the cryptocurrency sector. Particularly regarding money laundering and the financing of terrorism. Appropriate legislation will assist financial intelligence units in maintaining industry security. This entails adhering to established protocols for customer due diligence, reporting of suspicious activities, and the management of politically exposed persons.

Promote Innovation

Regulation of cryptocurrency can facilitate organic growth within the industry. It will also foster innovation among both startups and established enterprises. A definitive regulatory framework will elevate the cryptocurrency markets through innovation.

Market Stability

Numerous critics contend that Bitcoin prices are significantly controlled. This diminishes market confidence and engenders speculative and turbulent trading circumstances. An effective regulatory structure, such to US securities regulations, can establish enduring market stability.

Risks of Regulating Cryptocurrency Market

Although regulation can elevate the cryptocurrency business, it also presents several disadvantages to contemplate.

- **Cost Implications:** Regulatory red tape can be costly for crypto stakeholders. Specialised compliance teams are required to ensure adherence to regulations. This may adversely affect new market entrants.
- **Privacy Concerns:** The best cryptocurrencies to buy offer a level of anonymity when sending, storing, and receiving funds. Excessive regulation may result in privacy issues. The UK now mandates domestic exchanges to gather information from clients initiating wallet transfers.
- **Market Barriers:** The cryptocurrency markets are open and global. Nonetheless, heightened rules may establish entry obstacles that could impede expansion.
- **Enforcement:** It can be difficult to enforce crypto regulations at the consumer level. This is particularly true when utilising decentralised products, like as exchanges and self-custody wallets.

Conclusion

Cryptocurrency rules are a dynamic domain, with numerous nations instituting novel norms and legislation to safeguard consumers. Governments are especially focused on mitigating cryptocurrency fraud, unethical practices, and access to high-risk financial goods. Furthermore, there is enhanced concordance on anti-money laundering and taxes regulations. Future regulations will facilitate greater growth in the business. Regulation should be pragmatic, effectively mitigating risks while fostering innovation.

5.1.1 Stakeholders

The cryptocurrency sector has expanded swiftly over the last ten years, transforming from a specialized field into a worldwide phenomenon with considerable financial and technological ramifications. This expansion has been propelled by a varied coalition of stakeholders, generally termed "crypto players," who are essential in influencing the market. The participants comprise developers, investors, exchanges, miners, regulators, and users, each contributing uniquely to the ecosystem. This article will examine the many categories of cryptocurrency participants, their functions, and their influence on the cryptocurrency market.

Developers: The Architects of Blockchain Technology

Developers constitute the foundation of the cryptocurrency ecosystem, tasked with the creation and maintenance of the underlying blockchain technology.

These individuals or teams develop the code that underpins cryptocurrencies, smart contracts, decentralized apps (dApps), and diverse blockchain protocols.

- **Core Developers:** Core developers focus on the essential components of a blockchain, including consensus techniques, network security, and protocol enhancements. They guarantee the blockchain's security, efficiency, and scalability. The core developers of Bitcoin are tasked with the maintenance and enhancement of the Bitcoin network.
- **Smart Contract Developers:** These developers design and implement smart contracts—self-executing agreements with the terms encoded directly in the programming. Platforms such as Ethereum have popularized smart contracts, facilitating the creation of decentralized applications (dApps) that operate on blockchain technology.
- **dApp Developers:** Decentralized application developers build applications that run on blockchain networks. These applications may encompass decentralized finance (DeFi) systems and non-fungible token (NFT) marketplaces. dApp developers are instrumental in broadening the applications of blockchain technology beyond mere transactions.

Investors: Fueling the Crypto Economy

Investors are crucial participants in the cryptocurrency economy, supplying the funds essential for fostering innovation and facilitating adoption. Cryptocurrency investors encompass individual retail traders and substantial institutional investors, each possessing distinct tactics and risk tolerances.

- **Retail Investors:** Retail investors are individuals who buy and sell cryptocurrencies on exchanges, often driven by the potential for high returns. They generally invest lesser sums than institutional investors, however collectively exert a considerable influence on market dynamics. Retail investors frequently depend on social media, news outlets, and forums for information and may engage in activities such as day trading, staking, or yield farming.

- **Institutional Investors**: Institutional investors encompass hedge funds, venture capital firms, and family offices that allocate significant capital to cryptocurrencies. Their participation has increased markedly in recent years, with numerous institutions seeing the potential of digital assets as an alternative investment category. Institutional investors frequently possess access to exclusive investment prospects, including exclusive token sales and stock interests in blockchain businesses.
- **Whales:** "Whales" are individual or institutional investors who hold large amounts of a particular cryptocurrency. Their trading operations can substantially impact market prices owing to the considerable volume of their transactions. The crypto community regularly monitors whales, as their activities can induce price volatility or indicate market trends.

Exchanges: The Gateways to the Crypto Market

Cryptocurrency exchanges are platforms that enable the acquisition, disposition, and exchange of digital assets. They are an essential element of the cryptocurrency ecosystem, facilitating liquidity and allowing users to exchange fiat currency for bitcoin and vice versa.

- **Centralized Exchanges (CEXs):** Centralized exchanges such as Binance, Coinbase, and Kraken are the predominant venues for cryptocurrency trading. They serve as mediators, managing users' funds and conducting trades on their behalf. Centralized exchanges provide substantial liquidity, an extensive array of trading pairs, and sophisticated functionalities such as margin trading and futures contracts. Nonetheless, consumers must place their trust in the exchange regarding their funds, which poses a security risk.
- **Decentralized Exchanges (DEXs):** DEXs such as Uniswap, SushiSwap, and PancakeSwap function autonomously, enabling users to engage in direct trading using smart contracts without a central authority. Decentralized exchanges offer enhanced privacy and control over assets, as users maintain custody of their funds. Nonetheless, they may exhibit reduced liquidity and possess greater complexity in utilization relative to centralized platforms.
- **OTC Desks:** Over-the-counter (OTC) desks enable substantial transactions between purchasers and vendors outside conventional exchange order books. Over-the-counter (OTC) trading is frequently utilized by institutional investors and large stakeholders seeking to conduct substantial transactions without inducing price slippage in the public market.

Miners and Validators: Securing the Blockchain

Miners and validators ensure the security of blockchain networks through the verification and processing of transactions. Their efforts guarantee the integrity and permanence of the blockchain, rendering it impervious to fraud and manipulation.

- **Miners:** In proof-of-work (PoW) blockchains like Bitcoin, miners use computational power to solve complex mathematical puzzles, which allows them to add new blocks to the blockchain. Miners receive newly generated bitcoin and transaction fees as compensation for their services. Mining necessitates substantial investment in hardware and electricity, resulting in the concentration of mining power in areas with low energy costs.

- **Validators:** In proof-of-stake (PoS) and various consensus procedures, validators are tasked with proposing and verifying new blocks. PoS networks necessitate that validators possess and "stake" a specified quantity of bitcoin as collateral, rather than depending on processing power.

  Validators receive compensation through transaction fees and, on sometimes, freshly issued coins. Proof of Stake (PoS) is seen as more energy-efficient than Proof of Work (PoW) and is increasingly favored, exemplified by networks like as Ethereum migrating to PoS.

Regulators and Policymakers: Shaping the Legal Framework

Regulators and policymakers are essential in the cryptocurrency ecosystem, as they create the legal and regulatory framework that oversees the business. Their activities can profoundly influence the adoption, innovation, and stability of the cryptocurrency market.

- **Financial Regulators:** Financial regulators oversee the activities of cryptocurrency exchanges, wallet providers, and other financial intermediaries. They mandate adherence to anti-money laundering (AML) and know-your-customer (KYC) requirements to avert illicit activities including money laundering, terrorism financing, and fraud.
- **Central Banks:** Central banks influence the crypto market by shaping monetary policy and exploring the development of central bank digital currencies (CBDCs). Some central banks perceive cryptocurrencies as a risk to financial stability, while others are investigating methods to incorporate digital assets into the conventional financial system.
- **Legislators:** Legislators draft and enact laws that govern the use of cryptocurrencies within their jurisdictions. These regulations can encompass various matters, including taxes, consumer protection, and the categorization of cryptocurrencies as assets or securities.

The Interplay of Crypto Players in the Ecosystem

The bitcoin ecosystem is a multifaceted and interrelated network in which the activities of one group of participants can have a ripple effect throughout the entire market. Developers' innovations might create new investment opportunities for traders, but regulatory actions can influence exchange operations and user behavior. The cooperative essence of the ecosystem implies that many participants frequently collaborate to attain shared objectives. Developers and miners cooperate to enhance and protect blockchain networks, whereas investors and exchanges collaborate to ensure liquidity and promote adoption. Cryptocurrency participants are the catalyst for the expansion and evolution of the cryptocurrency market.

Every group—developers, investors, exchanges, miners, regulators, and users—contributes uniquely and significantly to the evolution of digital money. The ongoing evolution of the industry will shape the dynamics among these entities, influencing the trajectory and prosperity of the bitcoin ecosystem. Comprehending the responsibilities and motivations of these principal stakeholders enables us to have a more profound grasp of the dynamics influencing the cryptocurrency landscape and the opportunities it offers.

5.1.2 Roots of Bitcoin

(A) Cash

Prior to the widespread awareness of the Internet, cryptographer David Chaum was preoccupied about online anonymity. In his 1982 work "Blind Signatures for Untraceable Payments," Chaum invented the concept of "blind signatures," an anonymous payment mechanism for the Internet. Similar to how currency facilitates anonymity in actual financial transactions, blind signatures provide anonymity in electronic transactions, thus the term eCash. "You can pay for access to a database, buy software or a newsletter by email, play a computer game over the net, receive $5 owed you by a friend, or just order a pizza. The possibilities are truly unlimited." — David Chaum describing eCash at the first CERN conference in 1994

In 1989, Chaum established a company named DigiCash, using eCash as its principal product. At that time, interest in digital currency and payment systems was already substantial. In 1995, eCash received licensing from the Mark Twain Bank. In 1996, Deutsche Bank and Credit Suisse became involved. Subsequently, Norske Bank and Bank Austria also complied. The banks were conducting experiments but did not fully advance the technology. "Securing sufficient merchant acceptance to attract an adequate consumer base, or the reverse, proved challenging," Chaum stated to Forbes in 1999, following DigiCash's bankruptcy filing. This observation underscores the importance of the network effect in promoting a novel financial system.

Currently, coin-mixing providers employ blind signatures, in contrast to Bitcoin. From a design standpoint, Bitcoin and eCash share little similarities. eCash was centered on DigiCash. Financial institutions were essential for account reconciliations and transaction verifications. eCash offered privacy; nevertheless, it lacked the censorship resistance of Bitcoin. Despite lacking popularity, eCash established a foundation for subsequent iterations of electronic currency as the inaugural electronic cash system.

Hashcash

Adam Back, a British cryptographer, concentrated his postdoctoral research on combating internet spam. In 1997, a 26-year-old named Back posted his Hashcash proposal to The Cypherpunks email group. In his reply, he outlined a stamp equivalent for emails referred to as a "partial hash collision-based postage scheme." "The idea of using partial hashes is that they can be made arbitrarily expensive to compute, and yet can be verified instantly." — Adam Back

Hashing converts any data into a hexadecimal number of specified length. The ability to verify cryptographic hashes instantaneously, but incurring a generation overhead, underpinned the strategy of becoming spam computationally prohibitive to transmit. Incorporating a hashing stamp into a solitary email was imperceptible to an average user. However, hashing millions of spam emails rendered the operation computationally prohibitive, making it impossible to execute within a reasonable timeframe. Back expanded upon his proposal in the Hashcash white paper five years later.

Currently, we refer to the technology that underpins Hashcash as proof-of-work. The evident drawback of Back's technique was the inability to reuse hashes, rendering them irredeemable in monetary terms. Over the years, we have acclimated to the digital abundance of the Internet, where every resource can be effortlessly replicated. Proof-of-work established digital scarcity independent of a central authority. Scarcity, a fundamental requirement for currency, is established by linking digital resources to processing power constrained by the laws of physics. The security of Bitcoin is contingent upon proof-of-work, rendering any assault on the network prohibitively costly. It is a straightforward strategy, readily comprehensible. Best of luck comprehending the security aspects of the proof-of-stake consensus protocol.

(B) Money

Wei Dai, an anonymous cryptographer, recognized the inherent issues with monetary systems reliant on a central ledger, which permits governmental control over the monetary flow via regulation, and subsequently presented two alternative options. "Efficient cooperation requires a medium of exchange (money) and a way to enforce contracts" — Wei Dai in 1998.

One idea was that, rather than a central authority managing the ledger, all participants maintain individual copies of the identical ledger. Subsequent to each transaction, all individuals amend their records. These decentralized ledgers encompass public cryptographic keys linked to corresponding amounts. This method inhibits any individual entity from obstructing a transaction. A decentralized ledger is essential to the design of Bitcoin, announced a decade later by Satoshi Nakamoto.

Dai deemed the initial b-money approach unrealistic, citing its reliance on a synchronous and unjammable anonymous broadcast channel. The initial b- money concept failed to address the double-spending issue. In the second approach, Dai suggested that not all individuals uphold a version of the ledger. We have two categories of users: regular users and servers, with solely the servers responsible for maintaining the ledgers. Users authenticate the transaction by cross-referencing it with a random subset of these servers. Dai suggested that "each server must deposit a specified sum into a designated account to be utilized for potential penalties or incentives for evidence of misconduct." The second b-money concept is analogous to what is currently referred to as proof-of-stake. B-money exhibited substantial divergence from Bitcoin in its monetary policies.

Dai envisioned b-money as a stablecoin with a theoretical backing of a basket of things. The issuance of new coins was predicated on computational proof-of- work linked to the worth of a basket of products. The initial individual to generate a proof-of-work demonstrating the basket value would receive new b- money as a reward. The monetary policy of Bitcoin is straightforward. To introduce coins into circulation, it initially issued 50 new bitcoins each block, a figure that has been halved twice and presently stands at 6.25 BTC. The quantity will persistently diminish every 210,000 blocks till 2130, at this point the total issuance of bitcoin will attain 21 million. B-money was never realized, and Dai conceded that "b-money was not a fully practical design at that time." He did not anticipate b-money to gain significant traction and observed b-money operating alongside the fiat financial system: "I think b-money will at most be a niche currency/contract enforcement mechanism, serving those who don't want to or can't use government sponsored ones" —Wei Dai

Bit Gold

Nick Szabo is a computer scientist, cryptographer, and legal scholar, renowned for his introduction of the notion of "smart contracts" in an essay for Extropy magazine. His writings are profoundly influenced by economist Friedrich Hayek and present smart contracts as foundational elements for digital marketplaces. In smart contracts, sophisticated cryptography obviates the necessity for trusted intermediaries. "Trusted third parties are security holes." —Nick Szabo

Next to digital contracts, Nick Szabo also explored digital Money, as Internet money was a Holy Grail for Cypherpunks. "The problem, in a nutshell, is that our money currently depends on trust in a third party for its value. (...) As many inflationary and hyperinflationary episodes during the 20th century demonstrated, this is not an ideal state of affairs." — Nick Szabo

Clearly noticing the problem, Szabo wanted his creation to be both digital and scarce—a digital gold. "Precious metals and collectibles have an unforgeable scarcity due to the costliness of their creation. This once provided money the value of which was largely independent of any trusted third party. Precious metals have problems, however. [...] Thus, it would be very nice if there were a protocol whereby unforgeably costly bits could be created online with minimal dependence on trusted third parties, and then securely stored, transferred, and assayed with similar minimal trust. **Bit gold**." —Nick Szabo

Szabo initially conceived Bit Gold in 1998 and thoroughly articulated his concept in 2005. Bit Gold was founded on a proof-of-work method developed by Adam Back in Hashcash. Szabo proposed a digital ownership register to monitor the ownership of digital assets, drawing inspiration from Hayek. The ownership was to be monitored by specialized servers, akin to Wei Dai's second b-money proposal. Szabo proposed a "Byzantine Quorum System," utilized in security-critical systems, as an alternative to Dai's proof-of-stake technique. For the system to function properly, the majority of connected computers must perform correctly.

In 2008, Szabo inquired on his blog whether anyone was willing to assist in implementing his proposal. No one publicly responded to his inquiry, and the original plan of Bit Gold was never executed. Bit Gold was a significant source of inspiration for Satoshi Nakamoto, who subsequently published the Bitcoin white paper within the same year. Bit Gold relied on third parties for its servers and timestamp services, but Bitcoin addresses this issue comprehensively by utilizing proof-of-work as both a reward system and a consensus mechanism: the hash chain with the greatest proof-of-work is deemed the authentic historical record. Furthermore, Bitcoin possesses a predetermined inflation timetable, representing a considerably more straightforward monetary model than that suggested by Szabo.

Reusable Proofs of Work

In the 1980s, subsequent to his graduation from the California Institute of Technology, Hal Finney participated in the techno-libertarian movement known as the Extropians. Members of this group were influenced by Austrian economists and libertarian writers, using advanced technologies as instruments to advance humanity to the next evolutionary phase. Finney was an early proponent and aficionado of the Web, seeing both the potential and the dangers inherent in open online communication and transactions, which he perceived as a potential threat to human liberty. In his perspective, the transition to digital currency was unavoidable. "One concern I have is that the move to electronic payments will decrease personal privacy by making it easier to log and record transactions. Dossiers could be built up which would track the spending patterns of each of us"— Hal Finney in his 19 August 1993 essay.

The internet obviously needed digital money. When Finney discovered that David Chaum is already working on eCash he explained the project in Extropy, the magazine at the heart of the Extropians movement. "Cryptography can make possible a world in which people have control over information about themselves, not because government has granted them that control, but because only they posses the cryptographic keys to reveal that information" — Hal Finney, 1992.

As a founding member of The Cypherpunks, Hal Finney reviewed numerous early digital cash systems. In Adam Back's Hashcash proposal for an anti-spam mechanism, each proof-of-work was individually linked to a specific email, so preventing a Hashcash recipient from reusing the same proof-of-work in other contexts. From Finney's perspective, the absence of proof-of-work reusability represented a potential squandering of limited energy resources. In 2004, Finney introduced a digital currency system known as Reusable Proofs of Work (RPOW), which was a streamlined iteration of Bit Gold and utilized Hashcash's proof-of-work mechanism for money creation. Szabo and Dai did not execute their suggestions, although Finney developed a prototype.

In his approach, tokens symbolizing a singular proof of work might perpetually circulate as a reusable proof of work. The evident drawback of his implementation was its reliance on the trustworthiness of the RPOW server operator (to validate the absence of duplicate spending), which may be subject to censorship or deactivation, hence rendering the circulating tokens ineffective. Finney sought to prevent users from placing their trust in the operator of the RPOW server, regardless of whether that operator was himself. While Szabo and Dai endeavored to address the inflation issue by increased complexity, Finney just acknowledged the inflation. This streamlined design may have hindered the project's initiation. In the absence of financial incentive, there was no rationale for retaining RPOW tokens initially, resulting in the project encountering the chicken-and-egg dilemma and failing to establish the networking effect.

Bitcoin

In October 2008, Satoshi Nakamoto proclaimed Bitcoin on The Cypherpunks email group. Bitcoin was founded on Hashcash's proof-of-work process; however, it did not rely on any central server, unlike RPOW. The Cypherpunks paid little heed to Bitcoin, having quickly seen that: transactions were not instantaneous, opponents possessing substantial computational resources might dominate the system, and the solution seems to lack scalability. Despite those evident flaws, Bitcoin appeared highly promising to Finney. He particularly appreciated the concept of grounding security on the premise that the computational capacity of legitimate players surpasses that of the adversary. I believe there is potential value in a type of unforgeable token with a known production rate that cannot be manipulated by corrupt entities.

RPOW tokens had a decline in value over time, while Bitcoin addressed a significant issue. While reflecting about Bitcoin, Finney stated: "As an amusing thought experiment, imagine that Bitcoin is successful and becomes the dominant payment system in use throughout the world. Then the total value of the currency should be equal to the total value of all the wealth in the world. Current estimates of total worldwide household wealth that I have found range from $100 trillion to $300 trillion. With 20 million coins, that gives **each coin a value of about $10 million.**" — Hal Finney

Finney observed that the tokens possessed potential value. Even if initially merely speculative in value. Upon its inception in early 2009, Bitcoin saw Finney emerge as one of the initial miners on the network, making him the first individual globally to receive a Bitcoin transaction from Satoshi Nakamoto.

Magic Money

The earliest origins of Bitcoin may be traced to the late 1980s. The early digital currency initiatives were not failures; they provided valuable lessons that Satoshi Nakamoto assimilated. Bitcoin represents a technological balance that intensifies over time.

5.1.3 Legal Aspects

The distinctive innovations and progress in India's technology sector, particularly amid the challenges presented by the swift proliferation of COVID- 19, have yielded encouraging outcomes in the fintech industry. There has been an increase, primarily driven by curiosity and popularity, among the population of India in cryptocurrencies such as Bitcoin, Ripple, and Dogecoin, leading many individuals to invest a significant portion of their time and resources in these digital currencies. In India, the principal financial authority, the Reserve Bank of India ("RBI"), acknowledged cryptocurrency, specifically characterized as a type of digital or virtual currency generated through a sequence of coded instructions based on cryptography, thereby lacking any central issuing authority. Cryptocurrency is facilitated by blockchain technology, which creates a peer-to-peer issuance system that use private and public keys for authentication and encryption, ensuring secure transactions.

Growing Popularity of Cryptocurrency

As an unregulated industry with a potential exceeding one trillion dollars, India has experienced a significant increase in cryptocurrency exchanges. Observing the rapid rise in cryptocurrency usage within a year and the potential revenue loss to the Government of India, regulators and authorities began to take action. Consequently, in 2013, the RBI issued a press release cautioning the public against engaging in virtual or digital currencies.

Restrictions Imposed By RBI

In November 2017, the Government of India constituted a high-level Inter-Ministerial Committee to examine concerns pertaining to virtual currency. Subsequently, in July 2019, this Committee submitted its report recommending a comprehensive prohibition on private cryptocurrencies in India. The imminent threat of revenue loss prompted the RBI to issue a circular in April 2018, prior to the submission of the Inter-Ministerial Committee's report, prohibiting all commercial and cooperative banks, small finance banks, payment banks, and NBFCs from engaging in virtual/digital currencies and instructing them to cease services to entities involved in such currencies. This impeded the growth of the cryptocurrency sector in India, as exchanges necessitated banking services for the transfer of funds. The banking service is crucial for bitcoin conversion and subsequently for disbursing salaries, compensating vendors, and covering office expenses.

On 4th March 2020, the Hon'ble Supreme Court of India issued a well-reasoned verdict that annulled the prior prohibition placed by the RBI on cryptocurrencies and their usage. The Hon'ble Supreme Court of India primarily scrutinized the issue through the lens of Article 19(1)(g) of the Indian Constitution, which pertains to the right to engage in any profession or to conduct any occupation, trade, or business, alongside the notion of proportionality. The Apex Court observed that there is consensus among all regulators and foreign governments that, although virtual currencies have not attained the status of legal tender, they do exhibit digital representations of value and can operate as a medium of exchange, unit of account, and/or store of value. The court acknowledged the RBI's authority to undertake pre-emptive measures; nevertheless, it determined that the proportionality of such an action was absent in this instance, as RBI's regulated firms did not incur any direct or indirect damage or loss due to VC trading. Consequently, for many reasons, including the principle of proportionality, the contested Circular dated 06-04-2018 was annulled.

Developments In the Crypto-World

The Government of India is currently contemplating the enactment of a new legislation entitled "Cryptocurrency and Regulation of Official Digital Currency Bill, 2021" ("New Bill"), which bears resemblance to its preceding iterations. The New Bill aims to prohibit private cryptocurrencies in India, with some exceptions, to promote the underlying technology and cryptocurrency trading within a framework for establishing an official digital currency issued by the RBI. The New Bill addresses the challenge posed by the absence of cryptocurrency regulations and proposes a complete prohibition of all private cryptocurrencies. The New Bill's approach presents a paradox as the RBI remains uncertain about whether types of cryptocurrencies will be classified as private cryptocurrency. If the New Bill enacts a total prohibition on private cryptocurrencies, it will compel bitcoin investors to engage in transactions inside an entirely unregulated sector. The objective of implementing cryptocurrency legislation is to facilitate trading and possession within a more secure technological framework. Nonetheless, despite the implementation of state-owned cryptocurrency under the oversight of the RBI, the investment and holding risks associated with cryptocurrencies would persist unchanged.

Present The State of Cryptocurrency in India

In late March 2021, the Government of India mandated, per the recent modifications to Schedule III of the corporations Act, 2013, that corporations must report their cryptocurrency investments starting with the next financial year. Companies are now required to disclose profits or losses from bitcoin transactions, the quantity held, and information regarding deposits or advances from individuals engaged in cryptocurrency trading or investment. This action has been highly valued by those in the cryptocurrency field, as it will enable all Indian enterprises to include cryptocurrency on their balance sheets.

Conclusion

The analysis of the aforementioned facts and the current global context regarding cryptocurrencies reveals a significant absence of clarity on cryptocurrency law in India. Prioritizing well-structured and clear rules concerning cryptocurrency trading exchanges, blockchain technology, investors, and personnel within the sector is essential, since the cryptocurrency landscape is enduring and requires increased scrutiny. The Draft National Strategy on Blockchain, 2021, produced by the Ministry of Electronics and Information Technology, emphasizes the advantages of bitcoin.

Consequently, prohibiting a virtual currency that has significantly influenced numerous countries would not be the optimal course of action for our nation's development. The government must implement comprehensive measures for the regulation and enforcement of cryptocurrency to instill trust among investors and the general populace in the nation's development. On March 16, 2021, Union Finance Minister Nirmala Sitharaman said that there will not be a total prohibition on cryptocurrency, stating, "we will allow a certain amount of window for people to experiment with blockchain, bitcoins, and cryptocurrency."

It would be prudent to halt, reflect, and await the Government's establishment of explicit legislation regarding cryptocurrency before engaging in ambiguous activities.

5.1.4 Cryptocurrency Exchange

The cryptocurrency market is currently valued at over one trillion, experiencing a fervor for digital currencies and decentralized finance. Occasionally, numerous virtual currencies are emerging. Consequently, inquisitive cryptocurrency investors must acquire knowledge about an appropriate platform that facilitates rapid trading of diverse digital assets. Similar to conventional stock and commodities exchanges, cryptocurrency exchanges serve as platforms that enable participants to trade various cryptocurrencies. In light of the recent controversies surrounding prominent cryptocurrency exchanges, FTX and the ongoing Binance-SEC dispute, there is a heightened interest in gaining a deeper understanding of these platforms. Forbes Advisor India has compiled a comprehensive guide on cryptocurrency exchanges, detailing their operations, varieties, advantages and disadvantages, and, crucially, identifying potential red signals that a cryptocurrency exchange may present to prospective customers.

Meaning of A Cryptocurrency Exchange

A cryptocurrency exchange operates similarly to stock exchanges, facilitating investors in the buying and selling of digital currencies such as Bitcoin, Ethereum, or Tether. These platforms operate in digital marketplaces, such as mobile applications or desktop interfaces, akin to e-brokerages. They also offer a variety of trading and investment instruments to their users. The cryptocurrency exchanges also offer numerous trading alternatives, including margin trading, lending trading, and futures and options trading. To provide consumers with these numerous services, crypto exchanges impose various fees on transactions, which may be contingent upon the transaction volume or the specific sort of trade executed.

Prior to the advent of cryptocurrency exchanges, investors could only acquire cryptocurrency through mining or by facilitating trades in various online and offline forums. Currently, numerous cryptocurrency exchanges operate globally, providing a diverse array of digital currencies with differing security measures and pricing structures. In contrast to conventional stock or commodities markets, where fees have diminished in recent years, cryptocurrency trading typically incurs higher charges. The optimal cryptocurrency exchange will facilitate the trading of desired currencies with a streamlined cost structure and robust security measures.

How Does A Cryptocurrency Exchange Functions?

Cryptocurrency exchanges, both controlled and decentralized, are a relatively novel notion. They operate on the principle of facilitating a match between buyers and vendors. Establishing an account with a cryptocurrency exchange enables the acquisition and disposal of cryptocurrencies, including Bitcoin (BTC), Ethereum (ETH), Litecoin (LTC), Cardano (ADA), and Dogecoin (DOGE), among others. Individuals wishing to execute trades on cryptocurrency exchanges in India must first register and fulfill the Know-Your- Customer (KYC) procedure. Upon the establishment and verification of the user's account, they may transfer funds in fiat currencies, such as INR, or digital currencies into the platform, which can then be utilized for purchases.

So, if suppose you want to buy your first cryptocurrency via crypto exchange, here are the basic steps:

Step 1: Explore and choose a trustworthy and sound cryptocurrency exchange.

Step 2: Register with the exchange and open an account with them.

Step 3: Fund your account or crypto wallet either by depositing fiat or digital currencies.

Step 4: Now, select the cryptocurrency you want to buy and how much. For instance, if you wish to buy Bitcoin worth INR 10,000.

Step 5: Follow the necessary steps to initiate and complete a transaction.

Step 6: Check your account to verify that the transaction was a success.

Pros and Cons of Cryptocurrency Exchanges

Pros

- Very easy and hassle-free for users to buy cryptocurrencies.
- Exchanges allow you to place a legitimate trade on cryptocurrencies.
- There are many exchanges which offer their users with tax forms, making it easier to compute crypto taxes.

Cons

- Too much vulnerable to hacks and cyber theft.
- If the exchanges go bankrupt, users will not be able to access their funds or place trades.
- In most of the exchanges, users do not have the right to hold their private keys.

Types of Cryptocurrency Exchange Centralized Exchanges

These exchanges operate similarly to traditional equity stock exchanges or full- time brokerages. The centralized exchange is governed by a singular authority that monitors all accounts and exerts complete control over every transaction.

Pros

- Excellent liquidity.
- The recovery of the user's funds is feasible.
- Capable of processing transactions more swiftly.

Cons

- Centralized servers facilitate easier access for hackers due to the storage of valuable user data by CEX.
- Have been accused of manipulating trading volume previously.

Decentralized Exchanges or DEX

These types of exchanges are entirely contrary to centralized exchanges. They operate on the foundation of distributed ledger technology. Such exchanges facilitate the trading of cryptocurrencies without any governing authority. Decentralized exchanges operate autonomously, granting users ownership over their keys and digital assets. Furthermore, users are not obligated to undergo any KYC procedures, hence enhancing their privacy in safeguarding transactions.

Pros

- Complete control over their assets.
- Enhanced security and privacy.
- Distributed hosting mitigates the threat of cyber attacks.

Cons

- Insufficient liquidity.

Hybrid Exchanges

A hybrid exchange combines elements of both centralized (CEX) and decentralized (DEX) exchanges, aiming to provide the advantages of each type. They facilitate the convenience of a centralized exchange while also ensuring the privacy and security characteristic of a decentralized exchange.

Pros

- Enumerates the advantages ofboth decentralized exchanges (DEX) and centralized exchanges (CEX).
- Ensures a superior degree of confidentiality.

Cons

- A comparatively novel concept.
- There has been limited volume to date.
- Forbes Advisor India has compiled a list of the leading exchanges functioning in India. Consult our post on the Best Cryptocurrency
- Exchanges in India to obtain detailed information regarding particular exchanges and their essential characteristics.

Things to Check Before Selecting a Crypto Exchange

Exercise caution while selecting a cryptocurrency exchange, as an unwise choice may lead to complications. A cryptocurrency exchange is essentially a platform for the buying and selling of various cryptocurrencies. However, due to the inherent complexity of the cryptoverse, exchanges can be intricate and necessitate greater examination than ordinary stocks, as they are predominantly unregulated. Here are few crucial measures that could significantly mitigate your risk of fraud or exposure to a precarious cryptocurrency exchange: Verify if a specific firm is registered as a securities broker. Select the exchange that is incorporated or registered in India. This could prove beneficial if relevant authorities scrutinize the exchange.

The exchange is obligated to disclose the utilization of your funds. If the exchange is manipulating or commingling your cash, recovering your assets may be exceedingly difficult or impossible in the event of the exchange's bankruptcy. Poor lending practices resulted in the collapse of FTX and posed significant risks to its global users. The exchange ought to maintain a legitimate presence on social media platforms such as LinkedIn, Twitter, or Facebook. Prior to picking a cryptocurrency exchange, it is imperative to evaluate their customer care system by attempting to contact them through toll-free lines or their chat service. Prior to choosing the exchange, also identify the exchange's wallet. A properly running exchange often reveals its bitcoin reserves. However, if an exchange attempts to conceal this information, it may indicate an undercapitalized or fraudulent operation.

5.1.5 Black Market

A black market, or underground market, is an economic structure functioning beyond government-sanctioned avenues. Black markets entail the illicit exchange of goods and services, frequently to circumvent taxation or regulatory scrutiny. These transactions occur clandestinely and involve both illegal goods and services, as well as legal items sold unlawfully. The black market is characterized by efforts to circumvent governmental regulations, such as price controls and tariffs. Black markets typically feature unlawful commodities such as narcotics, counterfeit goods, and banned species, as well as legal things sold without appropriate taxation. Black markets are prevalent in areas characterized by economic instability, corruption, or stringent legal regulations.

Reasons for Black Market Existence

Black markets flourish in contexts where governments enforce stringent limitations or regulations on specific commodities and services. These markets provide consumers things that may be unattainable or prohibitively expensive through authorized channels. In nations with elevated taxation, stringent currency regulations, or restricted product availability, consumers resort to illicit markets to satisfy requirements inadequately addressed by official avenues.

Moreover, illegal marketplaces are motivated by the intent to evade substantial taxes and regulatory expenses. Individuals may acquire untaxed cigarettes or alcohol from illicit sources to economize. Likewise, currency trades in nations with stringent financial regulations—such as Venezuela or Iran—frequently function within illegal markets owing to inflated exchange rates.

Examples of Black Market Activities Illegal Goods and Services

Black markets are associated with the trade of illicit commodities and services. Frequently trafficked items encompass narcotics, guns, counterfeit currency, human organs, and endangered animals. Human trafficking persists as a significant illicit enterprise, facilitating the movement of individuals for coerced work or sexual exploitation. This market produces billions of cash each year, while circumventing law enforcement and taxation. In 2021, human trafficking figures indicated that around 40 million individuals were ensnared in various forms of contemporary slavery. These illicit operations occur clandestinely, complicating governmental efforts to regulate or fully acknowledge the scope of their harm.

Legal Goods Sold Illicitly

In addition to illegal products, black markets frequently encompass the distribution of legitimate commodities via unlawful methods. This encompasses things such as electronics, apparel, or alcohol sold without the requisite taxation or customs duties. A key factor contributing to these sales is tax avoidance. For example, individuals might sell imported commodities on the black market to evade taxes, or consumers may acquire untaxed products such as tobacco or alcohol. An illustration of this is evident in the commerce of luxury items, including designer handbags and electronics. These commodities, while not unlawful, are frequently sold without disclosure to tax authorities, resulting in black market transactions.

The Impact of Black Market Activities Economic Consequences

Black markets subvert normal economies by diverting transactions from conventional economic channels. This undermines government tax income, affects the official gross domestic product (GDP), and may mislead the actual economic condition. When a substantial segment of a nation's economic activity transpires clandestinely, official economic indices may underestimate the true magnitude of the economy, since black market transactions remain undetected. For instance, nations characterized by significant black market activity—such as certain regions in Africa or Latin America—frequently exhibit a substantial fraction of their GDP that remains unrecorded.

Social Consequences

Socially, illicit markets can yield severe repercussions. The lack of regulation in these sectors fosters potential for exploitation and deceit. Products offered may be fraudulent, inferior, or potentially detrimental. The absence of quality control can be fatal, particularly for counterfeit pharmaceuticals or tainted food products. Moreover, involvement in illicit market activities subjects individuals to legal hazards, with penalties varying from monetary fines to incarceration. Black markets exacerbate corruption, as officials may be persuaded to overlook illicit activities, hence deepening inequality and instability.

Pros and Cons of Black Markets

Pros

- Provides access to goods and services not available through legal channels
- Can stimulate informal economies
- Offers employment opportunities in regions with high unemployment rates

Cons

- Deprives governments of tax revenue
- Encourages criminal activity and corruption
- Poses significant risks to consumers, such as fraud or unsafe products

Types of Black Markets

Human Trafficking

Human trafficking represents one of the most egregious forms of black market activity. Individuals, including minors, are trafficked worldwide for coerced labor, sexual exploitation, or illicit adoption. The market for human organs represents a sinister facet of this commerce, when victims are frequently compelled to sell their organs or have them forcibly extracted. Human trafficking is especially prevalent in areas characterized by poor law enforcement and high poverty levels.

Counterfeit Goods

Counterfeiting constitutes a significant black market sector. Counterfeit luxury items, including designer handbags, watches, and apparel, are frequently exchanged. These products adversely impact genuine manufacturers and can lead to substantial financial losses for consumers who purchase substandard items. The counterfeit industry erodes customer trust and facilitates criminal organizations involved in various illicit operations.

Illegal Wildlife Trade

The illicit wildlife trade is an expanding segment of the worldwide black market. Endangered species, such as tigers, elephants, and rhinoceroses, are illicitly traded for their body parts, pelts, and tusks. The illicit trade in wildlife significantly endangers biodiversity and undermines conservation initiatives. This unlawful commerce is frequently associated with organized crime, and the revenues generated by wildlife trafficking support additional illicit endeavors.

The Evolution of Black Marketplaces Across Many Economies

Black markets adjust to the particular economic contexts in which they function. In underdeveloped countries characterized by fragile financial systems and elevated corruption, black markets flourish due to insufficient state oversight and the scarcity of vital commodities. In nations experiencing hyperinflation, illicit currency exchanges thrive as individuals pursue alternatives to volatile government currencies. In contrast, in more developed countries, black markets typically focus on heavily regulated or taxed commodities such as tobacco, alcohol, and electronics, providing these products at reduced rates by circumventing taxes or tariffs.

Digital Black Markets and The Dark Web

As digital technology have advanced, black markets have shifted from physical transactions to online platforms. The dark web, an unindexed segment of the internet, has emerged as a center for illicit market activity. Individuals can acquire illicit things such as narcotics, forged documents, and firearms with a certain level of secrecy by utilizing digital currency like Bitcoin. Prominent internet black marketplaces, like Silk Road, have been dismantled by law enforcement; yet, new platforms persistently arise, posing continual challenges for authorities.

The Role of Cryptocurrency in Black Markets

Cryptocurrencies, including Bitcoin and Monero, have become essential for online black market transactions. The decentralized characteristics of these digital currencies render them attractive for illicit transactions due to their capacity for anonymity and the challenges associated with tracing them. In conventional black market environments, currency served as the principal means of transaction to evade paper trails; however, cryptocurrencies increasingly provide a comparable function in digital black markets. This transition has complicated the ability of law enforcement agencies to monitor and terminate illicit transactions.

Government Responses to Black Markets

Governments globally adopt several strategies to counteract black markets. Some emphasize enhancing law enforcement and implementing more severe penalties for participants in illegal commerce, while others seek to tackle underlying issues, such as poverty and regulatory constraints. Furthermore, certain governments endeavor to diminish black market operations by legalizing formerly illicit commodities, such as marijuana, and incorporating them into the regulated economy. This technique has demonstrated efficacy in diminishing black market operations in regions where legalization has been enacted. Obstacles in quantifying the dimensions of the illicit market Measuring the magnitude of black markets is challenging due to the clandestine nature of the activities involved. As black markets function outside conventional economic frameworks, official metrics such as GDP frequently neglect to include these transactions. Estimates indicate that black markets may account for as much as 36% of GDP in poor countries and approximately 13% in wealthy nations. Nonetheless, these figures are only estimations, as the actual extent of black market operations remains predominantly unquantified.

Conclusion

The black market is a continual and adaptive component of the global economy, propelled by economic instability, stringent regulation, and consumer demand for unavailable or illicit commodities. Although it provides immediate remedies, such as access to limited resources, the enduring repercussions of black market operations encompass economic imbalances, corruption, and the expansion of criminal organizations. Governments must equilibrate regulation with accessibility to mitigate black market activity, tackling the root causes while enforcing laws that safeguard consumers and the economy. With the ongoing expansion of the digital era, novel obstacles emerge in monitoring and deconstructing black market transactions, especially on the dark web and via cryptocurrency. Comprehending and tackling the complex nature of illicit markets is essential for preserving economic stability and ensuring consumer safety.

5.1.6 Global Economy

We will analyze the influence of bitcoin on the global economy, addressing one facet at a time.

1. Remittances and Cross-Border Transactions

A. Breaking Down Barriers

Cross-border money transfers have consistently been a protracted and costly endeavor. However, the emergence of cryptocurrencies such as Bitcoin is altering the landscape. Cryptocurrencies facilitate rapid, economical, and borderless transactions, simplifying remittances and international payments.

B. Empowering the Unbanked

Cryptocurrencies are providing opportunities for unbanked and underbanked populations globally. Cryptocurrencies facilitate financial inclusion for millions who previously lacked access to financial services by offering a decentralized financial system independent of traditional institutions.

2. Banking and Financial Services

A. Disrupting Traditional Banking

Cryptocurrencies are disrupting the financial sector by providing alternatives to conventional banking services. Cryptocurrency wallets, decentralized finance (DeFi) systems, and peer-to-peer lending services exemplify the transformative impact of cryptocurrencies on the storage, borrowing, and management of financial resources.

B. The Rise of Central Bank Digital Currencies (CBDCs)

As cryptocurrencies proliferate, central banks globally are investigating the creation of their own digital currencies, referred to as CBDCs. Government- supported digital currencies possess the capacity to enhance monetary policy efficiency and bolster global financial stability.

3. Investment and Wealth Management

A New Asset Class

Cryptocurrencies have developed as a novel and intriguing asset class for investors. Cryptocurrencies, due to their distinctive characteristics and potential for substantial returns, are captivating both retail and institutional investors, thereby transforming the financial environment.

B. Diversifying Portfolios

As investors endeavor to diversify their portfolios, cryptocurrencies are gaining popularity. Cryptocurrencies provide access to a novel market, serving as a buffer against conventional financial risks and perhaps improving overall portfolio performance.

4. Commerce and Payments

A. Crypto-Enabled Commerce

An increasing number of enterprises are beginning to accept bitcoins as a payment method. This trend not only provides consumers with enhanced options in payment methods but also assists businesses in accessing new markets and client demographics.

B. Reducing Transaction Costs

Cryptocurrency transactions typically incur reduced fees in comparison to conventional payment methods, such as credit cards. This may provide substantial cost reductions for consumers and organizations alike, rendering cryptocurrency payments a more appealing alternative.

5. Privacy and Security

A. Enhancing Privacy

A distinguishing feature of cryptocurrencies is their capacity to offer enhanced anonymity relative to conventional financial transactions. Cryptocurrencies, through the application of cryptography and decentralized networks, provide consumers enhanced control over their personal information and financial data.

B. Securing Transactions

Cryptocurrency transactions are safeguarded by intricate cryptographic procedures and decentralized networks, rendering them exceptionally resistant to fraud and cyberattacks. This augmented security can foster trust in digital transactions and mitigate the danger of financial fraud.

6. Regulation and Compliance

A. Navigating the Regulatory Landscape

As cryptocurrencies rise in prominence, governments and regulatory agencies globally are contending with the regulation of this emerging technology. The regulatory framework is fast expanding, encompassing anti-money laundering (AML) measures and taxation, with substantial ramifications for individuals and organizations in the cryptocurrency sector.

B. Promoting Transparency and Accountability

As regulatory frameworks evolve, cryptocurrencies are increasingly exhibiting transparency and accountability. This can alleviate certain hazards linked to cryptocurrencies, such market manipulation and fraud, and promote more trust in the technology.

7. Innovation and Economic Growth

A. Fueling Technological Advancements

The emergence of cryptocurrencies has catalyzed a surge of innovation across multiple sectors. Blockchain technology, the foundation of cryptocurrencies, is being utilized across various sectors, including financial services and supply chain management, to develop innovative and transformative solutions to enduring problems.

B. Driving Economic Growth

By encouraging innovation and enhancing efficiency across sectors, cryptocurrencies possess the capacity to facilitate economic growth and job creation worldwide. As the adoption of cryptocurrencies by businesses and individuals increases, the technology may emerge as a significant catalyst for economic progress.

8. Environmental Impacts

A. The Energy Debate

Cryptocurrencies, especially those dependent on energy-intensive mining methods such as Bitcoin, have faced criticism for their environmental consequences. The ongoing discourse over the sustainability of cryptocurrencies has prompted certain projects to investigate more environmentally friendly alternatives, including proof-of-stake (PoS) consensus processes.

B. Encouraging Sustainable Practices

In reaction to apprehensions regarding the environmental repercussions of cryptocurrencies, many initiatives are implementing measures to enhance sustainability. The cryptocurrency sector is investigating methods to reduce its ecological impact, ranging from carbon offset programs to the advancement of sustainable mining technologies.

Conclusion

The emergence of cryptocurrencies is undeniably influencing the global economy in multiple dimensions. Cryptocurrencies are transforming existing institutions and promoting innovation across remittances, banking, investment, and commerce. As the world increasingly adopts this new technology, we can anticipate further significant transformations in our financial transactions and economic management.

5.2 BLOCKCHAIN APPLICATIONS

Blockchain is decentralized, signifying that each participant possesses a copy in the context of a public blockchain. Modifying data in the blockchain is exceedingly challenging, as it necessitates altering every copy across all locations, which is nearly impossible. This characteristic renders blockchain both distributed and immutable while ensuring transparency, as the data within the block remains fully accessible. The attributes of blockchain guarantee superior security, which accounts for its widespread popularity in applications that emphasize security and transparency. Currently, enterprises extensively utilize Blockchain applications. Let us examine many real-world applications of Blockchain technology.

1. Asset Management

Asset management represents a significant application of blockchain technology. Blockchain significantly influences the financial sector, particularly in asset management. Asset management often entails the administration and trading of various assets owned by a person, including fixed income, real estate, equities, mutual funds, commodities, and other alternative investments. Conventional trading procedures in asset management can be exceedingly costly, particularly when transactions encompass numerous nations and cross-border payments. In such circumstances, Blockchain can be highly beneficial as it eliminates the necessity for intermediaries such as brokers, custodians, and settlement managers. The blockchain ledger offers a straightforward and transparent mechanism that eliminates potential for error.

2. Cross-Border Payments

Have you ever utilized any Blockchain applications that facilitate cross-border payments in various currencies between countries? This process may be lengthy and intricate, potentially requiring several days for the funds to reach their destination. Blockchain has facilitated the simplification of cross-border payments by offering comprehensive remittance services devoid of intermediaries. Numerous remittance providers provide Blockchain services that facilitate international transactions within 24 hours.

3. Healthcare

Blockchain can significantly influence healthcare through the utilization of smart contracts, making it one of the most prominent applications of this technology. These smart contracts facilitate an agreement between two parties without the necessity of a middleman. All parties involved in the contract are aware of its details, and the contract is executed automatically upon fulfillment of its terms. In healthcare, personal health records can be encoded using Blockchain technology, ensuring access is restricted to main healthcare practitioners with a key. They also assist in maintaining the HIPAA Privacy Rule, which guarantees the confidentiality of patient information and restricts access to authorized individuals only.

4. Cryptocurrency

One of the most prevalent applications of Blockchain is in Cryptocurrency. Who is unaware of Bitcoin and its remarkable popularity? One of the numerous advantages of bitcoin utilizing blockchain technology is its absence of geographical constraints. Cryptocurrencies can facilitate transactions globally. The first consideration is exchange rates, acknowledging that individuals may incur financial losses during this procedure. This choice far surpasses regional payment applications like Paytm in India, which are confined to a specific country or geographical area and cannot facilitate transactions with individuals in other nations.

5. Birth and Death Certificates

A significant number of individuals globally lack a valid birth certificate, particularly in impoverished nations. UNICEF reports that one-third of all children under five lack a birth certificate. The issue is analogous to that of death certificates. Blockchain can address this issue by establishing a secure repository of validated birth and death certificates, accessible solely to authorized individuals. Isn't it an impressive implementation of Blockchain technology?

6. Online Identity Verification

Online verification and identity are required for the completion of any financial transactions online. This applies universally to all potential service providers within the financial and banking sector. Blockchain can consolidate the online identity verification process, allowing individuals to verify their identity once and thereafter share it with any desired service provider. Users may select their identity verification methods, including user authentication and facial recognition. Among the several applications of Blockchain, this particular application is extensively utilized across the entire business.

7. Internet of Things

The Internet of Things is a network of networked devices that communicate with one another and gather data with the purpose of deriving valuable insights. Any system of objects qualifies as IoT once it is interconnected. The most prevalent illustration of IoT is likely the Smart Home, wherein various household equipment, including lights, thermostats, air conditioners, and smoke detectors, may be interconnected on a unified platform. What is the role of Blockchain applications in this context? Blockchain is essential for ensuring security in this extensively distributed system. In IoT, the security of the system is contingent upon the least secure device, which represents the vulnerable link. Blockchain can guarantee that the data collected by IoT devices is secure and accessible solely to authorized entities.

8. Copyright and Royalties

Blockchain applications have also impacted the creative industry. Copyright and royalties pose significant challenges in creative industries such as music and film. These are artistic media, and they appear to lack any connection to Blockchain. This technology is crucial for maintaining security and transparency in the creative sectors. Numerous occurrences exist where music, films, art, and similar works are plagiarized, with insufficient acknowledgment afforded to the original creators. This issue can be resolved using Blockchain, which maintains a comprehensive database of artist rights. Blockchain is transparent and can offer a secure record of artist royalties and agreements with major production corporations. Royalties can also be administered through digital currency such as Bitcoin.

5.2.1 Internet of Things

How does IoT work with blockchain?

The Internet of Things (IoT) facilitates devices on the internet to transmit data to private blockchain networks, thereby establishing tamper-proof records of shared transactions. IBM Blockchain® facilitates the sharing and access of IoT data across your business partners without necessitating central control and management. Every transaction can be authenticated to avert disputes and foster trust among all authorized network participants.

Benefits of IoT and Blockchain

1. Build trust in your IoT data

Every transaction is documented, compiled into a data block, and appended to a secure, immutable data chain that is unalterable, permitting only additions.

2. Rely on added security

The IBM® Watson IoT® Platform allows for the selection of data to be managed, analyzed, personalized, and shared across authorized clients and partners.

3. Gain greater flexibility

The IBM Blockchain technology is open, interoperable, and designed for a multicloud environment, utilizing the latest iteration of the premier Hyperledger Fabric technology, tailored for Red Hat® OpenShift®.

4. Develop novel efficiencies

IBM Blockchain optimizes processes and generates new business value throughout your ecosystem by utilizing data provided by IoT devices, sensors.

Applications of Iot and Blockchain

1. Freight Transportation

Transporting freight is a multifaceted procedure that entails various stakeholders with divergent agendas. A blockchain integrated with IoT can record the temperatures, locations, arrival times, and statuses of shipping containers during transit. Immutable blockchain transactions facilitate trust among all parties, enabling prompt and efficient product movement.

2. Component Tracking and Compliance

The capacity to monitor components utilized in aircraft, vehicles, or other items is essential for safety and regulatory adherence. IoT data recorded in shared blockchain ledgers enables all parties to see component provenance throughout a product's life. Disseminating this information to regulatory bodies, shippers, and manufacturers is secure, efficient, and economical.

3. Log Operational Maintenance Data

IoT devices monitor the safety status of essential machinery and its upkeep. Blockchain offers an immutable database of operational data and subsequent maintenance, applicable from engines to elevators. Third-party repair partners can oversee the blockchain for preventive maintenance and document their activities on the blockchain. Operational records may be disseminated to governmental agencies to confirm adherence to regulations.

5.2.2 Medical Record Management System

Traditional medical record systems encounter intricate administrative procedures for data processing to safeguard patient privacy, resulting in significant waste of human resources. This architecture is evidently inefficient for the sharing of medical records. The blockchain approach has lately been utilized to enhance the security of medical data exchange and management. The cryptography feature of blockchain networks ensures patient privacy. Data integrity and incorruptibility safeguard medical data against tampering. The blockchain can be seen as a distributed database that saves data across each network node to circumvent the halting problem. It thus offers enhanced stability, uniformity, and resistance to attacks. The issue of distributed denial- of-service assaults (DDoS) inside the traditional centralized framework can be addressed with blockchain technology. The implementation of blockchain in the medical record system enhances reliability and accelerates the interchange of medical records. Due to decentralization, ownership of the medical record is reverted to patients, enabling them to directly manage their records and oversee their health.

Biofeedback is a method that use electrical sensors to quantify physiological activities of the human body, including blood pressure and heart rate. Biofeedback seeks to enhance understanding of one's physiological state and its functioning. Biofeedback training is available in clinics, medical facilities, and hospitals. These measurements regarding biofeedback are therefore crucial for future therapy. Consequently, such data storage or management is essential and may be incorporated into the medical record system. This chapter examines blockchain-based medical record management solutions in the literature. A new medical record structure is designed and deployed using the open-source platform, Ethereum. The Ethereum platform permits any anyone to create applications within blockchain networks. The Ethereum Virtual Machine (EVM) performs smart contracts within the virtual environment. Utilizing the smart contract, developers can deploy these codes onto the blockchain. The codes will be executed automatically following the formation of the blockchain. The medical record management system is designed with the smart contract. The proposed architecture would get the desired level of health care through the implementation of smart contracts.

5.2.3 Domain Name Service

The emergence of blockchain and Web3 has fundamentally transformed the registration, management, and resolution of domain names. The Web2 domains have been utilized till the present, as blockchain technology gains prominence. The Ethereum Name Service (ENS), affiliated with Ethereum, is one of the most prominent on-chain domain registration services. Recently, emerging blockchains are creating their own DNS protocols, indicating that this sector is still in its nascent stages.

What is Blockchain DNS?

A DNS functions as an access point to the internet and is crucial universally, particularly for enterprises, as it establishes your company address. In this context, blockchain DNS refers to a decentralized DNS server that facilitates the registration, management, and resolution of domain names on theblockchain. The network operates in a decentralized manner, with files saved and shared on a peer-to-peer server system. The primary members in the network function as nodes, interconnecting directly without middlemen. The various domain registry platforms utilize smart contracts. Upon purchasing a domain from a blockchain DNS, the domain is owned by you, and censorship by others is not permissible without your consent. In numerous instances, blockchain domains are expected to constitute web addresses that operate as bitcoin wallets. Here are the seven premier blockchain domain name services to explore in 2022.

Top 7 Blockchain DNS Software

1. Namecoin

Namecoin is the inaugural split of Bitcoin and has emerged as one of the most inventive cryptocurrencies. It is the inaugural altcoin to incorporate merged mining and a decentralized DNS. The website employs. bit as its domain name and functions similarly to conventional DNS systems. As a site user, you can register, renew, and transfer domains using fiat and bitcoin. Upon acquiring the domain, it is need to install distinct software to handle the bit domain as a browser extension. Namecoin can enhance decentralization, security, censorship resistance, privacy, and the efficiency of DNS and other identities. Namecoin possesses the capability of decentralizing DNS, IDs, and other technologies.

2. Blockstack

Formerly known as OneName, Blockstack has a decentralized DNS that establishes a decentralized website on the Bitcoin Blockchain. They also eliminate the intermediaries responsible for managing identification systems, databases, and web servers. Blockstack is a trailblazer in the decentralized application (DApp) domain as it employs blockchains to create a DNS counterpart and a Public Key Infrastructure (PKI). As a result, they do not depend on root servers or centralized authorities. An individual can register a name and exercise ownership over it. Furthermore, there are no assaults, DNS service disruptions, hacking incidents, or restriction of certain websites.

3. Ethereum Name Service (ENS)

The Ethereum Name Service is a prominent blockchain domain name system. There has been a rise in registrations, totaling 1.12 million names and 406,000 owners. It represents a novel blockchain-based DNS integrated with a conventional system, enabling users to reap the advantages of both frameworks. Ethereum DNS possesses a distinctive feature that enables users to transfer domains. For instance, one may migrate their conventional domains to the blockchain DNS service. The transfer can proceed provided that one supplies their DNSSEC registration. A domain is registered with the .eth extension through an auction process. A user can store addresses and receive any cryptocurrency, token, or NFT.

4. Emercoin – EmerDNS

Emercoin employs a Proof of Stake mechanism that integrates proofs of labor and ownership. It functions as a substitute for DNS, facilitating the advancement of Decentralized Software Development Kits (dSDKs). These tools are vital as they aid users in creating service and software solutions, including APIs, technical documentation, and domains, without the necessity of technical coding. Emercoin possesses the advantage of supporting four domain zones as well as any additional zone. Nevertheless, the DNS is resistant to censorship and obstruction. Moreover, the DNS is entirely decentralized, rendering information impervious to substitution or obstruction. Users may designate the domain rental duration upon registration. Finally, users may end their domain by removing it from the blockchain without awaiting its expiration or lease duration.

5. Peername

Peername offers a user-friendly blockchain plugin compatible with Chrome, Opera, and Firefox. The platform is constructed using XNR, Namecoin, and Emercoin cryptocurrencies. It facilitates the resolution of .bit, .emc, .coin, .lib, and .bazar domains. The cost of registering a domain is $7 per domain, which is little higher than its rivals. Peername transfers all domains at no cost to entice users to the platform and offers users the subsequent year free with each registration. Upon transferring their domains, users can relocate them to their private wallets, thereby granting them substantial control. Furthermore, upon registration, all data is preserved in cold storage, thereby mitigating the dangers of cyberattacks and hacking attempts.

6. NEM Blockchain DNS Extension

The NEM Blockchain DNS is a Chrome addon that enables users to access websites with the .nem domain extension. While the platform is not as complete as others, it provides certain valuable capabilities that enable users to get domain names from the NEM Blockchain naming system. NEM is a user-friendly software that necessitates no additional downloads. The platform is constructed using blockchain technology and is open-source. Upon installation of the extension, the domain owner can effortlessly execute updates. Similar to previous blockchain DNS extensions, it is inherently uncensorable, allowing owners to publish material without requiring approval.

7. Handshake

Handshake depends on network members to authenticate DNS zones. The development signifies a movement towards a tool that fosters a more decentralized internet. One advantage of utilizing Handshake is the opportunity to engage in a safe decentralized open naming platform facilitated by a peer-to- peer network. Upon registering a name, the cryptographic key controlled by the owner is capable of creating ordered records. Handshake employs its blockchain to decentralize and sequence events.

Conclusion

Blockchain technology is nascent within the domain industry, hence a predominant domain has yet to emerge in the market. Each registry site possesses distinct offerings. Nonetheless, constraints persist, such as the absence of browser integration, rendering them somewhat distinct. Consequently, when enterprises increasingly develop, you get the opportunity to evaluate new features. This approach enables you to ascertain which registry is most suitable for your needs.

5.3 FUTURE OF BLOCKCHAIN

Certain individuals may harbor skepticism concerning the necessity of understanding blockchain trends. The promise of blockchain as an advanced technology is a key incentive to be informed about current developments in the blockchain sector. By neglecting prevalent blockchain developments, you may overlook the next significant innovation in industries such as gaming or financial services. Awareness of blockchain trends also facilitates understanding of technological advances that benefit consumers and developers. Blockchain trends elucidate the potential trajectory of blockchain technology in the future. Crucially, awareness of current trends in the blockchain domain can facilitate informed decision-making about cryptocurrency investments and decentralized application projects.

What Trends Will Prevail in the Blockchain Landscape in 2025?

The discourse surrounding themes poised to significantly impact the blockchain sector highlights emerging technologies, the evolution of decentralized finance, improved interoperability solutions, and the adoption of central bank digital currencies (CBDCs). One can investigate innovative prospects to leverage the capabilities of blockchain technology by utilizing insights regarding significant blockchain trends. Emerging tendencies in blockchain will facilitate a decentralized, interconnected, and more sustainable future. Emerging important trends will redefine industries and generate new opportunities to revolutionize the digital world.

All Eyes on Bitcoin

The current Crypto Bull Run and favorable occurrences for Bitcoin have propelled the inaugural cryptocurrency to its historical zenith. Bitcoin surpassed the $100,000 threshold in December 2024, subsequent to Donald Trump's triumph in the Presidential elections.

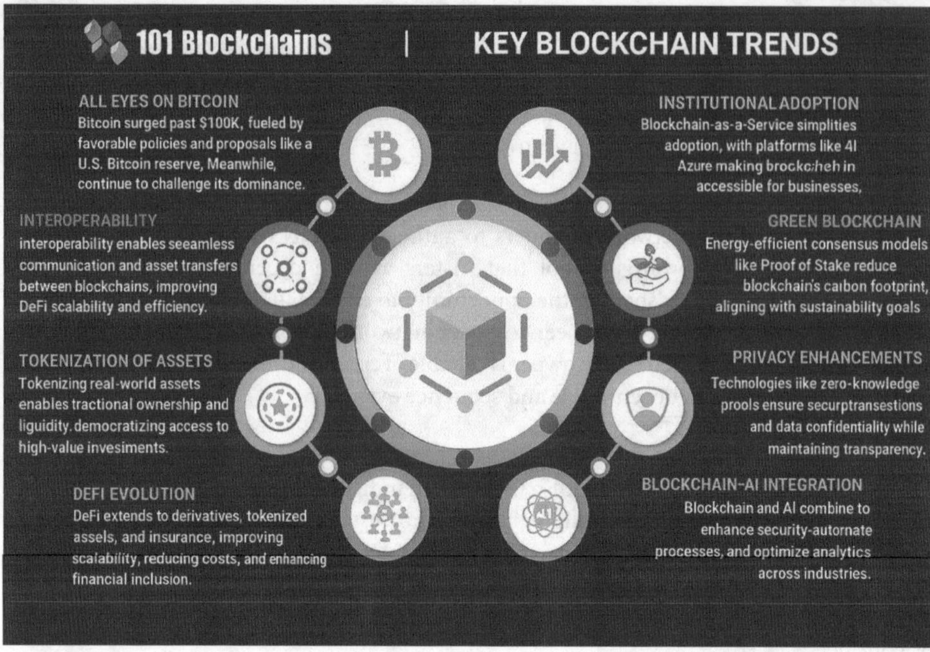

Fig. 5.1

The most significant development for Bitcoin is the proposed national Bitcoin reserve by a Republican Senator in the United States. The idea for the Bitcoin reserve posits that Bitcoin will function as a safeguard against currency devaluation, inflation, and geopolitical risk. A strategic Bitcoin reserve will be established by acquiring 200,000 Bitcoin year to amass one million tokens. Advocates of the Bitcoin reserve assert that it will mitigate financial deficits without raising taxes.

Certain proponents argue that the Bitcoin reserve will facilitate a reduction of the United States' debt by fifty percent over about two decades. Simultaneously, it is crucial to monitor the prospective emergence of altcoins as contenders for Bitcoin's supremacy in the cryptocurrency market.

Interoperability Becomes a Priority

The future of blockchain technology significantly relies on interoperability among various blockchain systems. Interoperability will be a paramount priority in the blockchain ecosystem to provide seamless asset transactions and data sharing among blockchain networks. The necessity for interoperability will foster a resilient blockchain ecosystem with interconnected platforms, hence guaranteeing improvements in efficiency and scalability. Interoperability with cross-chain solutions facilitates collaboration among several networks, including Ethereum, Solana, Arbitrum, and Polkadot. Prominent initiatives that facilitate interoperability encompass Polkadot and Cosmos.

The two blockchain platforms provide integrated ecosystems and common communication protocols to guarantee compatibility. The emphasis on interoperability will facilitate the development of innovative solutions for DeFi that enhance overall system scalability.

Tokenization of Real World Assets

Real World Assets (RWA) represent a significant trend poised to influence the future of the blockchain sector. The tokenization of physical assets enables the realization of benefits including fractional ownership and enhanced liquidity. Tokenization can encompass any tangible assets in the physical realm, including real estate or precious metals. Blockchain will facilitate the tokenization of real- world assets and permit the trade of these tokenized assets in secondary marketplaces. It can enhance liquidity by diminishing the financial obstacles to accessing particular assets. Fractional ownership of tokenized real-world assets enables several investors to collectively share ownership of high-value assets.

Evolution of Decentralized Finance

Decentralized finance will undergo significant transformations in accordance with prominent trends. The relevance of DeFi in the future of blockchain will not be limited to lending and borrowing protocols. As the blockchain ecosystem expands, DeFi intends to introduce increasingly sophisticated financial instruments, including tokenized assets, derivatives, and insurance. The primary advantage of DeFi is in enhancing financial inclusion, especially for the unbanked demographic. The advanced DeFi will resolve issues related to scalability and elevated transaction costs. Anticipate a more secure, efficient, and accessible DeFi ecosystem characterized by enhanced user experiences and diminished obstacles to entry. A prominent illustration of DeFi's progress is found in the liquidity pools of the Aave protocol, which provide staking solutions for under-collateralized loans.

Institutional Adoption of Blockchain Technology

Any enumeration of significant trends in the blockchain domain for 2025 will be deficient without emphasizing institutional usage of blockchain technology. Anticipate intermittent expansion in the quantity of Blockchain-as-a-Service solutions in the future. Enterprises of all scales can utilize the BaaS concept for implementing blockchain technologies. The Blockchain-as-a-Service concept will allow every enterprise to access blockchain prospects without incurring substantial costs. It will promote blockchain adoption by guaranteeing user- friendliness and accessibility of the technology. Reliable BaaS solutions are available from Amazon Web Services and Microsoft Azure, which will simplify the development of blockchain applications from the ground up.

Green Blockchain Initiatives

Green blockchain efforts will prominently feature among blockchain trends capable of exerting significant influence. Sustainability has been a significant concern for blockchain adoption because to the substantial carbon footprint associated with traditional approaches like Proof of Work. With the increasing demand for sustainability in 2025, the blockchain environment may experience the emergence of new consensus mechanisms. The novel consensus processes will prioritize enhanced energy efficiency. Green blockchain initiatives will facilitate adherence to global climate objectives by minimizing carbon footprints. Innovative mechanisms like Proof of Stake and Proof of History can diminish energy consumption and mitigate the environmental impact of blockchain platforms. Eco-friendly methods can enhance the long-term sustainability of blockchain protocols and foster innovative solutions. The move of Ethereum to Proof of Stake exemplifies a prominent green blockchain endeavor.

More Emphasis on Privacy

Privacy has become a significant issue inside the blockchain domain. Innovations in privacy-enhancing technologies will be essential in the future of the blockchain landscape. This is a significant trend in blockchain technology that protects user privacy while enabling secure transactions. Prominent privacy-enhancing technologies anticipated to gain traction in 2025 encompass ring signatures and zero-knowledge proofs. Cryptographic approaches enhance data secrecy and may influence the future of interactions with blockchain protocols and decentralized applications (dApps). Projects like Zcash and Monero are leading a revolution to improve privacy. The principal objective of privacy-enhancing technologies is to attain an optimal equilibrium between privacy and transparency.

Integration of Blockchain with AI

Artificial intelligence is a significant trend that will impact the future of blockchain technology, offering promising benefits. The integration of the two technologies can provide adaptive, highly secure, and intelligent systems. The integration of blockchain with AI can facilitate the development of solutions capable of analyzing extensive datasets and ensuring process automation. The integration of blockchain and AI will merge the immutability of blockchain with the analytical capabilities of AI. It will establish a robust basis for enhancing security and refining decision-making abilities. The integration of blockchain with artificial intelligence will present significant opportunities for enterprises across various sectors, including gaming, banking, and supply chain management.

Conclusion

The projections for blockchain technology in 2025 depict an optimistic outlook for the sector. Emerging trends in the blockchain sector generate new opportunities. It is time to transition from inquiries such as 'Is blockchain the future?' to contemplating the revolutionary improvements inside the blockchain scene. Prominent trends anticipated for 2025 indicate the potential establishment of a national Bitcoin reserve in the US, the advancement of DeFi, and the emergence of cross-chain solutions. Anticipate developments including the integration of blockchain with artificial intelligence and the use of privacy-enhancing technology. As the blockchain industry progresses, it is essential to be informed about the current trends to maintain a competitive edge and seize opportunities. Explore further significant trends anticipated in the future of blockchain.